Public Land Mulies

David W. Long

Eastmans' Publishing, Inc.

POWELL, WYOMING

Eastmans' Publishing, Inc.
P. O. Box 798, Powell, Wyoming 82435
© 2006

All rights reserved. Published 2006
First Edition

First Printing July 2006
Second Printing October 2006
Third Printing January 2008

Printed in Canada

Front cover photograph by David W. Long
Back cover deer photograph by Mike Eastman
Illustrations by Darcy Tate
Book and cover design by Scott Larsen

ISBN (hardcover) 0-9778837-1-X
Library of Congress Control Number: 2006929942
9 8 7 6 5 4 3 2 1

Dedication

First and foremost I want to thank my wife, Cheryl. Without her patience and understanding, this book would have never been possible. There have been many of times over the years that she has had to manage all of the household duties and take care of the kids while I have been off pursuing mule deer. For that I thank her.

Second, I would like to thank my children for being very understanding of me missing a lot of their school sporting events, etc. in order to spend more time hunting the high country.

Last but not least, I would like to thank my mom and dad for getting me started hunting when I was young. Thanks to them, I was able to start pursuing mule deer at a very early age which ultimately turned out to be one of my passions in life.

Once again, thanks to all of you!

Contents

Section 4   Backpacking

Section 5   Early Season Hunting

Section 6   Mid-Season Hunting

Section 7   Late Season Hunting

Section 8   On the Horizon

About the Author

David Long was born in Tooele, Utah on April 28, 1966. He spent his childhood years growing up in the small community of Stockton, Utah. David learned to hunt at a very early age and could always be found pursuing jackrabbits in the foothills just east of town. Even at this young age, David didn't hesitate to venture off by himself while hunting.

David's family relocated to Big Piney, Wyoming when he was 12 years old. Two years later, he was old enough to hunt mule deer and took on several small jobs to make enough money to buy a .270 Remington Model 700 ADL.

A couple of years later, David was already investing in backpacking equipment and doing solo backcountry trips before he was even out of high school. The high country was David's place of choice to pursue trophy mulies. He has never looked back since.

David now pursues trophy mulies in two, sometimes three, western states every fall. It doesn't matter what time of year it is, David generally can be found doing something to do with mule deer. Whether it be scouting in the spring and summer, hunting in the fall or filming bucks in the winter, you can bet that David will be in the field trying to learn more about mule deer behavior.

David is currently an official measurer for the Boone and Crockett Club and the North American Shed Hunters Club. His extensive "hands on" experience measuring antlers, as well as viewing literally hundreds of bucks per year, gives David the expertise and background necessary to compile a book of this category.

In addition, David is a field editor for *Eastmans' Hunting Journal* and has made

several appearances on *Eastmans' Hunting TV* to discuss mule deer strategies and the proper backpacking equipment needed to pursue bucks in the backcountry. David has written numerous hunting and how-to articles for *Eastmans' Hunting Journal* over the years and has appeared on the cover twice.

In 1998, David co-authored the tremendously successful book, *Wyoming's Finest Mule Deer*. The book included photos and stories of all of the biggest mule deer bucks ever killed in the state of Wyoming. The book was limited to a production of 4,000 copies and is currently out of print. The book is a must for anyone wanting to pursue mule deer in the state of Wyoming.

David didn't stop there. In 2000, He released his first mule deer video, *In Pursuit of Magnum Mulies*. Two years later, the second video in the series, *Magnum Mulies 2 – The Pursuit Continues* was released. Then in 2003, the final installment in the series, *Magnum Mulies – The Final Pursuit* was released. After the third video was released, David gave up packing the video camera because he wanted to focus all of his efforts on hunting, rather than filming.

Over the years, David has had tremendous success hunting public land mulies. He has developed a public land hunting method that obviously works. In this book, he will share that hunting method as well as the tips and tactics he has learned over the last 25 years of pursuing trophy bucks in the high country.

Preface

I can remember back as a child looking through an old copy of the Boone and Crockett Club's all-time record book, known only to us kids as "the book." The book seemed to be larger than life and I would often sit for hours browsing through the listings imagining what it must be like to have been fortunate enough to have taken such a specimen. I would try to imagine how the events of their hunts played out. Did they have the buck scouted before the season? How many shots did it take? Were they backpacking? Questions such as these made my imagination run wild. It was then that I told myself if there was one thing I wanted to accomplish in hunting, it was to harvest a buck large enough to make the book.

That goal has since become a reality. Not only have I been fortunate enough to put a deer in the book, but I have been fortunate enough to harvest many nice mule deer bucks. They did not come easy. Each and every hunt that I was able to be successful on took a lot of time and hard work. I have always been told that nothing worth having comes easy. I believe this is true with mule deer hunting. Along with the hard work, I have had to make sacrifices over the years as well. The biggest sacrifice has been the lack of time spent with my family because of all of the time I have spent in the field. Thankfully, they have been very understanding.

I want to make one thing clear. I don't claim to be a mule deer expert. But I do love to hunt them and have been lucky enough to have taken some exceptional deer throughout the years. Over the past 25 years of hunting mule deer, I feel that I have learned a little bit about this amazing animal. Sometimes they can be very predictable, while other times, not predictable at all.

I have always felt that the most difficult thing to do in hunting is to kill a mule deer buck that has a four point typical frame that gross scores 195 B&C. With that being said, I have been fortunate enough to have taken two of them, a 197²/₈ and the other a 202⁶/₈ B&C. Although luck always plays a big factor, I believe with the right equipment and a little bit of mule deer behavior knowledge, you can increase your odds of taking a trophy buck immensely. Throughout the eight sections of this book, I will discuss in great detail the habits of this amazing animal that just may help you harvest the buck of a lifetime.

During your pursuit of trophy mule deer, there is one thing to remember and that is mule deer are very adaptable. This is very evident when you consider the diverse terrain they can be found inhabiting—from the arid hot deserts all the way up among the majestic peaks above timberline, which is my favorite place to pursue them. I can't even put it in words of how I feel when I am chasing timberline bucks. There is nothing like it. Although this book covers mule deer hunting at all elevations, the main focus will be on high country public land hunting.

Over the years, my equipment has evolved from "not so good" to the best equipment made. During my early years of mule deer hunting, it is amazing that I ever survived. Looking back, I was never prepared for emergencies or adverse weather changes. I used to wear denim jeans and cotton T-shirts, along with a cotton base layer. That is a dangerous combination when you get wet and the temperatures cool down. After a long day in the field, my jeans used to be frozen all the way up to just below my knees. If I would have been forced to spend the night in the field, I would have been in trouble.

Not only was all my clothing made from cotton, I never carried any water or packs with any supplies. The only thing I would have is a candy bar in my coat pocket. Thankfully, I made it through those years and have learned from it and nowadays, I am always well prepared. Later on in this book, we will take a good hard look at the equipment that I use, and why.

I feel that I have gained a lot of knowledge in my 25 years of hunting mule deer. This great creature has definitely taught me a thing or two throughout my years in the mountains. In the hunting sections I will discuss how mule deer change their behavior and eating habits during the early, mid and late seasons. Not only does their behavior change, so do their eating habits. I will explore some of the different foods mule deer eat, as well as where the food can be found.

I will also discuss the mule deer's future. What it holds, and what needs to be done as far as hunting pressure, habitat and poaching. I will also mention how important it is that we take our younger generation hunting. The kids of today will be our game managers of tomorrow. It is critical that they learn conservation and proper hunting ethics, along with the importance of hunting at an early age. I recently took my youngest daughter hunting this past year and had the time of my life. You will read about it in the last section of this book. It was very special indeed.

I love hearing details of other people's successful hunts and sharing the memories of my past hunts, which is why I was excited when Mike and Guy Eastman approached me about writing a mule deer book. It gave me a chance to relive all of my past hunting memories and share information with other hunters that may make their future hunts more enjoyable. Not only did I use stories of my hunts, but I have called upon many of my friends who have taken large bucks over the years to include their stories to help reinforce hunting techniques and deer behavior.

There are a couple of reasons why I feel this book is so unique. First of all, every story, picture and buck harvested in this book is on public land. There are no guided hunts. These are all do-it-yourself public land hunts. This, in my opinion, is the toughest way to harvest a trophy class mule deer, which makes it that much more enjoyable and satisfying when you do. Second, is I am honored the foreword to the book was written by Dr. Valerius Geist, who is known worldwide as being the authority on mule deer behavior. Dr. Geist is a professor of environmental sciences on the Faculty of Environmental Design at the University of Calgary in Alberta Canada.

Hopefully you can find a tip or two in this book that may help you in your own pursuit of public land mulies. If nothing else, I hope you find it an enjoyable read. So sit back and relax, grab something cold to drink and come along with me in pursuit of my favorite animal—the mule deer.

David W. Long

Acknowledgements

There are many people who contributed to this book. Without them, this book would not have been possible.

Mike Eastman
Guy Eastman
Dr. Valerius Geist
Robby Denning
Scott Mansor
Hall Sawyer
Victor Clark
Jed Lowe
Gil Winters
David Woodhouse
Gary Fralick
Gavin Lovell
Danny Adams

Tracy Tolbert
Kyle Paxman
Paul Pennie
Steve James
Bill Tanner
Rick Costello
Bill McEwen
Darcy Tate
Mark Gocke
Arizona Game and Fish
   Department
Colorado Division of
   Wildlife

Idaho Fish and Game
   Department
Nevada Division of
   Wildlife
New Mexico Game and
   Fish
Montana Fish, Wildlife &
   Parks
Utah Division of Wildlife
   Resources
Wyoming Game and Fish
   Department
Boone & Crockett Club

"Boone and Crockett Club's score charts for typical and non-typical mule deer reproduced with the express written permission of Boone and Crockett Club, 250 Station Dr., Missoula, MT 59801.

To learn more about the Club and the many activities it is involved in, please visit their web site at www.booneandcrockettclub.com or call (406) 542-1888."

Foreword

Dear David,

This book is a jewel. Nobody can help learning when they follow the clear prose of a hunter as observant, as dedicated and as reflective as you with over a quarter century of firsthand experience in hunting and filming trophy mule deer. I must also confess that I am a sucker for anecdotes innocently told without hype or preaching, as in following the trials and tribulations of the hunter I seem to always pick up something of real interest and value. And this book has enough of just such stories. However, the book is better still. Much better!

Please note: bucks like those illustrated in this book do not grow just anywhere. It takes special circumstances to grow them, and the attentive reader can find that in this book. That is, one can by closely reading this book decipher the kind of environment that is needed to grow huge bucks with monster antlers. Antler growth is closely tied to the quality of nutrition just prior to and during the growth of the velvet antlers. Clearly, these monstrous bucks enjoyed exquisite nutrition, a nutrition far better than mule deer bucks enjoy in different landscapes. Have you noticed in looking at the fine photographs of the landscapes that the hills and ridges are rounded with smooth contours? That means that the underlying rock is soft and weathers readily into small pieces and particles. Hard granitic rock does not do that, but creates cliffs and disintegrates into steep boulder fields almost void of vegetation.

What's the significance of rock weathering into small particles?

It means that plants have plenty of spaces to grow their roots in, but above all, they come in contact with a very fertile soil weathering out of that rock. Consequently, green plants cover virtually all the land in summer. Did you see that the mountains inhabited by these monster mule deer are all green to the very top? In short, rock which weathers into smooth-contoured hills and ridges is ideal for plant growth due to both soil structure and fertility.

The ridges and hills so favored by the big bucks project high above the tree line. And that means when springtime arrives to these mountains, and ascends slowly the slopes towards the peaks, it will take a long time getting there, for Wyoming's mountains and tree lines are high! And that means that as plants spout in response to increased warmth, there is a wave of early plant growth ascending the mountain. Deer feed of course within that wave, consuming the plants at their nutritional best, when they are young, highly digestible and full of protein and minerals. Consequently, the higher the mountains the longer bucks can feed on the very best of plant food while their antlers grow. Reaching the top, plant growth is so nutritious that it leads to the velvet antlers expanding at every opportunity. Thus the taller the mountains the longer beamed and longer tined the antlers.

However, as good as the food was while getting up there, at the top the food is best of all. Why? First of all, because snow accumulation and good soils lead to water retention. And plants like that! There is an additional important factor: at high elevation summer nights are cooler and days are longer than in the valley. This means long periods of photosynthesis by plants, followed by a near shut-down of the metabolism at night. Consequently, the sugars produced during the day cannot be metabolized away at night. This results in thin-fibered, exceptionally rich plant forage just as antler growth is racing toward completion. High growth of antlers in velvet due to superior food leads to huge, long-tined, massive antlers. Just look at the huge extent of high quality sub-alpine and alpine range in Dave's pictures! That's real antler-growing country.

Even that is only part of the story. Please notice the intermediate ranges between winter and summer ranges that David repeatedly draws attention to. In springtime these ranges break out in vegetation superior to that on the dry winter range allowing surviving bucks a rich food source and excellent recovery of condition before growing the new antlers. That's very important because the bucks use body stores to kick-start antler growth. Bucks in good condition just before the velvet antlers start to grow again can put a lot more into antler growth than bucks fresh off a depleted winter range. Good body condition just before the start of antler growth insures big, massive beams. In short, where bucks can move uphill into excellent forage because of timely spring weather and plant growth just as their antlers begin growing are on the way to become trophy bucks.

Similarly, on the way down from the mountains in fall, stopping to feed in the aspen groves, insures that they fatten up not only for the rut, but also for the poor winter ranges lower down. Getting fat and staying fat is very important in survival and subsequent body growth. The intermediate ranges thus help spring and fall to insure good antler growth.

Finally, no decent antlers ever grew on the head of poorly developed buck-fawns. Superior antler growth is predicated by well-developed fawns and well-fed dams producing plenty of rich milk for fawn growth. David points, quite rightly, to females living along creeks and drainages, and how important it is to keep these from despoiling by overgrazing. Again, right on. Mule deer throughout their distribution concentrate in stream-edge vegetation, or riparian vegetation. Look after that vegetation and you cannot but generate healthy, large bodied deer—the only kind that grows large antlers. David's book is vitally important for understanding how trophy bucks develop in what is undoubtedly the finest mule deer habitat in North America. For those bent on record book mulies there is no better source of information than David's book. Years ago I visited Big Piney and the mountains David hunts and while I was thrilled as a naturalist by what I saw, smelled and heard, I never saw a monster mulie. Had I had David's insights, I might have!

Mule deer occupy a huge range in North America, exceeded in relatively recent times by the white-tailed deer's race to the north. It is now in the Yukon, poised to enter Alaska!

Mule and black-tailed deer vary greatly through their huge range, offering another kind of trophy hunting, namely that focusing on regional variants. Mule deer in central British Columbia live in low mountains covered over completely by dense interior rain forest. They grow beautiful, compact rugose antlers, but their most astonishing characteristics are their small, narrowly set eyes and narrow, whitetail-like skulls. In the Alberta foothills mule deer have eye sockets as large as those of pronghorns, and widely spaced to boot. These prairie type mule deer range far north into British Columbia along the mountain front. Mule deer in the Yukon are so wolf-attuned that even seeing one is a feat, as they are so secretive. The mule deer's ancestor, the black-tailed deer varies vastly over its range. Vancouver Island blacktails grow big, occasionally huge rosettes that flare out over their eyes protecting these from the antler points. These deer are usually forks, but in fighting the tines of those forks penetrate deeply and big, flaring rosettes protect the eyes. Getting here a little four point swamp buck is a feat! Even more so getting a good buck from the dense forests wherever such may be, but especially from steep, completely forested mountains.

I recommend this book, and yes, David, I had as much fun reading it as you did writing it.

Sincerely,
Valerius Geist, PhD., P. Biol.
Professor Emeritus of Environmental Science
The University of Calgary

SECTION 1

TROPHY HUNTING

The Passion ~~Passion~~ *Obsession*

Snow continued to fall as I worked my way through the small patch of quaking aspen. The once dry and noisy leaves that blanketed the ground were now wet and soft, allowing me to sneak quietly towards the spot where I missed a trophy buck the day before. I'm not exactly sure why I missed because the buck was standing broadside at 150 yards staring at me through an opening in the quakies. Granted, it was an offhand shot, but I still felt that I shouldn't have missed—but I did! The buck bounded through the trees and disappeared in a matter of seconds.

I wasn't sure if I would ever lay eyes on the buck again, but the next day found me on the same mountain once more. I felt confident that if I worked my way through the patch of quakies the buck was in the day before, and was patient, I would have a second chance at the buck if he was still in the area.

The going was slow. I kept picking the trees apart with my binos, but there was no sign of the buck. When I approached the exact spot that I had seen the buck the day before, I slowed down to a snail's pace. Finally, my slow pace and patience paid off. Seventy-five yards ahead I could just make out parts of a deer standing broadside. It was him. Even as slow as I was going, the buck already had me pegged. I didn't have a shot, but if I took two steps to my right I would have a good shooting lane. I took one slow step, the buck remained dead still. I took the second and luckily, the buck still remained motionless. I slowly raised my rifle and pressed it against a four-inch diameter quakie tree. I eased the safety off and settled the crosshairs just behind his front shoulder and pulled the trigger. As the rifle recoiled, I lost sight of the buck momentarily. When I regained sight of him, he disappeared behind a couple of tall pine trees.

Knowing that there was no way I could miss the buck for a second time, I slowly walked up to where he was standing and just as I thought, there were large amounts of blood in the snow where he had stood. After following his tracks for about 40 yards, I could see him laying on the ground up ahead behind the two large pine trees.

I had taken several nice bucks in the past, but this was the first buck I had taken that would score over 185 B&C. The buck was only 25 inches wide, but was very tall. The buck took first place in the typical mule deer category in a contest held by the North American Hunting Club that year. I was hooked. Ever since that day, I have wanted to take it to the next level.

Since then, mule deer hunting has become my passion. I can honestly say that there are not many days that go by that I don't think about mule deer. Just ask my wife and kids. It is definitely a passion to me. According to my wife, Cheryl, it is an obsession. She's probably right. I guess when you think of something 365 days a year that would qualify as an obsession. Luckily, Cheryl has been very understanding over the years. Considering the amount of time I spend in the hills, it's a miracle that our marriage has survived.

I can tell you right now, upfront, that public land trophy hunting for mule deer is not for everyone. It is not nearly as glamorous as most people make it out to be. Not only do you need to be physically fit, but you need to be mentally strong as well. It takes a totally different mindset to be successful at trophy hunting. But if it is something you want to try, continue reading on and we will take a look at several important items, as well as get to know mule deer a little bit better.

Public land trophy mule deer bucks have become one of the most sought after big game animals in the last 10 years. Most people who set out after a trophy mule deer, however, return home empty-handed or with a lesser buck than what they initially set their sights on. What makes killing a trophy mule deer so tough? One reason is because very few public land deer live long enough to grow a trophy sized set of antlers. The odds are stacked against them from day one. Between predators, hunting seasons, poachers and harsh winters, only a small percentage will make it to maturity. Proof of this is a radio collar study conducted in Idaho back in the 1980's. Radio collars were put on 30 deer of which eight were bucks. Within three years, seven of the eight bucks were dead. Four of them were harvested during hunting seasons, one was illegally taken by a poacher, one winter-killed and one road-killed. That left one sole survivor, which incidentally, spent all summer and fall in an adjacent state.

Although some mule deer grow trophy racks at the age of 4½ years old, most bucks start growing trophy antlers at the age of 5½ years old. They will normally grow four to five good sets of antlers before dying of old age. Most bucks in the Rocky Mountains simply do not live past 10½ years of age. One of the main reasons for this is most bucks at that age don't have any teeth left. Their teeth are worn completely down to the gum line, which results in them not getting enough nutrition to survive the winter. One of my bucks, the buck I call Curly, was aged at 9½ years old and his teeth were worn all the way down to the gum line. Even if I hadn't harvested him, there is absolutely no way he would have made it through another winter.

When a buck reaches the ripe old age of 5½ years, he is a veteran of many hunting seasons and chances are he won't be harvested. I talked with a game and fish biologist several years back and he told me that he believed that 80% of the bucks that live to be 5½ years old will never be harvested. I firmly believe this. I have confirmed this while watching bucks on the winter range as well. Most of the mature bucks on the winter range return year after year without being harvested, only to die of old age. Is this because they are super smart? No, they are not super intelligent. They simply have found ways of avoiding hunting pressure. They are true survivors. They don't necessarily live in the most rugged, out of the way places. Instead, they will seek out areas with the least amount of hunting pressure. Sometimes, this might be right next to a road, house or even a subdivision.

The buck I harvested in 1989 was only 25 inches wide, but extremely tall. The buck took first place in an annual competition held by the North American Hunting Club.

What is the Bottom Line?

The subtitle of this book is *The Bottom Line*. I picked it for a reason. There is no great secret to harvesting big bucks year after year. You simply have to do two things. If you do these two things, you will have a great advantage over every other hunter on the mountain. The Bottom Line—you simply need to hunt *harder* and *smarter* than everyone else. That's it in a nutshell. As simple as it sounds, that is the key to putting your tag on trophy bucks on a regular basis.

Hunting harder is pretty self explanatory. You need to get up early and be on the hill by first light. If you don't, you already have two strikes against you. If this means skipping your regular cup of coffee in the morning, then skip it. If it means eating breakfast on the go, or better yet, eating after you're already on top of the hill, then do it. After the morning glassing session is over, you need to continue hunting hard all day long. Don't return to camp and hang out and wait for the evening hunt, stay on the mountain all day long.

Not only do you need to be the first one on top of the mountain in the morning, but it is just as important to make sure you are the last one off the mountain in the evening. Most people start heading down an hour before dark so that they arrive in camp just as it gets dark. This doesn't cut it. Stay on the mountain until it is dark and then hike to camp using your headlamp. Maximize your chances by spending every minute of available daylight on the hill.

Most people find they can do this for one or two days, but what separates a successful trophy hunter from everyone else is that they can repeat this day in and day out. This is where all of your off season training that we will talk about later will pay off dearly. Without it, you simply cannot hunt as hard as you need to give yourself the best possible chance at harvesting a trophy buck. One thing you need to keep in mind is that sometimes trophy mule deer hunting is not fun. Sometimes it wears on you physically and mentally and you find yourself questioning your sanity for putting yourself through such punishment day after day. There have been times that I have told myself that I should just give it up and take up something a lot easier, like stamp collecting. But there's something about trophy hunting mulies that keeps bringing me back year after year.

Hunting hard by itself is not enough to be successful year after year because there are a lot of other hunters out there that also hunt very hard every year. In order to separate yourself from everyone else, you will need to hunt smart as well. This is the part that if you read this book and apply what I say, I believe it will make a difference in your ability to harvest trophy mule deer bucks.

One of the main reasons people are unsuccessful at putting their tag on a trophy mule deer buck is because they are unwilling to adapt their hunting styles to fit the season in which they are hunting. The hunting method you use in early September, doesn't necessarily work during late October. You have to change your hunting methods according to varying deer behavior and weather. Think about it—what is going to separate you from the thousands of other hunters scouring the mountains during the hunting season?

Hunting smarter also means that you must get to know your quarry's habits. The more you learn about his capabilities and limitations, the better success you will have at hunting him. You must literally learn when he eats, sleeps and drinks. You need to pit your strengths against his weaknesses. Think about it, when a coach prepares for a big game or a boxer for a fight, they study their opponent and learn their weaknesses. You need to do the same.

That is the basis of this whole book—pitting your strength against the mule deer's weaknesses. What is the mule deer's greatest weakness? He has to eat. This is the one thing that will make him leave the security of his hidey hole in the timber during the hunting season. He has to eat. What is your strength? Optics! I feel that the quality optics available nowadays have given hunters a huge advantage over their quarry. What does all this mean? It should be fairly clear. Your best odds of finding that buck of a lifetime are to spot him while he is feeding. That is where this book comes in. Throughout the pages of this book I will not only be talking about how to glass effectively, but a little bit about mule deer behavior, which will help you with where and when to glass.

Jim Hamilton

The Mule Deer

(Odocoileus hemionus)

Mule deer has the broadest distribution of any antlered game animal in western North America. They range from northern Canada all the way down to central Mexico. They inhabit the arid deserts, the high mountain peaks, as well as every type of habitat in between. While deer behavior and habits differ from region to region, their needs for survival remain the same. I pick up every article, scientific paper and radio collar study that I can in order to learn more about them and how they utilize their habitat from day to day and how that routine changes at different times of the year.

As mentioned earlier, deer are true survivors. Every action and movement they perform is merely a function of survival. Deer do not just wander around the high country aimlessly. They do not simply get up from their bed and decide to take a stroll to see what is going on in their neighborhood. When they are moving, they are moving for a reason. Every function they perform requires the burning of energy, and in order to survive, they must take in more energy than they burn during their daily routine. Therefore, they know where to find the best available food sources that require the least amount of energy and movement. They also know what cover provides the best protection from predators.

Habitat

To better understand mule deer behavior, you must first learn a little bit about habitat. Habitat is where the mule deer lives and can vary greatly from one area to another. There are so many types of mule deer habitat that it would be impossible to cover them all, so I would recommend when researching the area you plan on hunting, to take the time to learn a little bit about the type of habitat that the deer utilize in that *region*. One thing to keep in mind is that although habitat can vary greatly in its appearance, all good mule deer habitat has four things in common: space, cover, water and food. As seasons change, so does the types of habitat they use.

Capture of a mule deer for a telemetry study in southwestern Wyoming.

Space

All good habitats must have enough space to support the mule deer population that inhabits it. If it doesn't, overgrazing can occur and the entire deer population can suffer because of it. Although this may have been a problem years ago, it isn't too much of a factor nowadays. It is rarely the case that you see the mule deer population at or above the carrying capacity of the available habitat. The overgrazing nowadays normally is because of domestic livestock, rather than too many deer.

Cover

Cover is very important in all habitats. It doesn't matter if you're hunting the desert or at 12,000 feet, deer need to have cover. Cover is important for two reasons. The most obvious reason is to provide protection from predators—both two-legged and four-legged. The second is it provides protection from the elements. In the summer, cover provides important shade that allows deer to keep from overheating. During hot weather, the only place you will find deer is in the shade of available cover. They will normally bed down with their front legs extended out to help dissipate body heat which helps keep them cool.

Water

Water is usually not a problem in the high country, but in the lower more arid places, such as Arizona and southern Utah, water availability is a big factor in where you will find deer. Sitting on a water source in those areas can be very productive.

Jim Hamilton

During hot weather, the only place you will find deer is in the shade of available cover.

In the higher country, deer seem to get enough water out of the plants that they eat. You could sit on a water source for days and never see a deer utilize it. That is another reason why you must take the time to learn each individual area you will be hunting. What works in one area, will almost certainly not work in another.

Food

That brings us to the most important of the four—food. A few years ago there was a radio telemetry study done in Colorado that showed mule deer selected habitats primarily based on forage availability, while cover proved to be secondary. Deer are no different than you and I in the fact that they must eat several times throughout the day. They simply cannot remain bedded from sunup to sundown without grabbing small bites to eat throughout the day. They might not be up for long, but they will get up and eat. This is the greatest weakness of the mule deer that I have found. Therefore, to be successful at mule deer hunting, you must learn a little bit about their eating habits.

Deer are browsers and rely on many different plants to get the nutrition they require. Researchers have identified close to 800 different plant species that the mule deer in the Rocky Mountains use for food. Of these 800 plants, 60% are forbs, 25% are shrubs or trees and 12% are grasses. Mule deer very rarely concentrate on any one plant, they will move while feeding taking advantage of several different

29

species.

The plants a deer will eat varies throughout the year. This can dictate where you find them at different times of the year. During the spring, mule deer will be found eating mainly grasses and forbs which are greening up as the temperatures become warmer. As the grasses dry in the summer, deer will tend to stop eating them and start eating more forbs and shrubs. In late summer, deer will still eat forbs, but they will start to browse more and more on shrubs. During hunting season, shrubs will make up about 75% of their food intake, while forbs will fill the remaining 25% of their diet.

Since deer are mainly browsing on shrubs in the fall, I am constantly looking and trying to identify the ones that they tend to favor. After all of my years in the field, I believe the two most important shrubs in their diet are antelope bitterbrush and mountain mahogany. I normally find the antelope bitterbrush at the higher elevations, while the mountain mahogany is usually found at mid to low elevations. Willows, when present, always seem to attract deer as well.

A Mule Deer's Senses

Of all his senses, a mule deer relies the most on his sense of smell.

Another thing you must do to become a better hunter is learn to respect the senses of the mule deer. Mule deer have very keen senses. Their eyesight is amazing. They can pinpoint your location from very long distances if you are moving. Although they have tremendous eyesight, their vision does have a weakness. If you are stationary, they seem to have a hard time identifying you, but any movement at all and they will spot you instantly. It doesn't matter how far away you are, if you are moving, you are at a disadvantage.

Mule deer also have very good hearing. The reason they are called mule deer is because of their rather large ears that look like those of a mule. Trust me, they are not just for looks. With all of that surface area their ears are amazing and can pick up even the slightest sound. A good example to show you how effective their ears are is to cup your hands behind your ears with elbows out. The sounds will be amplified ten-fold. That goes to show you how good mule deer can gather sounds with their large, oversized ears.

Reading mule deer radio collar studies can be very valuable. The information you can learn regarding mule deer behavior will make you a much better hunter.

That brings us to their third sense—their sense of smell. To me, this is the mule deer's strongest sense. If you don't have the wind in your favor during a stalk, it will never be successful no matter how careful you are. Their sense of smell is probably the sense that mule deer rely on the most. Several times I have had the wind in my favor and had deer watch me move slowly through the trees at relatively close distances without having them panic and run. Then the wind changed directions and I could see them raise their nose in the air and they were gone immediately. They don't waste any time once they smell human presence.

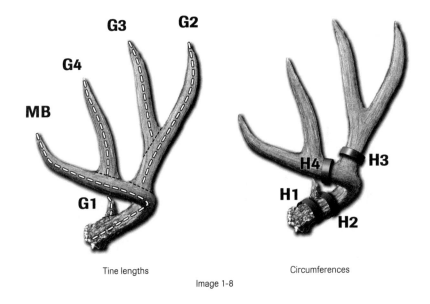

Tine lengths   Circumferences

Image 1-8

B&C Scoring System

Throughout this book, all of the scores I refer to will be tabulated according to the Boone and Crockett Club scoring system. This system has long been the standard for judging trophy mule deer. It is a system that rewards long tines, mass and symmetry.

The B&C Club was originally founded by United States president Theodore Roosevelt in 1887. At that time, there were no regulated hunting seasons for taking big game, but Roosevelt, along with several friends, fortunately had enough foresight to see the need. They built the club around the philosophy of "Fair Chase."

The club released its first record book in 1932, entitled, *Records of North American Big Game*. The book used a measuring system developed by Dr. James L. Clark. The system used very simple measurements to rank trophies such as, the length of skull, or the longer antler, plus a base circumference. The second book released by the club in 1939, also used very simple measurements to rank trophies. One of the chapters, however, was by Grancel Fitz and it covered his idea of a more complex system of measurements that would more appropriately rank the trophies.

In 1947, the club started annual Big Game Competitions with the winner being decided by a panel of judges. While these competitions were very popular, the results were merely the opinions of the judges. The club still saw a need to revamp the system to be fairer in the ranking of trophies.

Then in 1949, a committee was formed to devise a fairer scoring system. The committee combined certain parts of Clark's and Fitz's methods to form the measuring system which was adopted by the Boone and Crockett Club in 1950. Once this system was adopted, it quickly became the broadly accepted method of measuring North American big game.

The club publishes two sets of books: their Awards Program records book and their All-Time records book. The two books differ greatly in important ways. The awards program books are released every three years. The awards book only includes entries which were entered in that specific three year period. The awards book has a minimum entry score for mule deer of 180 for typicals and 215 for non-typicals. The all-time records book is only published every six years and includes all entries since the inception of the club. The all-time book has higher minimum scores: 190 for typicals and 230 for non-typicals. On the next few pages you will find copies of the most current B&C score sheets.

Boone and Crockett's scoring system for mule deer is based on the deer's typical frame. The typical frame score is comprised of 19 total measurements—nine measurements on each antler along with the inside spread of the main beams.

Image 1-8 shows where to properly take the nine measurements on each antler. These consist of five tine length measurements known as the G1, G2, G3, G4 and main beams, as well as four circumference measurements known as H1, H2, H3 and H4. When all 19 measurements are totaled, you will have the typical frame B&C gross score. Differences in measurements from side to side, along with the length of any non-typical points are then deducted; giving you the typical frame net B&C score. A non-typical is scored the exact same way except the non-typical points are added to the net typical frame, rather than deducted. The net score is the only score that B&C lists in their books.

Boone & Crockett Entry

So how do you go about getting your once-in-a-lifetime trophy scored for entry into the Boone and Crockett Club's record book? The first thing you will have to do is contact the Boone and Crockett Club to locate an official measurer in your area. You and the measurer will need to agree on a time and place to have your antlers scored. Remember, all measurers are volunteering their time, so you might have to work around their schedule. The measurer will score your antlers on the appropriate form (see typical & non-typical score sheets). If the antlers meet, or exceed, either the awards minimums, or all-time minimums, it qualifies for entry into the records book and you will have to submit the following to the B&C Club:

- Original score sheet signed and dated by official measurer.

- Four photos (front, rear, right & left sides) of the rack.

- Entry affidavit (back of score sheet) either witnessed by an official measurer or notarized.

- Completed Hunter, Guide and Hunt Information Form.

- Copy of hunting license.

- $25 registration fee.

Records of
North American
Big Game

250 Station Drive
Missoula, MT 59801
(406) 542-1888

BOONE AND CROCKETT CLUB®
OFFICIAL SCORING SYSTEM FOR NORTH AMERICAN BIG GAME TROPHIES

TYPICAL
MULE DEER AND BLACKTAIL DEER

MINIMUM SCORES	AWARDS	ALL-TIME
mule deer	180	190
Columbia blacktail	125	135
Sitka blacktail	100	108

KIND OF DEER (check one)
☐ mule deer
☐ Columbia blacktail
☐ Sitka blacktail

Detail of Point Measurement

Abnormal Points	
Right Antler	Left Antler

| SUBTOTALS | |
| TOTAL TO E | |

SEE OTHER SIDE FOR INSTRUCTIONS			COLUMN 1	COLUMN 2	COLUMN 3	COLUMN 4
			Spread Credit	Right Antler	Left Antler	Difference
A. No. Points on Right Antler		No. Points on Left Antler				
B. Tip to Tip Spread		C. Greatest Spread				
D. Inside Spread of Main Beams		SPREAD CREDIT MAY EQUAL BUT NOT EXCEED LONGER MAIN BEAM				
E. Total of Lengths of Abnormal Points						
F. Length of Main Beam						
G-1. Length of First Point, If Present						
G-2. Length of Second Point						
G-3. Length of Third Point, If Present						
G-4. Length of Fourth Point, If Present						
H-1. Circumference at Smallest Place Between Burr and First Point						
H-2. Circumference at Smallest Place Between First and Second Points						
H-3. Circumference at Smallest Place Between Main Beam and Third Point						
H-4. Circumference at Smallest Place Between Second and Fourth Points						
		TOTALS				

ADD	Column 1		Exact Locality Where Killed:
	Column 2		Date Killed: Hunter:
	Column 3		Trophy Owner: Telephone #:
	Subtotal		Trophy Owner's Address:
SUBTRACT Column 4			Trophy Owner's E-mail: Guide's Name:
FINAL SCORE			Remarks: (Mention Any Abnormalities or Unique Qualities)

OM I.D. Number

COPYRIGHT © 2006 BY BOONE AND CROCKETT CLUB®

B&C Scoring System

I, _____ , certify that I have measured this trophy on _____
   PRINT NAME   MM/DD/YYYY

at _____
   STREET ADDRESS   CITY   STATE/PROVINCE

and that these measurements and data are, to the best of my knowledge and belief, made in accordance with the instructions given.

Witness: _____ Signature: _____ I.D. Number ☐☐☐☐
                                              B&C OFFICIAL MEASURER

INSTRUCTIONS FOR MEASURING TYPICAL MULE AND BLACKTAIL DEER

All measurements must be made with a 1/4-inch wide flexible steel tape to the nearest one-eighth of an inch. (Note: A flexible steel cable can be used to measure points and main beams only.) Enter fractional figures in eighths, without reduction. Official measurements cannot be taken until the antlers have air dried for at least 60 days after the animal was killed.

A. **Number of Points on Each Antler:** To be counted a point, the projection must be at least one inch long, with length exceeding width at one inch or more of length. All points are measured from tip of point to nearest edge of beam. Beam tip is counted as a point but not measured as a point. **Point totals do not add into the final score.**

B. **Tip to Tip Spread** is measured between tips of main beams. **Tip to tip spread does not add into the final score.**

C. **Greatest Spread** is measured between perpendiculars at a right angle to the center line of the skull at widest part, whether across main beams or points. **Greatest spread does not add into the final score.**

D. **Inside Spread of Main Beams** is measured at a right angle to the center line of the skull at widest point between main beams. Enter this measurement again as the Spread Credit **if** it is less than or equal to the length of the longer main beam; if greater, enter longer main beam length for Spread Credit.

E. **Total of Lengths of all Abnormal Points:** Abnormal Points are those non-typical in location such as points originating from a point (exception: G-3 originates from G-2 in perfectly normal fashion) or from bottom or sides of main beam, or any points beyond the normal pattern of five (including beam tip) per antler. Measure each abnormal point in usual manner and enter in appropriate blanks.

F. **Length of Main Beam** is measured from the center of the lowest outside edge of burr over the outer side to the most distant point of the Main Beam. The point of beginning is that point on the burr where the center line along the outer side of the beam intersects the burr, then following generally the line of the illustration.

G-1-2-3-4. **Length of Normal Points:** Normal points are the brow tines and the upper and lower forks as shown in the illustration. They are measured from nearest edge of main beam over outer curve to tip. Lay the tape along the outer curve of the beam so that the top edge of the tape coincides with the top edge of the beam on both sides of point to determine the baseline for point measurement. Record point lengths in appropriate blanks.

H-1-2-3-4. **Circumferences** are taken as detailed in illustration for each measurement. If brow point is missing, take H-1 and H-2 at smallest place between burr and G-2. If G-3 is missing, take H-3 halfway between the base and tip of G-2. If G-4 is missing, take H-4 halfway between G-2 and tip of main beam.

ENTRY AFFIDAVIT FOR ALL HUNTER-TAKEN TROPHIES

For the purpose of entry into the Boone and Crockett Club's® records, North American big game harvested by the use of the following methods or under the following conditions are ineligible:

I. Spotting or herding game from the air, followed by landing in its vicinity for the purpose of pursuit and shooting;
II. Herding or chasing with the aid of any motorized equipment;
III. Use of electronic communication devices to guide hunters to game, artificial lighting, electronic light intensifying devices (night vision optics), sights with built-in electronic range-finding capabilities, thermal imaging equipment, electronic game calls or cameras/timers/motion tracking devices that transmit images and other information to the hunter;
IV. Confined by artificial barriers, including escape-proof fenced enclosures;
V. Transplanted for the purpose of commercial shooting;
VI. By the use of traps or pharmaceuticals;
VII. While swimming, helpless in deep snow, or helpless in any other natural or artificial medium;
VIII. On another hunter's license;
IX. Not in full compliance with the game laws or regulations of the federal government or of any state, province, territory, or tribal council on reservations or tribal lands;

I certify that the trophy scored on this chart was not taken in violation of the conditions listed above. In signing this statement, I understand that if the information provided on this entry is found to be misrepresented or fraudulent in any respect, it will not be accepted into the Awards Program and 1) all of my prior entries are subject to deletion from future editions of **Records of North American Big Game** 2) future entries may not be accepted.

FAIR CHASE, as defined by the Boone and Crockett Club®, is the ethical, sportsmanlike and lawful pursuit and taking of any free-ranging wild, native North American big game animal in a manner that does not give the hunter an improper advantage over such game animals.

The Boone and Crockett Club® may exclude the entry of any animal that it deems to have been taken in an unethical manner or under conditions deemed inappropriate by the Club.

Date: _____ Signature of Hunter: _____
                                 (SIGNATURE MUST BE WITNESSED BY AN OFFICIAL MEASURER OR A NOTARY PUBLIC.)

Date: _____ Signature of Notary or Official Measurer: _____

35

Records of
North American
Big Game

250 Station Drive
Missoula, MT 59801
(406) 542-1888

BOONE AND CROCKETT CLUB®
OFFICIAL SCORING SYSTEM FOR NORTH AMERICAN BIG GAME TROPHIES

NON-TYPICAL
MULE DEER AND BLACKTAIL DEER

MINIMUM SCORES		
	AWARDS	ALL-TIME
mule deer	215	230
Columbia blacktail	155	155
Sitka blacktail	118	118

KIND OF DEER (check one)
- ☐ mule deer
- ☐ Columbia blacktail
- ☐ Sitka blacktail

Abnormal Points	
Right Antler	Left Antler
SUBTOTALS	
E. TOTAL	

Detail of Point Measurement

SEE OTHER SIDE FOR INSTRUCTIONS		COLUMN 1	COLUMN 2	COLUMN 3	COLUMN 4
A. No. Points on Right Antler	No. Points on Left Antler	Spread Credit	Right Antler	Left Antler	Difference
B. Tip to Tip Spread	C. Greatest Spread				
D. Inside Spread of Main Beams	SPREAD CREDIT MAY EQUAL BUT NOT EXCEED LONGER MAIN BEAM				
F. Length of Main Beam					
G-1. Length of First Point, If Present					
G-2. Length of Second Point					
G-3. Length of Third Point, If Present					
G-4. Length of Fourth Point, If Present					
H-1. Circumference at Smallest Place Between Burr and First Point					
H-2. Circumference at Smallest Place Between First and Second Points					
H-3. Circumference at Smallest Place Between Main Beam and Third Point					
H-4. Circumference at Smallest Place Between Second and Fourth Points					
	TOTALS				

ADD	Column 1		Exact Locality Where Killed:	
	Column 2		Date Killed:	Hunter:
	Column 3		Trophy Owner:	Telephone #:
	Subtotal		Trophy Owner's Address:	
SUBTRACT Column 4			Trophy Owner's E-mail:	Guide's Name:
	Subtotal		Remarks: (Mention Any Abnormalities or Unique Qualities)	
	ADD Line E Total			
	FINAL SCORE			

OM I.D. Number

I, _____ , certify that I have measured this trophy on _____
        PRINT NAME   MM/DD/YYYYY

at _____
   STREET ADDRESS   CITY   STATE/PROVINCE

and that these measurements and data are, to the best of my knowledge and belief, made in accordance with the instructions given.

Witness: _____ Signature: _____ I.D. Number ▢▢▢▢
                                              B&C OFFICIAL MEASURER

INSTRUCTIONS FOR MEASURING NON-TYPICAL MULE DEER AND BLACKTAIL

All measurements must be made with a 1/4-inch wide flexible steel tape to the nearest one-eighth of an inch. (Note: A flexible steel cable can be used to measure points and main beams only.) Enter fractional figures in eighths, without reduction. Official measurements cannot be taken until the antlers have air dried for at least 60 days after the animal was killed.

A. Number of Points on Each Antler: To be counted a point, the projection must be at least one inch long, with length exceeding width at one inch or more of length. All points are measured from tip of point to nearest edge of beam as illustrated. Beam tip is counted as a point but not measured as a point. **Point totals do not add into the final score.**

B. Tip to Tip Spread is measured between tips of main beams. **Tip to tip spread does not add into the final score.**

C. Greatest Spread is measured between perpendiculars at a right angle to the center line of the skull at widest part, whether across main beams or points. **Greatest spread does not add into the final score.**

D. Inside Spread of Main Beams is measured at a right angle to the center line of the skull at widest point between main beams. Enter this measurement again as the Spread Credit if it is less than or equal to the length of the longer main beam; if greater, enter longer main beam length for Spread Credit.

E. Total of Lengths of all Abnormal Points: Abnormal Points are those non-typical in location such as points originating from a point (exception: G-3 originates from G-2 in perfectly normal fashion) or from bottom or sides of main beam, or any points beyond the normal pattern of five (including beam tip) per antler. Measure each abnormal point in usual manner and enter in appropriate blanks.

F. Length of Main Beam is measured from the center of the lowest outside edge of burr over the outer side to the most distant point of the main beam. The point of beginning is that point on the burr where the center line along the outer side of the beam intersects the burr, then following generally the line of the illustration.

G-1-2-3-4. Length of Normal Points: Normal points are the brow tines and the upper and lower forks as shown in the illustration. They are measured from nearest edge of main beam over outer curve to tip. Lay the tape along the outer curve of the beam so that the top edge of the tape coincides with the top edge of the beam on both sides of point to determine the baseline for point measurement. Record point lengths in appropriate blanks.

H-1-2-3-4. Circumferences are taken as detailed in illustration for each measurement. If brow point is missing, take H-1 and H-2 at smallest place between burr and G-2. If G-3 is missing, take H-3 halfway between the base and tip of G-2. If G-4 is missing, take H-4 halfway between G-2 and tip of main beam.

ENTRY AFFIDAVIT FOR ALL HUNTER-TAKEN TROPHIES

For the purpose of entry into the Boone and Crockett Club's® records, North American big game harvested by the use of the following methods or under the following conditions are ineligible:

   I. Spotting or herding game from the air, followed by landing in its vicinity for the purpose of pursuit and shooting;

   II. Herding or chasing with the aid of any motorized equipment;

   III. Use of electronic communication devices to guide hunters to game, artificial lighting, electronic light intensifying devices (night vision optics), sights with built-in electronic range-finding capabilities, thermal imaging equipment, electronic game calls or cameras/timers/motion tracking devices that transmit images and other information to the hunter;

   IV. Confined by artificial barriers, including escape-proof fenced enclosures;

   V. Transplanted for the purpose of commercial shooting;

   VI. By the use of traps or pharmaceuticals;

   VII. While swimming, helpless in deep snow, or helpless in any other natural or artificial medium;

   VIII. On another hunter's license;

   IX. Not in full compliance with the game laws or regulations of the federal government or of any state, province, territory, or tribal council on reservations or tribal lands;

I certify that the trophy scored on this chart was not taken in violation of the conditions listed above. In signing this statement, I understand that if the information provided on this entry is found to be misrepresented or fraudulent in any respect, it will not be accepted into the Awards Program and 1) all of my prior entries are subject to deletion from future editions of **Records of North American Big Game** 2) future entries may not be accepted.

FAIR CHASE, as defined by the Boone and Crockett Club®, is the ethical, sportsmanlike and lawful pursuit and taking of any free-ranging wild, native North American big game animal in a manner that does not give the hunter an improper advantage over such game animals.

The Boone and Crockett Club® may exclude the entry of any animal that it deems to have been taken in an unethical manner or under conditions deemed inappropriate by the Club.

Date: _____ Signature of Hunter: _____
                                              (SIGNATURE MUST BE WITNESSED BY AN OFFICIAL MEASURER OR A NOTARY PUBLIC.)

Date: _____ Signature of Notary or Official Measurer: _____

This buck is right at the 30-inch mark. I simply couldn't pass him up. These days, I don't care how wide a buck is. I am looking for a buck with a high scoring typical frame.

Setting Your Standards

In trophy hunting, one of the first things you will have to do is set a realistic standard for yourself. When I turned 14 and was old enough to hunt, I already had the mentality that I wanted to harvest the biggest buck on the mountain. The problem was, at that age I found it rather tough to pass up smaller bucks. I simply could not pass up a mature four-point buck. This was not all bad. I feel that harvesting the smaller bucks early on in my hunting career helped hone my hunting skills and gave me valuable shooting experience.

This is where most people struggle. When most hunters see that first 170 B&C mature four point on opening morning, it's over. It took me several years to get past shooting the first mature buck I saw. Now, I don't have any problems passing up bucks. There have been several occasions that I have passed up bucks over 30 inches wide because they either didn't score well, or they were willow horned and not very impressive.

The most important thing I am looking for is a big typical frame. I will take a 24-inch 190 buck any day over a 30-incher that scores 170. Keep in mind that those are the standards that I have set for myself. A lot of people I talk to are just looking for a buck that breaks the magical 30-inch mark. It doesn't matter if the buck scores 160, 170 or 180, as long as it is wide. And that's fine. Everybody has to set his or her own standards.

The bottom line is that it doesn't matter what you set your standards at. The main thing is once you have your standards set, stick to them. If you don't and you continually shoot deer that are below the standards you have set, odds are, you will never harvest a true, trophy-sized mule deer.

The standard that I see most people set for themselves is the magical 30-inch mark. If a 30-inch buck is your goal, you have your work cut out for you. How rare are they? Let's take a look at some historical data to determine how few 30-inch bucks are actually harvested.

The first set of data we will look at was taken on the Kaibab between 1936 and

1951. During this 16-year period, antler spread measurements were taken on 8,781 deer which were harvested from the famous Kaibab deer herd in Arizona. Out of the 8,781 mule deer bucks, 93.7% of them measured less than 30 inches wide. Only 6.3% of the bucks reached, or exceeded, the magical 30-inch mark. Keep in mind, this data was collected from one of the premiere mule deer areas of the Rockies. Most areas will be considerably less than the six percent. The Wyoming Game and Fish Department also collected similar data on its Wyoming Range mule deer herd since 1989.

Gary Fralick, a wildlife biologist from Thayne, Wyoming, was kind enough to provide me with all of the data that the WGFD has collected. The Wyoming Range mule deer herd (Hunt Areas 134, 135, 143-145, 147) is managed as a special management deer herd with a postseason buck to doe ratio of 30-45 bucks per 100 does. Hunting seasons during the 1993-1996 seasons were designed to minimize harvest in order to allow the population to increase toward the postseason population objective of 50,000 deer. Beginning in 1989 a concerted effort was made to collect antler width measurements and incisor teeth from harvested buck deer for aging

Wyoming Game and Fish Department Check Station Data

Spread (Inches)	1989–1995 (781 Total Bucks)				1996–2001 (905 Total Bucks)			
	# Heads Measured	Avg. Age	Range of Ages	Heads Measuring Less (%)	# Heads Measured	Avg. Age	Range of Ages	Heads Measuring Less (%)
8	1	2	2	0.0%	1	1	1	0.0%
9	1	2	2	0.1%	2	1	1	0.1%
10	0	N/A	N/A	N/A	3	1	1	0.3%
11	4	1.5	1-2	0.3%	9	1.5	1-3	0.5%
12	8	2	1-3	0.8%	5	1	1	2.0%
13	13	2	1-3	2.0%	18	2	1-3	2.0%
14	23	2	1-3	3.0%	16	2	1-6	3.0%
15	42	2	1-4	6.0%	22	2	1-3	4.0%
16	54	2	1-4	12.0%	37	3	1-6	7.0%
17	53	3	2-5	19.0%	52	2	2-5	11.0%
18	63	3	2-4	25.0%	51	3	2-5	17.0%
19	43	3	2-6	33.0%	46	3	2-7	23.0%
20	55	3	2-9	39.0%	51	3	2-6	28.0%
21	53	3	2-7	46.0%	57	3	2-10	33.0%
22	67	4	2-10	53.0%	82	4	2-9	40.0%
23	55	4	3-8	61.0%	53	4	2-8	49.0%
24	49	4	3-8	68.0%	86	4	2-9	54.0%
25	51	4.5	3-10	75.0%	79	5	2-9	64.0%
26	44	4.5	3-9	81.0%	55	5	3-9	73.0%
27	40	4.5	3-9	87.0%	62	5	3-9	79.0%
28	24	4.5	2-9	92.0%	42	5	3-9	86.0%
29	14	4.5	3-6	95.0%	27	5	3-8	91.0%
30	12	5.5	4-9	97.0%	20	5	3-8	94.0%
31	6	5	4-6	98.0%	16	5	3-8	96.0%
32	4	5	3-8	99.0%	11	4	3-7	98.0%
33	0	N/A	N/A	N/A	5	6	5-8	99.0%
34	0	N/A	N/A	N/A	2	4	4-5	99.3%
35	2	6	5-7	99.7%	1	7	7	99.5%
36+	0	N/A	N/A	100.0%	3	6	5-6	99.7%

Table 1-1

The 6% Rule

If a 30-inch buck is what you have your sights set on, more often than not, there is a good chance that you will be going home without punching your deer tag. As a general rule, only about 6% of the mule deer harvested in the West meet or exceed the magical 30-inch mark. Several sets of data collected in Arizona and Wyoming throughout the years show that at best, your odds of taking a buck of this caliber are 6% or less.

Between 1936 and 1951, antler data was collected from 8,781 deer harvested on the world famous Kaibab in Arizona. Of the 8,781 mule deer bucks harvested, only 6.3% of the bucks reached, or exceeded, the magical 30-inch mark.

The Wyoming Game and Fish Department has also collected similar data on its Wyoming Range mule deer herd since 1989. During the 13-year period between 1989 and 2001, antler width measurements were taken on 1686 harvested bucks. Only 4.8% of the bucks eclipsed the 30-inch mark.

The average between the two states is 5.5%. Keep in mind, this data was collected from two of the premiere mule deer areas of the West and that most areas will be considerably less than the six percent.

purposes using the cementum annuli method. During the 13-year period (1989-2001) a total of 1686 bucks were aged and their outside antler width measured. Table 1-1 shows the data separated into two different time frames. The first time frame is from 1989-1995. There were 781 bucks checked during this period and only 24 of them had an antler spread of 30 inches or better. That means that only 3% of the bucks reached the magical 30-inch mark.

The second set of data was taken from 1996-2001. A total of 905 bucks were checked with 58 of them that met or exceeded the 30-inch mark. Although the amount of bucks reaching the 30-inch mark was up from the previous period, only 6% of the bucks checked were 30 inches or better. During the entire period, 4.8% of the total bucks measured made the 30-inch mark. Now you can start to see how rare a 30-inch buck really is.

There is also a definite correlation between age and antler width according to the data collected. Although there were ages from 3 to 9 years of age for bucks that met or exceeded the 30-inch mark, according to this table, the 30-inch buck you are looking for will normally average 5 to 5.5 years of age.

It doesn't take much evaluation to determine that this buck's spread is over 30 inches. Bart Hamilton took this magnificent 36½-inch wide buck on opening morning in Wyoming.

Field Judging

So now that you have your standard set, how do you go about determining if a buck is 30 inches wide or will make the B&C minimum? Let's take a look at the characteristics that I am looking for to determine a 30-inch spread. Over the years I have measured the ear width on many mature bucks. The spread of the ears from tip to tip, when the ears are in their normal relaxed position, normally range between 18 and 22 inches wide from tip to tip. That means that most mature bucks will average 20 inches from tip to tip on their ears. With this average in mind, look at Image 1-11. I would be looking for a buck that has about 5 inches of antler that is out past the tips of the ears on both sides.

While a buck with a 30-inch spread is indeed a fine trophy, most hardcore mule deer hunters will agree that harvesting a buck large enough to qualify for the B&C book is the ultimate achievement. You've definitely got your work cut out for you if this is your goal. A 30-inch buck is rare, but a record book buck is extremely rare.

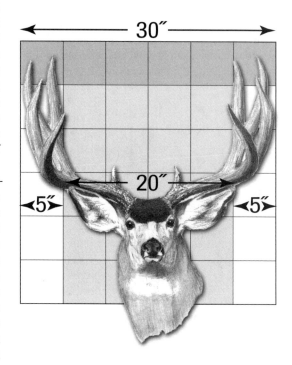

Image 1-11

How do you know if that buck you are looking at through your scope is large enough to make the book? In all of the years of pursuing and watching trophy mule deer, I have come to one conclusion: You know a Boone and Crockett buck when you see one. You don't have to sit there trying to figure out how long his tines are, how much mass does he have, how long are his main beams—there will be no doubt. I have been fortunate to have killed two bucks that have typical frames that exceed the B&C all-time minimums, and on both occasions, there was no hesitation or sizing them up. I knew instantly that they were *big*. If you do have to sit there and try to figure out if he is big enough, odds are, you'll be disappointed when you walk up to him laying there on the ground. This is where the term ground shrinkage came from.

Average Typical B&C Score Makeup

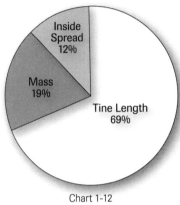

Chart 1-12

If I have plenty of time, I can normally estimate a buck's score within two inches. I can honestly say that when I am looking at a buck, I don't try adding any measurements in my head. I have simply looked at enough deer over the years that I can usually judge them very accurately just by looking at the overall antler configuration. There is no substitute for accurately judging mule deer other than looking over as many as you possibly can. I realize that not everyone has the luxury of observing as many mule deer during the year as I do, so we will cover the basics of what to look for: tine length, mass and inside spread.

In order to accurately field judge a buck's B&C score, you must realize the makeup of the score as far as mass, inside spread and tine length are concerned. The main message that I want to get across is that tine length is the most important thing to look for. Mass and inside spread, although important to the score, are not near as critical. There are a lot of bucks that make the B&C book that don't have much for mass, but have extremely long tines. You won't see very many bucks that qualify with a lot of mass and very little tine length. Tine length is definitely the most important.

Several years back I became an official measurer for the Boone and Crockett Club. Before that, I had the privilege to have scored for various other organizations. Over the years, I have been able to lay my hands on some pretty impressive racks. To show you how important tine length is, I dug through all of my files and got out all of my mule deer score sheets that I have filled out throughout the

Image 1-13

Image 1-14

years. All of the racks scored between 185 and 205 B&C typical. I ran the numbers on every score sheet and below is the average makeup of all the scores for the typical frames on the bucks.

A look at Chart 1-12 shows you just how important tine length (including main beams) is in the total score. It makes up 69% of the total B&C score, while mass and inside spread combined only make up 31% of the score.

So knowing how important tine length is in determining a buck's score, how do you go about judging the buck's score in a matter of seconds during the hunting season? First off, let's be realistic, are you going to sit there and try to guess and tabulate all of the 19 measurements that it takes to come up with a B&C gross score? I don't think so. Normally you don't have that much time.

One thing that can help with field judging is being familiar with different antler configurations. These configurations often have unique characteristics that you can rely on when sizing up a buck. You will have bucks with strong fronts and weak backs, bucks with strong backs and weak fronts and literally everything in between. I would like to point out some different traits between bucks with strong backs versus strong fronts.

If you will look at Image 1-13, this image depicts a buck that has weak fronts and strong backs. Bucks that normally have this antler configuration are usually narrow and tall. Their inside spread can often be less than 20 inches and their main beams are typically short. Because these bucks can be so tall, oftentimes their back forks are strong enough that they can make up for the weak fronts. But in order to do this, they must have back forks that appear huge.

Image 1-14 depicts a buck with big fronts and weak backs. When you see a buck with strong fronts, you really need to start paying attention. These bucks are a lot rarer than the buck with weak fronts and typically can score very well. They are usually wider and appear not to be quite as tall. Their inside spread is typically over 20 inches and so are their main beams.

Image 1-15

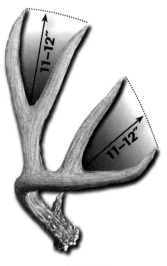

Image 1-16

This combination adds to the score drastically. As long as they don't have a super weak back fork, they will generally score very well.

Then you have the bucks with both strong fronts and backs like the buck in Image 1-15. These are a rarity indeed. This kind of buck should really jump out at you. As I said earlier, there should be no doubt when you see a buck of this caliber that has strong fronts and backs and reaches the B&C all-time minimum score of 190.

If there is one tip that I could give in sizing up a buck in a matter of seconds out in the field, if you only had time to look at one characteristic, it would be to look at how deep his forks appear to be. If you will look at Image 1-16, this is what I am looking for. If they appear to be 11 to 12 inches deep, both front and back, and everything else looks to be average for a mature buck, (no noticeable short points) I am confident that I am looking at a buck that will net right at or just over the B&C minimum of 190. It's that simple. I feel that this is the simplest approach to sizing up a buck that will be right at the B&C minimum typical score of 190.

Non-Typicals
THE "WOW" FACTOR

Non-typicals are just that – non-typical. They literally come in all shapes and sizes. Some have huge typical frames with lots of extras that score very well, while others don't score very well at all but are equally as impressive. The old saying, "The trophy is in the eye of the beholder," really comes into play as far as non-typicals are concerned.

One of the most common benchmarks for non-typicals I see people trying to reach is harvesting a buck that scores over the 200-inch B&C mark. To me, when it comes to non-typicals, the score is secondary to the buck's "Wow" factor. What is the "Wow" factor? It should be pretty self explanatory. It is also known as the "Holy #@$%" factor to some people. You get the point.

Although a well scoring typical frame is the main feature I am looking for in a buck's headgear, when it comes to a non-typical, character is the most important feature I am looking for. For example, I am willing to overlook the fact that a buck is missing a G3 on one side if his antlers are heavy and he has an 8-inch droptine on his right antler.

The best advice I can give you on field judging non-typicals is don't worry about the score, you should be more concerned about the buck's "Wow" factor.

Steve's buck has 21 total points and a 33¼-inch outside spread. The buck was large enough to qualify for the B&C all-time record book.

The 21 Point Buck

By Steve James

Oh no! This isn't the kind of deer I want to see first thing opening morning. A 27-inch four point with good mass was working his way toward me, across the base of an avalanche chute. He was one of those borderline bucks. I was tempted…but he wasn't the trophy I was hoping for. He finally saw me at 20 yards and made a hasty departure.

About 20 minutes later, after crossing the basin and working up the other side, I saw him.

This part of Wyoming is big country where you can see for miles. I was just doing my job, glassing a lot. At 500 yards, I caught a two second glimpse of something that looked real big. He walked into a tiny vertical finger of pines on a very steep northern exposure. I watched and waited, feeling very fortunate to have caught that glimpse.

A perfect place for a trophy buck! Three smaller bucks fed on the hillside below. From where I sat, he could not get off the hillside without me seeing him. But it was a very long shot. I hoped he would get up and come out into the open and feed.

It took about an hour before he finally stuck his head out of the pines. All I could see was the left side of his rack, his head and about half of his neck. He looked massive. Eagerly, I took a dead rest, held high and pulled the trigger. He came out of there like his ass was on fire. I chambered another round and touched off another shot just before he disappeared into the next finger of pines. It looked like he had stumbled a little bit…a good sign. But I couldn't see him.

Trophy Hunting

Not wanting to lose my vantage point, I waited 45 minutes. The suspense was killing me. Finally, I worked my way down the snow slides to the bottom and prepared to begin the "vertical part" up the other side when I saw him laying 30 yards away. He was in the bottom of a chute piled up against a downed tree. He had fallen down the mountain about 200 yards.

I thought, "He's got to have sticks caught in his rack – no, that's his rack." I screamed and danced around, and then I screamed and danced around some more. I couldn't believe it. He was gigantic! I haven't been the same since.

The rack was 33¼ inches wide and including the double eyeguards on both sides, had 21 points over one inch long. A four-inch drop tine growing out of the back of his rack had broken off in the fall. Miraculously it was still attached by a tiny six-inch piece of velvet, the only velvet left on his rack. Both my first and second shot hit him six inches apart in the chest. The Remington .270 with 140 grain reloads had done it again.

It took three hours to bone and cape him out. I loaded him into my empty pack and began the two-hour hike back to my tent. This country is steep. With a 100-pound pack, one slip and you're in big trouble. Ninety minutes after I arrived at camp, it began snowing so hard that the visibility dropped to 50 yards. I was really lucky.

I never saw another person that day until my hunting buddies arrived in camp about 4:00 p.m. Boy, did their jaws drop at the sight of my trophy. What a day. The next day, I spent six hours coming off the mountain with a 100 pound pack. I felt I had really earned my buck.

2003: 211⁷/₈ gross, 201²/₈ net B&C.

Back to Back

By Gavin Lovell

The Wyoming Range deer hunt opened the 15th of September, so Dale and I loaded up his horses and headed up on the 14th. On the way up to our spot we didn't run into anyone, which was a relief. Just before we got to our camp spot we saw a herd of elk on the far hillside just above camp with a big herd bull. We got camp set up just as it got dark and warmed up some MREs because Dale (he said it was me) forgot to bring the big bowl of pasta salad that my wife Nadine had made for us to eat that night. The next morning we got up before light and set up by a big log overlooking a deep canyon as the sun came up. We saw a few small bucks in the big canyon and on the hillside behind us, but nothing big enough to shoot. We decided to go over the hill to where we used to camp and where we have killed a few nice bucks and didn't see anything there either. We then decided to start working around the hill to a saddle where some aspens and a sagebrush opening were. As we worked around the edge I looked up and saw a buck moving away from us up the hill. I couldn't tell how big he was but could tell that he was a nice buck. I signaled to Dale but I think he had already seen the deer and was moving to get set up. I had to move around the base of a tree to get a clear look and when I did the big buck had stopped and was looking to the left with four other bucks. I could see his neck and the top of his shoulder and Dale didn't have a shot due to the four other bucks in front of the big guy.

The buck was about 200 yards, and next to a line of trees. I didn't think he was going to be around for long and seeing the incredible back forks on him I thought I better do something,

2004: 216⅛ gross, 206⁶⁄₈ net B&C.

so I put the crosshairs on his lower neck and pulled the trigger. After the boom of the .300 I heard a *thwaak!* and saw the big boy go down behind a big log and he didn't get up.

Dale and I started to walk over to it and we started to talk about what had just happened, still not knowing how big this guy actually was. I was anxious to get up there not only to see what he looked like, but just to make sure he was down for good. When we finally got up there we were both awestruck at the size of this dude. We were jumping around giving each other high fives and just about excited as we have ever been. After we finally settled down Dale said, "You just killed a book buck," and I didn't believe it. Dale said get the Leatherman out and he got a weed and my Leatherman and measured it at 210 gross B&C (within two inches of its official score). It was sure a pretty place where the deer was with the fall colors and the canyon and the big log, and believe it or not I had left the camera. Well, we got the deer all quartered out and went and got the horses and packed it back to camp. That night we went and looked for a buck for Dale but didn't see anything.

The next morning I went one way and Dale went the other and said we would meet after a while and go back over to the hill where I had killed the big buck the day before. We met up later and headed over the hill and got to the place where I had shot from. I told Dale that was the spot I had shot from and I found my brass and said I was going to keep it. Just as I said that we both looked up and saw a buck standing in the same place where I had killed mine. The other four bucks that were with mine where there also, as well as the bigger buck that had hooked in with them. The big buck had moved behind the tree line and was moving to the left toward a clearing but never made it all the way out in the clearing. The buck then turned and was moving to the right with only about an eight-inch gap in the trees for Dale to shoot through. Just at the last moment Dale could have shot he touched one off and I heard a thud, but didn't see him go down. We got up there and the buck was down. Dale had made an incredible shot and hit him through the front shoulders. The amazing thing was his buck was a genetic match to mine, just a little smaller. My buck had a set of regular eyeguards as well as an extra set coming out over his eyes and Dales buck had the same extra set of eyeguards starting, the same deep forks, and the same frame structure. It looked like the buck was either a little brother or a son to my buck.

We went through the same celebration and got his buck back to camp. We got camp all packed and headed up the trail. I was so paranoid my horns might get broke I packed them out on my back instead of on the horse just in case we had a horse wreck. The buck officially scored 211$^7/_8$ gross and 201$^2/_8$ net typical B&C.

It is neat that it's going to make the book, but the score isn't everything. I am just happy to be able to harvest a buck of that caliber. I have to say that without Dale letting me go with him to his spot it never would have happened. He is the best friend a guy could ask for and we have had some great times together. To my surprise my wife Nadine was also pretty stoked about the size of the buck. I also have to thank her for letting me get out and hunt. The stars lined up and the sun shone down on me that fall being able to harvest a mule deer of that caliber as well as see my daughter Neshia kill her first antelope and mule deer.

After harvesting a 200+ net typical mule deer last year, I never thought I would ever see another 200-inch typical buck let alone have a shot at one. I wasn't anticipating being able to hunt the early rifle season this year since my friend Dale had just had knee surgery five days before and had not planned on going. Since this is Dale's spot, if he couldn't make it, I would wait and hunt the later opener in October. The day before the early opener Dale called and said he had decided to go and asked what my schedule was. I told Dale I had to go to a sage grouse meeting in Green River the day before the opener, but might be able to leave just a little early so we could get to the hills in time for opening morning. I left the meeting as soon as I could and met Dale to load the horses and we were ready to go.

As we rode in, big storms were rolling in from the west and by the time we got close to camp, it was raining and hailing with lightning hitting all around the ridge we were riding down. We were glad to get to camp and get the tent set up as the weather showed no signs of letting up. We weathered out the storm by eating the majority of three days worth of pasta salad my wife had sent in with us, and went to bed anticipating what the next morning would bring. We decided that we would get up a few minutes earlier than usual to give Dale time to get ready and get to our spot since his leg had just been operated on.

We were in our spot when the sun came up and we started to glass some deer across the canyon from where we were. As I moved the spotting scope from deer to deer I thought I was seeing things when I saw a huge buck that looked like it was still in the velvet.

I moved the spotting scope back into position and my jaw dropped as I saw the big dude feeding uphill with an impressive full velvet rack swaying from side to side. I told Dale that the buck was even bigger than the one I got last year and to get set up for the shot. The buck was close to the timber and we knew that if we didn't do something quick he would be gone in the timber just like other bucks we had seen in the past. I asked Dale if he happened to miss the shot if he wanted me to try to take him and he said, "YEAH."

I was watching the buck in my scope as he moved and fed in the clearing. I asked Dale a few times if he was going to take him. Dale tried to get set up and get a good rest but just didn't feel good about the shot, and sure enough the big buck made it in the timber. I have to give Dale credit for not taking a shot he didn't feel good about on a buck that size. I told Dale that the biggest deer we had ever seen just slipped out from under us. We hurried and moved a little and Dale got a better rest. I put my gun over a rock pile with my pack underneath and settled in for the shot in case Dale missed.

We watched the tree line in hopes that the buck would show his face one more time, and believe it or not after a few minutes, he did. There was one more little opening he was working through before he went into another patch of timber. The buck kept moving and stopping and I remember asking Dale if he was going to shoot because I was thinking he was going to get in the timber for good this time and I really wanted Dale to get him. The buck was almost in the timber and stopped to feed for just a moment and Dale touched one off. The buck just stood there looking around so I shot and the buck moved down hill untouched. Just before the buck got to the timber he stopped one last time and looked back up across the canyon to where we were. Dale was a little to my left and didn't have a clear shot so I thought it was now or never. I felt good about the shot even though it was a long ways off, so I pulled the trigger and he dropped out of my sight in the scope. After I fired the shot I heard a THWAAK that sounded like a solid hit but I wasn't sure. We were looking and looking, but couldn't see the deer anywhere and it never came out of the timber. I decided to get the spotting scope out and look real careful where he was when I last shot. After a few minutes I thought I could see a big velvet antler laying horizontal, so I let Dale take a look and he thought it was an antler too.

We were both pretty excited to know the buck was down. Since it would take about two hours to go get the horses and ride around to where the deer was, we watched it for a while longer making sure it was down for good.

After we were satisfied it wasn't going anywhere, we went and got the horses and made the longest hour and a half ride I had ever been on. We were both anticipating how big he actually was and when we got to where he was, we weren't disappointed. He wasn't as symmetrical as last year's buck but had a lot more mass and was wider. Thank goodness I remembered to bring a camera this year since I have never lived down not having one last year. We got some photos and took care of the deer trying to keep the velvet intact since it was close to coming off. We got everything back to camp alright and still couldn't believe what had just happened. I can honestly say I wish Dale could have got this one since I killed that buck last year and it was Dale's area. I carried the horns and head out on my back just as I did last year making sure we didn't have a horse wreck and break them. Dale didn't have much sympathy for me when we got back to the truck after about an eight mile trip when I complained about my aching back (he has more faith in horses than I do).

After the 60-day drying period the buck officially scored $216\frac{1}{8}$ gross and $206\frac{6}{8}$ net typical Boone and Crockett points with a $31\frac{5}{8}$-inch outside spread. My buck from last year was close at $211\frac{7}{8}$ gross and $201\frac{2}{8}$ net typical B&C. I never in my wildest dreams thought I would ever kill a 200-inch typical mule deer, let alone do it in back to back years on a general tag on public land. Without Dale it never would have happened. I just tell everyone they need a little luck and a good friend like Dale.

The Bottom  Line

Trophy hunting mule deer can be very satisfying and rewarding at times, but it can also be flat-out hard work. It can be tough on a person not only physically, but mentally. At times you will question your sanity for putting yourself through such pain and mental anguish, but other times it will provide you with great memories that will last a lifetime.

Trophy mule deer are extremely rare. Even in the best areas in the West, they can be extremely difficult to locate. Why are they so hard to locate? Simply put, there are not many trophy class bucks out there. Not many bucks survive the required amount of years it takes to grow a trophy-sized rack, and the ones that do are true survivors and have found ways of avoiding hunting pressure.

Currently, trophy mule deer bucks are one of the most sought after big game animals in the West. Each year, it seems there are more and more people wanting to put their tag on a trophy-sized public land mulie. So what can you do in order to separate yourself from everyone else on the mountain and increase your odds of success? The bottom line—you must hunt harder and smarter than everyone else.

You can hunt harder by being the first one on top of the mountain in the morning, as well as being the last one off the mountain in the evening. You simply need to spend more time in the field than everyone else. You must also hunt smarter than everyone else. Pick up every article, scientific paper, etc. that you can find on mule deer and read them over and over. Get to know your quarry. Learn when he eats, drinks and sleeps. The more you know about him, the more you will be able to hunt him effectively.

Finally, everyone has to set his or her standards based on their individual expectations. It doesn't matter what you set your standard at, the main thing is that you stick to it. If you continually keep lowering your standards and shooting lesser bucks, odds are you will never kill that true, once-in-a-lifetime buck.

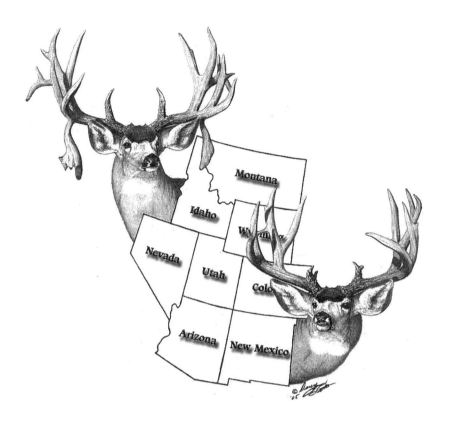

SECTION 2

RESEARCH

Beginning Your Quest

I enjoy researching trophy areas almost as much as I do actually hunting them. I love to spend hours reading record books, sifting through statistics and talking with people to gain any knowledge that I can on big buck areas. The nice thing about doing research is that you can do it all year long. I am constantly looking over maps and making phone calls to game biologists to better understand areas that I'm looking at possibly hunting.

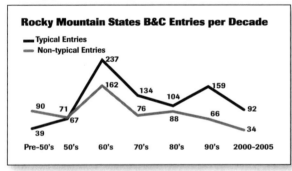

Rocky Mountain States B&C Entries per Decade

— Typical Entries
▬ Non-typical Entries

237
162
134
104
159
90
71
67
76
88
66
92
39
34

Pre-50's 50's 60's 70's 80's 90's 2000-2005

Chart 2-1

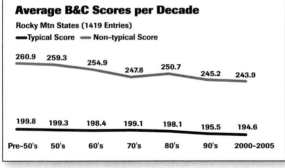

Average B&C Scores per Decade

Rocky Mtn States (1419 Entries)
— Typical Score ▬ Non-typical Score

260.9 259.3 254.9 247.8 250.7 245.2 243.9

199.8 199.3 198.4 199.1 198.1 195.5 194.6

Pre-50's 50's 60's 70's 80's 90's 2000-2005

Chart 2-2

I am not going to give out any specifics on areas, but the information in this section will definitely help you get started in the right direction. The states we will be concentrating on in this book are the eight Rocky Mountain States: Arizona, Colorado, Idaho, Montana, Nevada, New Mexico, Utah and Wyoming. All entries that I will be referring to are entries that qualify for the all-time B&C record book. Minimum score for typicals is 190 and for non-typicals it is 230. You may have heard the old saying "finding a B&C buck is like finding a needle in a haystack." Well, that could not be more true.

Consider the fact that between the eight states there are over 860,000 square miles of area and there has only been 1419 total entries into the record book from the eight states since Boone and Crockett Club started their record keeping system. One thing you will notice looking through the B&C record books is that the banner mule deer days were back in the 1960's. Chart 2-1 confirms that. Over one quarter (27%) of the 1419 B&C entries came from this decade. Although the majority of the largest bucks were killed many years ago, the good news is, the graph clearly shows that there are still plenty of B&C mule deer being harvested today.

There was a rather large decline in entries during the 70's and 80's as deer populations took a severe downward trend in the Rocky Mountains. One interesting note that Chart 2-1 shows is that since the 1980's, the number of non-typical entries is trending downward, while the number of typical entries has been trending upward.

Percentage of B&C Entries
FOR ROCKY MOUNTAIN STATES • 1419 TOTAL ENTRIES

COLORADO	33%
IDAHO	19
UTAH	13
WYOMING	10
NEW MEXICO	9
ARIZONA	8
MONTANA	5
NEVADA	3

Chart 2-3

Six years into this decade, the number of typical entries is on pace to have over 150 entries, which is encouraging. The projected number of non-typical entries will be in the mid-50's, which means that the downward trend will continue.

The same trends are very similar when you look at the average scores of all 1419 B&C entries. Chart 2-2 shows the average typical and non-typical scores for all 1419 entries per decade. You will notice that the average typical score has remained fairly constant over the years. The only drop in average was in the 1990's, but keep in mind, B&C lowered its minimum score which can account for this reduction in average score. The average non-typical score has pretty much been declining since record keeping has existed.

Now that we know when the B&C entries were taken and what the average scores are, let's find out where they came from. Chart 2-3 shows a pie chart that represents what percentage

Forest Service Acreage
(IN MILLIONS)

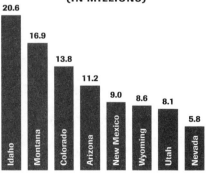

Chart 2-4

of the 1419 B&C entries came from what state. The most noticeable thing in the graphic is that a third of the entries have came from Colorado. Colorado and Idaho have combined for over half of the 1419 entries. That is an amazing statistic. Why have these two states produced more B&C deer than all of the other six states combined? Two words—habitat and genetics. When it comes to high country acreage, these two states are in the top three when it comes to total national forest acreage. Idaho has the most at 20.6 million acres, while Colorado comes in third with 13.8 million acres (Chart 2-4). Combine this with the genetics these two states have and you are going to have good amounts of trophy bucks.

Now that we know the percentage of B&C entries each state has produced since the inception of the B&C Club, let's figure out which states are currently producing B&C size deer. We need to do that because some states that may have historically produced big deer may not be producing them today.

First of all, before we start breaking down each individual state, let's take a look at Charts 2-5 and 2-6. Chart 2-5 shows the number of typical and non-typical entries from each state for all years. Chart 2-6 shows the number of B&C entries for each state since 1985. The first thing you will notice is that Colorado is at the top of both by a rather large margin. Not only has Colorado historically produced good bucks, it is still producing monster bucks today.

Idaho has maintained its second place rating as well. The only real big shake up is Utah has fell from third to fifth, while New Mexico has moved from fifth to third.

This information should help you to pick out a couple of states to apply for. After you have decided on which states you want to apply for, you need to study the tables in the individual state sections. Because the draw odds in the better units are so low, I recommend that you apply in several states. I normally put in for five of the Rocky Mountain States every year.

The next step is to narrow it down to one or two possible counties within each state that you want to focus on. In the following pages of the

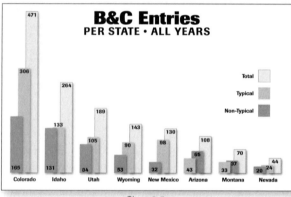

Chart 2-5

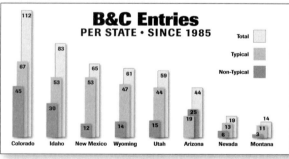

Chart 2-6

Maps

Maps are one of the most valuable pieces of research material that you can own. I have a collection of maps that I started collecting back when I was in high school. They have always intrigued me. I enjoy studying maps and can literally spend hours looking over maps of prospective mule deer areas.

If you don't have an extensive map library or a computer mapping software, I suggest that you logon to the Internet and checkout Topozone.com. This is the site that I use when I want to look at an area that I don't currently have a map for. Although you can pay a fee to get an upgraded package and get shaded relief maps and aerial photos, you can search and look at basic topo maps covering the entire US for free.

book, I have created individual sections for each of the eight Rocky Mountain States. I have prepared numerous tables showing which counties have produced the most B&C deer for all years since the inception of the B&C records and also separate tables showing which counties have still been producing record book since 1985. You will notice several things while looking at the stats. Some counties that produced big bucks back in the 50's and 60's are not currently producing very many. This has to do with several factors such as hunting pressure and land development, etc. Another thing you will see is that some counties that historically never produced B&C deer are now producing them. The main factor for this is usually limited quota areas where tags are extremely hard to get. This allows the deer to reach the age class when they can grow a trophy set of antlers. Then you have your top counties that historically produced B&C entries and are still producing top-notch heads.

Once the counties are decided on, you need to contact the game and fish biologists in those particular counties and pick their brains. Don't immediately start asking where you can find big bucks. Visit with them for a little while first and tell them exactly what your plans are, such as how long you plan to hunt, method of hunting (backpacking, horses or truck camp) and see if there are any areas they recommend that will suit your plans. Make sure to have any questions you want to ask written out so you are prepared and this way you won't forget to ask any of them. Also, make sure you have maps of the area in front of you, so that when they start talking about areas you can mark them on the map. Don't rely on your memory to remember this information, write it directly on your maps. Write down such things as names of drainages, mountains, lakes and other info they might give you. Keep in mind though, that you are not the first person to contact the biologist on information for that area. Every other person that has ever researched that area has probably contacted him and picked his brain. So don't think that you're the only one that he is giving this information to, but he can definitely get you going in the right direction.

Another good way is to purchase one of the state record books for the state that you plan to hunt. These are a great source of information for individual states. The main thing I like about these books is that they have a lot of deer in them that are not listed in the B&C record books. They also tend to list more specific areas on deer that have been harvested than B&C books, which normally only give you the county. Scott Mansor and I put out the mule deer state record book for Wyoming which is entitled Wyoming's Finest Mule Deer. The first edition, which was released in 1998, was limited to 4,000 copies and is sold out. Although there will not be any reprints of the first edition, we are currently working on the second edition.

One of the best tools out there is the Internet. The information that is currently available on the web seems to be endless. You can research just about anything including current mule deer hot spots, equipment, photos, maps and a lot more. One of the best features is the people searches; I use these all of the time when I need to talk to someone about mule deer hunting but don't know their phone number. You can plug in their name and they will generate you a list with all matches for the search criteria you have entered, such as nationwide, or by individual state.

Another great Internet research tool is the Boone and Crockett Club's "Trophy Search" which is located on their website at *www.booneandcrockettclub.com*. This is an incredible resource for researching trophy areas and historical trends. It is an online annual subscription, which allows you unlimited sessions accessing the Club's entire records database from 1830 to present. You can search by species, hunter, state, rank, county, etc. There is also an advanced search option which allows you to search a category, such as mule deer, for such criteria as highest score, greatest spread, most points and a lot, lot more. If you are serious about big mule deer, you owe it to yourself to subscribe to this great research tool. It is well worth the $50 subscription ($40 for Club members).

Once you decide on an area, you need to logon that particular state's fish and game website and start looking at the application process for that state. You need to do this as soon as possible because many states have application periods very early in the year.

This is where you will find it rather disappointing. In most of the good areas you will have to enter into a drawing in order to get a tag. And don't hold your breathe because some of the odds for the better areas are very, very low. Some lower than two percent. However, there are some exceptional mule deer areas out there that have draw odds that range from 30 to 60%. Trust me; those are good odds when it comes to drawing a good mule deer tag. The good news is that there are some good mule deer areas out there that actually have leftover tags available after the drawing has been conducted. You need to do your homework to find such areas but they do indeed exist.

Arizona

There are two world famous mule deer areas in Arizona—the Kaibab and the Arizona Strip. Don't get your hopes up too high on hunting these great hunting areas though. The draw odds for these two areas normally run less than two percent.

The Kaibab (which is Paiute for "mountain laying down") is bordered on the south by the Grand Canyon, and is without a doubt one of the single most famous mule deer areas in North America. It consists of Game Management Units 12A East and 12A West. If you are a serious mule deer hunter, you have heard of it. It has produced as many huge non-typicals as any other mule deer area out there, including two that score over 300 B&C. But one thing to keep in mind, most of those were taken many years ago. The Kaibab isn't what it used to be. Although it still produces a few big bucks, they are extremely rare. One of the most common misconceptions about the Kaibab is that there are big bucks everywhere; this is simply not the case. The hunter success rate over the past 10 years has been between 40 to 50%. If you do get lucky enough to draw a tag, make sure that you have realistic expectations, or you may come home disappointed.

The history of the Kaibab mule deer has definitely had its ups and downs as far as management goes. During the early 1900's, the mule deer population on the Kaibab Plateau was almost nonexistent. There was only between 3000 to 4000 deer living there, while the estimated carrying capacity was 10 times that. Drastic measures were needed in order to help the mule deer population recover. That help came on November 28, 1906, when Theodore Roosevelt designated the area as the Grand Canyon National Game Preserve and shut down all hunting within its boundaries. Government trappers were also called in to help control the predator population. The combination of no hunting and killing literally thousands of predators definitely succeeded in bringing back the mule deer. In fact, it worked too well. By 1923 the population was an amazing 100,000 mule deer, which was three times the carrying capacity of the area. Not only were there too many deer, the land had also been

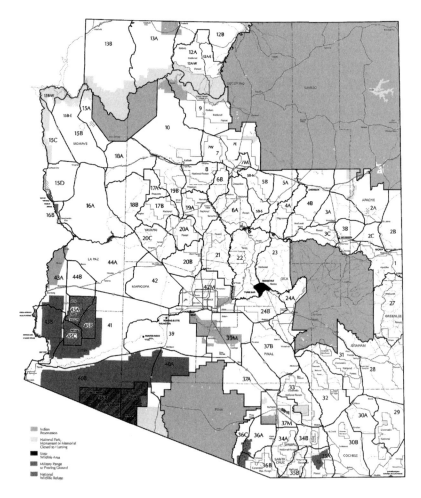

severely overgrazed by livestock. That winter, it is estimated that over 50,000 of the mule deer succumbed to starvation and died. Hunting was reinstated in the preserve and livestock grazing permits were drastically reduced. Nowadays, with proper game management and very limited tag quotas, the Kaibab will hopefully continue to produce some of the top B&C heads.

The Arizona Strip (Game Management Unit 13B) is in the northwest corner of Arizona. It borders Utah and Nevada and is extremely remote and is the most sparsely populated region of the state. The area has a current population of about 2,000 mule deer, which is only about half the population the area had in the mid 1970's. The hunter success rate is one of the best in the state, running close to 70%.

In 1995, the Arizona Game and Fish Department developed a management plan for Game Management Units 12A, 12B, 13A, 13B, 36B, 45A, 45B, and 45C entitled Wildlife 2000 Strategic Plan. Under the plan, the AGFD is to manage the above units to allow for "buck hunting opportunities that emphasize harvest of older age class animals, reduced hunter densities and have higher hunter success." One of their

60

objectives is for a harvest consisting of older mature bucks (5+ years old) in the following percentages: 20 to 30% in 12A and 12B, and 45 to 55% in 13A and 13B.

I'm really glad to see them managing certain areas for mature bucks. With these plans in place, the Kaibab and Arizona Strip will continue to provide those that are lucky enough to draw one of the coveted tags a chance at possibly harvesting the buck of a lifetime.

A look at Table 2-1 shows that Arizona has produced 108 total B&C entries. Of the 15 counties in Arizona, five of them have produced B&C caliber bucks. When you take a look at the numbers, it doesn't take a genius to figure out where the big bucks are coming from. Leading the way is Coconino County with an amazing 75 total entries. Both the state record typical and non-typical bucks came from Coconino County. The state record non-typical was taken in 1943 by William L. Murphy and scores $324^{1}/8$ and ranks number five in the world. The state record typical was killed by a mountain lion and was picked up in 1994. It scores $216^{2}/8$ and ranks number three in the world. Coconino County has produced more B&C non-typicals than any other county in the Rocky Mountain States.

A look at the second table shows that Coconino County is still producing the most record book heads. As a matter of fact, since 1985, it has produced nearly half of all of the B&C bucks to come from Arizona.

Mohave County comes in a distant second with a total of 21 B&C entries. Just like Coconino County, you are more likely to harvest a B&C non-typical there than a typical. Recent history confirms this fact. Since 1985, the county has produced 14 B&C heads, 11 of which are non-typicals. The largest of these was harvested in 2004 by Thomas Friedkin and scores a whopping $279^{4}/8$. Nick Papac was lucky enough to harvest the largest typical from the county in 1964 with a score of $203^{4}/8$.

Apache County fills the third spot. Prior to 1985 it had no B&C entries. Since 1985 it has produced seven heads that have been large enough to qualify for the B&C record book. The largest non-typical was taken by Lamell Ellsworth in 1992 and scores $257^{7}/8$. The largest typical was not harvested, but rather picked up in 1994, and scores $203^{7}/8$.

The only other counties to produce B&C mule deer are Pima and Yavapai with one entry each. Richard Cordova harvested a $238^{4}/8$ non-typical in 1989 for Pima County's lone entry, while Joseph Peca harvested a $200^{5}/8$ typical in Yavapai County during the 1983 hunting season.

Chart 2-7 shows a definite correlation between typical entries and non-typical entries. They both have followed the same pattern, except during the 70's when there were very few non-typical entries. Arizona is one of the few places that produces more B&C non-typicals than typicals. The

Arizona B&C Entries
PER DECADE
—— Typical Entries   —— Non-typical Entries

Chart 2-7

Arizona B&C Entries

All Years					Since 1985			
County	Typical	Non-typical	Total		County	Typical	Non-typical	Total
Coconino	30	45	75		Coconino	11	9	20
Mohave	6	15	21		Mohave	3	11	14
Apache	4	3	7		Apache	4	3	7
Unknown	2	1	3		Unknown	1	1	2
Pima	0	1	1		Pima	0	1	1
Yavapai	1	0	1		**Totals**	**19**	**25**	**44**
Totals	**43**	**65**	**108**					

Table 2-1   Table 2-2

most interesting factor is that the 90's has been the top producing decade for B&C entries. Unfortunately, since 2000, it is only on pace to produce 7 total B&C entries, which will make it the least productive decade in Arizona's history.

Top Producing National Forests

There are seven national forests in the state of Arizona. Five are completely within the state, while the other two are shared with New Mexico. Arizona has more than 11 million acres of national forest, which puts it in fourth place among the Rocky Mountain States.

Coconino National Forest

At 1.8 million acres, the Coconino is Arizona's second largest national forest. It has everything from semiarid desert all the way up to alpine tundra above 12,000 feet. Within its boundaries it contains all or part of 10 wilderness areas, including the Kachina Peaks Wilderness, which is where the highest point in the state is located at 12,633 on top of Humphrey's Peak in the San Francisco Mountains.

Both mule deer and whitetails can be found on the forest. The best places to look for mule deer are in the pinyon/juniper and ponderosa pines. According to the AZGF the two main foods that mule deer seek out on the forest is cliffrose and acorns on the Gambel oak.

Kaibab National Forest

The Kaibab National Forest is the top producing mule deer forest in the state. This is where you can find the world famous Kaibab herd. It is located in the northern portion of the state in Coconino County and is 1.5 million acres in size. Coconino County has produced 75% of the state's B&C deer and several of those have came from the Kaibab N.F. The Grand Canyon runs through the center of it, basically dividing the forest into two sections.

The Kaibab Plateau, which makes up most of the northern section of the forest, has been heavily logged throughout the years. The Plateau is 850,000 acres in size and is mainly covered with ponderosa pines.

Buck of a Lifetime

By Ned Smith (As told by Shane Adair)
Arizona Public Land, DIY

Originally appeared in Eastmans' Hunting Journal *issue 81*

After nine years of waiting, Jodee Adair finally drew her mule deer tag in a coveted unit north of the Grand Canyon. Being a lifetime Arizona resident and growing up hunting with her dad, she was excited. So was her husband, Shane. Finally they would be able to hunt instead of scouting with binoculars and camera.

Shane's good friend and taxidermist, Travis Roundy, helped narrow down a couple of areas in their unit where some monster sheds had been found over the last couple of years. Prior to her hunt they scouted in these areas, but each time they found it extremely tough and saw very few deer. They never spotted a buck, only does.

They had seen some articles and pictures of giant sheds found in the area they were scouting, so they knew a big buck was there somewhere. It's unusual for anyone to see these old monster bucks except maybe in the summer. By hunting season they become ghosts and are rarely seen. But knowing she had drawn the November hunt and the rut sometimes kicks in, they had high hopes that some of the bigger bucks known to exist in the unit would join the does.

One buck in the area where they were scouting and would be hunting had been seen a few rare times over the years, but not for very long. His sheds had been picked up for the past four years. In 1998 he scored 191. In 1999 he was at 207, by 2000 he had grown to 234 points and then the drought year of 2001 took its toll on antler growth and he dropped to 200 inches. No sheds were found in 2002 and most shed hunters and locals thought this buck was now either dead or on the downhill slide as far as antler growth was concerned.

But summertime sightings again in 2003 confirmed he was alive and even bigger. With his six-inch eye guards he was hard to mistake. Those that saw him said he was at least 40 to 50 inches bigger than his last found sheds! They figured his main frame was more than 28 inches wide and would score around 200 points. But with all the cheaters sticking out he would be close to 36 inches wide. He had cheaters off every main point with huge front forks. He would be in the 250-point range! He was a deer worth looking for.

Opening morning found Shane and Jodee set up behind their tripods looking through powerful 15x60 Swarovski binoculars. The first buck they found was pushing a small group of does: the rut was on. He had a tall rack and looked to be around 26 inches wide and big bodied. They moved in for a closer look and figured he was around 180 points. A nice buck!

But Jodee hadn't waited 10 years to harvest this size of buck opening morning. She decided to pass and keep looking for the phantom buck they had never seen, only heard about. They both watched the buck and does feed over the hill and they slipped away undetected, hoping they had made the right decision.

They glassed most of the day and saw no more deer. They decided it was time to push deeper into the brush. There was a storm coming in and it was extremely windy, so they figured the deer would be in the thick cedars. Most hunters avoid these thick areas, as it's tough to get off a shot. Usually you just hear them running off and if you're lucky you might get a glimpse of a big buck running through the brush. At the most, you might get a 50-yard shot.

As they slowly hunted the thick cedars, they jumped several deer and were unable to tell what they were but it kept up their excitement and kept them hunting. Finally, they spotted a herd of does through a small opening, feeding out about 150 yards in front. Jodee got out her Stoney Point shooting sticks, and resting her 25-06, watched the clearing as the does slowly faded into the thick cedars. They knew the rut was on and the possibility of a buck pushing these does was good, so they watched intently. It felt like forever, but really it was only a minute or two before a monster buck stepped into the opening.

Jodee pulled the trigger without hesitation and Shane watched the buck jump. They quickly climbed to the top of the ridge where they had seen the buck last and found blood on both sides of his tracks and knew he was hit hard. After 50 yards of easy tracking they found him folded up in the sagebrush. As they walked up to him they knew he was big, but the closer they got the bigger he got. Cheaters and points going everywhere -- both of them knew he was the buck of a lifetime!

You know the buck you dream about, but know you will never kill? Well, this buck was even bigger!! After many hugs and hollers, it was time to take pictures. The buck just got bigger by the minute. There wasn't any ground shrinkage with this bruiser!

Jodee's buck gross scored 253 B&C and nets 248 B&C points. He has an outside width of 36 inches and double six-inch eye guards on both sides. He has major cheaters off every point and stickers everywhere. His main beams are 26 inches long. The left side has 12 scorable points and the right side has 14 points. With tons of mass, his bases are seven inches around. He dressed out at 260 pounds and was aged at nine years old. He is truly a once-in-a-lifetime buck!

Arizona
THE BUCK OF A LIFETIME

Arizona is one of the few places that continually produces more record book non-typicals, than typicals. The state's premiere mule deer tags are some of the toughest to draw in the west and in some of the better units, such as the Kaibab and Arizona Strip, your odds of drawing are less than two percent. But as can be seen by this story, if you are lucky enough to draw a tag, you have the chance, although a very slim one, at harvesting the buck of a lifetime just as Jodee Adair did in 2003.

THE BOTTOM LINE
KEYS TO SUCCESS

Research • Jodee and Shane did their research. They followed up on stories of the monster buck being sighted and put themselves in the area the buck lived on opening morning. A good mule deer hunter will follow up on all mule deer stories. More often than not, they will result in a dead end, but you still must track them down.

Persistence • In order to be a successful trophy hunter, you have to be persistent. Those who give up easily, rarely kill big bucks. Even after Jodee and Shane scouted this area numerous times before the season and never laid eyes on a buck, they didn't give up on the area.

Setting Your Standards • Jodee passed on a 180-class buck on opening morning. It had taken her 10 years to draw the rare tag and she wasn't about to punch it on the first nice buck she laid eyes on. Set your standards and stick to them.

Hunt Areas Other Hunters Avoid • Jodee and Shane hunted the thick cedars, which is an area most other hunters avoid. This is key, because big bucks will often seek out areas that receive the least amount of hunting pressure. Keep in mind, this doesn't always translate to the most rugged, remote country you can find, often times it may be an overlooked piece of ground very near a road, trailhead, etc.

—David Long

Colorado

Like many other states, the mule deer population in Colorado has fluctuated greatly. During the early 1900's, mule deer were nearly extinct in Colorado, but by the late 1930's and early 1940's, mule deer were so prevalent that they were causing crop damage and were overbrowsing their winter ranges. Many winter ranges were supporting twice their carrying capacity. The population continued to grow and reached an all-time high in the 1940's and 1950's.

Today mule deer numbers are once again on a downward trend. They have been steadily declining since the banner mule deer days of the 1950's and 1960's. It is estimated that the total mule deer population in Colorado today is only half of what it was back at its peak in the 1940's.

Colorado has 63 counties and 42 of them have produced record book bucks. It is the number one state for book heads by a rather large margin. With 471 total record book entries, it has over 200 more entries than the next closest state, which amounts to 33% of all B&C entries. Unlike some other states that only produce B&C heads in certain regions, Colorado has pretty much produced good mule deer from everywhere in the state.

A look at Table 2-3 shows that there are well over a dozen counties that have B&C entries in the double digits. Leading the way is Eagle County with 30 typical entries and 21 non-typical entries. The number three typical buck from Colorado came from Eagle County in 1967. It was taken by Paul Muehlbauer and scores 214$\frac{3}{8}$ and ranks number 7 in the world. The number four non-typical buck from Colorado came from Eagle County in 1962. It was taken by James Austill and scores 303$\frac{6}{8}$ and ranks number 17 in the world. Table 4 shows that Eagle County has remained the top producing county over the past 20 years.

Mesa County runs a close second to Eagle County with 50 total entries. The largest typical from the county was taken in 1960 by Robert Zaina and scores 208$\frac{5}{8}$, while the largest non-typical was by George Blackmon, Jr. in 1961 and scores 300.

Garfield County is third all time with 39 total entries. But when you look at the last 20 years, it has not kept pace with the top two counties. The largest typical from Garfield County was taken in 1971 by Errol Raley and scores 212$\frac{7}{8}$, while the best

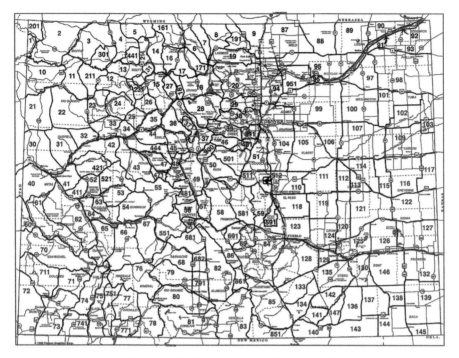

non-typical was taken by Larry Prehm in 1967 and scores 276^{4}/$_{8}$.

With 32 total entries, Montrose County is the fourth best county in Colorado for B&C entries. But when you look at the last 20 years, it has only had seven entries which drops it into a tie for fifth in recent years. The top typical from the county was taken in 1974 by Mike Thomas and scores 209^{5}/$_{8}$. The top non-typical was taken in 1961 by Keith Thaute and scores 278^{7}/$_{8}$.

At number five is Gunnison County with 30 total entries. Although Gunnison County ranks number five overall, it is tied for second since 1985. The top typical from the county was taken by William Peacock in 1962 and scores 205^{4}/$_{8}$. The top non-typical was taken by Gordon Blay in 1975 and scores 264^{3}/$_{8}$.

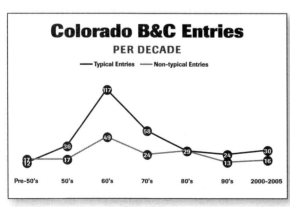

Chart 2-8

There are two counties that tie for sixth: Archuleta and Delta Counties with 25 total entries each. Archuleta has a tendency to produce mainly typical bucks. As a matter of fact, 23 of its 25 entries are typicals, while Delta County produces both typicals and non-typicals.

The one thing you will notice by looking at the listings for Colorado is that

Colorado B&C Entries

	All Years		
County	Typical	Non-typical	Total
Eagle	30	21	51
Mesa	36	14	50
Garfield	24	15	39
Montrose	27	5	32
Gunnison	23	7	30
Unknown	8	19	27
Archuleta	23	2	25
Delta	13	12	25
La Plata	13	4	17
Rio Blanco	7	10	17
Moffat	12	4	16
Dolores	12	1	13
Grand	8	5	13
Montezuma	7	5	12
Routt	8	4	12
San Miguel	3	5	8
Summit	4	3	7
Yuma	2	5	7
Larimer	4	2	6
Pitkin	3	3	6
Douglas	2	3	5
Hinsdale	2	3	5
Las Animas	5	0	5
Ouray	4	1	5
Jackson	4	0	4
Saguache	2	2	4
Adams	2	1	3
Boulder	2	1	3
Huerfano	3	0	3
Jefferson	2	1	3
Pueblo	2	1	3
Arapahoe	2	0	2
Clear Creek	1	1	2
Morgan	0	2	2
Cimarron	1	0	1
Costilla	0	1	1
Custer	1	0	1
Del Norte	1	0	1
Elbert	1	0	1
Fremont	1	0	1
Otero	0	1	1
Park	1	0	1
Rio Grande	0	1	1
Totals	**306**	**165**	**471**

Table 2-3

most of the top trophies were taken in the 60's and 70's. As a matter of fact, if you look at the top 20 typical deer from Colorado, there has only been one entry since the 1970's and it was taken in 1982. On the non-typical side, there were four bucks in the top 20 taken in the 1980's. But since 1989, there has not been a single entry that has cracked the top 20 for Colorado.

The first thing you will notice when you look at Chart 2-8 is that the banner mule deer days in Colorado were definitely back in the 1960's. Thirty-five percent of the state's entries came from that decade. In the first six years of the 2000's, the state has already produced 46 entries. At this current rate, by the end of the decade there will be 77 entries, which will make it the top producing decade since the 70's. The future definitely looks bright for the state of Colorado.

Top Producing National Forests

There are 12 national forests in the state of Colorado. Eleven are completely within the state. The other is shared with Utah. Colorado has 13.8 million acres of national forest, which puts it in third place among the Rocky Mountain States.

Routt National Forest

The Routt National Forest is located in the northern part of the state and is 1,125,564 acres in size. There are nine wilderness areas in the forest's boundaries, Byers Peak, Flat Tops, Mount Zirkel, Neota, Never Summer, Platte River, Ptarmigan Peak, Rawah and Sarvis Creek. The forest is located in the following counties, Garfield, Jackson, Larimer, Moffat, Rio Blanco and Routt.

Colorado B&C Entries

Since 1985

County	Typical	Non-typical	Total
Eagle	7	3	10
Gunnison	6	3	9
Mesa	4	5	9
Unknown	3	5	8
Montezuma	4	3	7
Montrose	7	0	7
Yuma	2	5	7
Archuleta	5	0	5
Las Animas	5	0	5
Garfield	3	1	4
Adams	2	1	3
Delta	1	2	3
Douglas	2	1	3
Larimer	2	1	3
Moffat	1	2	3
Pitkin	1	2	3
Pueblo	2	1	3
Dolores	2	0	2
Morgan	0	2	2
Summit	1	1	2
Arapahoe	1	0	1
Clear Creek	1	0	1
Costilla	0	1	1
Elbert	1	0	1
Grand	0	1	1
Hinsdale	0	1	1
Huerfano	1	0	1
Jefferson	0	1	1
La Plata	1	0	1
Otero	0	1	1
Ouray	0	1	1
Routt	1	0	1
Saguache	1	0	1
San Miguel	0	1	1
Totals	**67**	**45**	**112**

Table 2-4

San Juan National Forest

The San Juan National Forest (located in the southwestern part of the state) is approximately 1,869,931 acres in size and covers parts of 10 counties, Archuleta, Conejos, Dolores, Hinsdale, La Plata, Mineral, Montezuma, Rio Grande, San Juan and San Miguel. Several B&C entries have came from these counties, not to mention the current world record typical which came from Dolores County in 1972. There are four wilderness areas within its boundaries, Lizard Head, Mesa Verde, South San Juan, and Weminuche.

At 500,000 acres in size, the Wenimuche Wilderness comprises nearly one third of the San Juan N.F. and is the largest wilderness area in the state of Colorado. The South San Juan Wilderness Area is known as Colorado's most rugged terrain. This area was home to the last known grizzly bear in the state, which was killed in 1979. Although none have been seen since, there are a lot of people who still believe this great bear roams these extremely rugged mountains.

Uncompahgre National Forest

The Uncompahgre National Forest is located in western Colorado and is 944,922 acres in size. It has three wilderness areas, Lizard Head, Mount Sneffels and the Uncompahgre. Although the forest has several peaks that are over 14,000 feet high in the Telluride and Ouray area, the highest being Uncompahgre Peak at 14,309, probably the best known part of the forest for mule deer would be the Uncompahgre Plateau.

The Uncompahgre Plateau is located within Mesa and Montrose counties and covers an area of 2290 square miles. The Plateau rises from 4600 feet in elevation, up to 10,300 feet at the top of Horse Fly Peak. It is 90 miles in length and runs southeasterly and ends at the base of the San Juan Mountains. Over the years, this area has produced numerous bucks that have been large enough to qualify for the B&C all-time record book.

White River National Forest

Located in the north-central region of the state, the White River National Forest is one of the oldest national forests in the United States, and at 2.3 million acres in size, it is also one of the largest. Eight wilderness areas are located within its boundaries, Collegiate Peaks, Eagle's Nest, Flat Tops, Holy Cross, Hunter-Fryingpan, Maroon-Bells Snomass, Ptarmigan Peak and Raggeds Wilderness.

The White River N.F. has a great history as far as B&C bucks are concerned. The forest falls within nine counties, including Eagle, Garfield, Gunnison, Mesa, Moffat, Pitkin, Rio Blanco, Routt, and Summit counties. A quick look at the two tables for Colorado shows you that the top three all-time and the top three counties since 1985, all come from this group of nine counties.

Timberline Memories

By Rick Hendrix
Colorado Public Land, DIY

Originally appeared in Eastmans' Hunting Journal *issue 93*

The plans for my high country mule deer hunt began, of all places, on a sheep hunt. I was helping Joe Wyman on a desert bighorn hunt in my home state of California. I had met Joe a few years earlier while playing on a traveling fastpitch softball team. Joe had drawn a sheep tag in the same unit I hunted in 2001. Also helping were Joe's dad Corky Wyman, and Joe's cousin Joe Stroh (Joe S.), both from Colorado. After a successful hunt for Joe, in which he took a great 161-inch desert bighorn, talk around the campfire lead to mule deer hunting in Colorado. I soon learned that Joe Stroh was a high country mule deer fanatic. We talked on the phone all winter, and we decided my best chance for a tag, with the preference points I had, was a muzzleloader hunt. Finally, the results were posted and the hunt was on. Joe Wyman (Joe W.) had drawn a muzzleloader tag for the unit next to mine so we decided to go together and camp where we would both have access to our units. We arrived on Wednesday three days before the opener.

The first evening Joe W. and I had decided to scout my unit first. After a four-mile ride and a short hike over the hill we were sitting at 13,000 feet and looking at the most beautiful country I had ever seen. We instantly started spotting deer. Before we headed back to camp we had spotted 21 bucks, and of those 21 bucks there were four that I would be more than happy putting my tag on. Joe S. pulled into camp on Thursday night and we talked about the bucks we had seen. Joe S. had done some previous scouting and knew of the bucks we had described to him. Joe said, "Before you decide on going after one of those bucks, let's see if we can't find another buck I've seen in a different part of the unit," so the next morning we headed out to the other side of the unit. After three hours of some of the roughest trails you can imagine we were finally there. We had no sooner gotten there when the clouds rolled in and it started to storm. In the high country the weather can change in an instant. If you're not prepared for these changes your trip can turn into a nightmare real fast. The basin we had hoped to check out was now totally covered with clouds, so we headed for some shelter in the timber to eat a little breakfast and sit out the storm. After about an hour the storm passed and we were able to start glassing our basin. Joe S. spotted a couple of deer feeding about three quarters of a mile up the basin. After setting up the spotting scope Joe S. could see they were both bucks and he was pretty sure they were two of the seven bucks that he saw with the big buck he was hoping to show me. A closer look revealed six more bucks bedded down and the buck we were after was laying there sound asleep soaking up the morning sun. He was everything Joe S. had said he was. He had a great main frame with deep forks and a four or five-inch inline on his right side and a couple of stickers on his left side. Joe guessed he would be close to the 200-inch mark. He was without a doubt the biggest buck I had ever laid eyes on, and I knew instantly he was the one I wanted. We watched him for the rest of the afternoon and talked over plans on how we were going to get close enough for a shot with my muzzleloader if we could find him in the morning.

We awoke on opening morning to the sound of rain pounding down on our wall tent. Not wanting to make the 26-mile trek in the rain if we didn't have to, we opted to wait out the storm. Finally, after a three-hour wait, the three of us were off. Joe W. had decided to give up his opening morning hunt to help me on mine. It was 10 o'clock when we were in position to start glassing and picking apart the basin in hopes of finding my buck. We immediately spotted a few bucks but soon found out they weren't the ones we were looking for. We had glassed the whole basin, and though we had spotted a number of bucks, we couldn't locate the group of bucks we were after. We were starting to get worried they had left the area when Joe S. spotted some deer feeding on the hillside that we hadn't noticed before. Joe said, "There he is Rick. That's him." and as if they had appeared out of thin air, there was the group of eight bucks we had been searching so hard for. Our spotting scopes were locked on the big buck as we watched and waited, hoping he would bed down in a spot where we could put a stalk on him. An hour passed, and one by one each buck found the spot he wanted and bedded down. We decided Joe W. would stay and watch the buck through the spotting scope, then we went over the signals Joe would give us if the buck moved before we could get into position. Joe S. and I grabbed our gear and headed up the mountain.

About an hour and a half into the stalk we were able to see Joe W. and he was signaling to us that the buck had moved. Once we figured out where Joe was trying to tell us the buck went we had to get to a place we could glass from and find the buck before we tried another stalk. We glassed from every spot we could get to but we couldn't locate the buck. We could spot the other bucks, but not the one we were after. What we didn't realize, and Joe W. was trying to tell us, was that the big buck, sensing something wasn't right, had split off from the group and bedded in some thick brush by himself. Once we figured this out Joe S. spotted him through a small opening in the brush. I don't know how Joe spotted him. All you could see was a part of his face and a little bit of his antler. There was no way we could get close to him from our location so we had to back track and start over from the other side of the basin. After crawling through thick willows and wet spongy ground (much like you would encounter on a Caribou hunt) we could see the buck was still lying down and didn't seem to be alarmed. We were 300 yards from the buck and trying to figure out how to get within muzzleloader range (I was hoping my shot would be 100 yards or less but I had been practicing all summer long and felt confident up to 150 yards), when all of a sudden he sprang to his feet and started looking around. The wind must have swirled on us and he caught our scent. You could tell all his senses were in high gear and he wanted to bust out of there but wasn't sure where we were. I think the only thing that saved us was another buck and doe came up out of the bottom and started feeding near the buck. He finally bedded down again and we knew it was now or never. In order to get above him for a shot we had to go through an open area about 50 yards long. We waited until the other buck and doe fed behind some brush and we made our move. We made it across the opening and headed straight up the hill, staying behind a small rise that was between the buck and us. Once we had the elevation we needed, we started to side hill toward the buck. We came to a 30-foot cliff that had a few small pines at the end of it. Joe crawled out to the edge of the cliff and spotted the deer. The buck was up and feeding with the other two deer. I crawled out on the edge and got ready to shoot. The brush was thick and I had to wait for the buck to come into an opening. The doe came out first and we ranged her at 115 yards. Joe could see the bucks were coming and told me to get ready. The other buck came into the opening next, and I put my sights right where he came out of the brush and waited for the big buck to step into the opening. At the last minute the big buck decided he didn't like that opening and headed back into the brush. I caught movement down and to the left of where the other deer had come out. Joe caught the same movement and when the buck stepped into the clearing Joe ranged him at 129 yards. I took a deep breath, slowly let it out and squeezed the trigger, making a great shot.

After taking pictures, we went to work caping and quartering the deer. It was well past dark when we finished so we decided to spend the night on the mountain and pack everything out the next morning. What a way to end it, three friends spending the night above timberline eating MRE's and loving every minute of it.

The next day Joe S. rough scored the buck at just over 202 inches with a 30-inch spread. We spent the rest of the week hunting Joe W's unit and he scored on a beautiful velvet covered four-point on the 5th day of his hunt. After spending 11 days on a DIY hunt in the high country you are physically and mentally beat, but there is no place I would rather be. A special thanks goes out to Joe Stroh and Joe Wyman for all of their help, as this hunt wouldn't have been possible without them.

Colorado
TIMBERLINE MEMORIES

One-third of the listings in B&C's all time record book have came from the state of Colorado. That's a whopping 471 total entries. With 13.8 million acres of national forest land, Colorado has plenty of high country in which to pursue mule deer. If you are lucky enough to draw a tag, you just may harvest a monster buck like Rick Hendrix did that will give you high country memories that will last a lifetime.

THE BOTTOM LINE
KEYS TO SUCCESS

Scouting • Rick's friend Joe Stroh, had made numerous preseason scouting trips into the area and had located Rick's buck prior to the season.

Arrive Early • Rick Hendrix and Joe Wyman arrived several days before the opener. This gave them a jump on everyone else. It gave them enough time to locate the monster buck that Joe Stroh had preseason scouted and they knew where they needed to be setup on opening day.

Wait Until Bucks Bed • I feel one of the best choices Rick and his friends made, was that once they located the bucks, they waited for them to bed down before they began their stalk. This is critical. If you don't, you won't know the buck's exact location when you arrive at your shooting point and there is a good chance the stalk will fail.

Teamwork • Hand signals work great while doing stalks. While doing your stalk, having a friend stay behind on a vantage point to keep an eye on the buck is extremely effective. You can communicate back and forth with hand signals to inform the person doing the stalk of the buck's location. The most important consideration here is to make sure that you are very clear of your hand signals before beginning your stalk. There is nothing more frustrating than being in the middle of a stalk and your partner is trying to tell you something, but you are unable to figure out what it is.

—David Long

Idaho

Mule deer are the most abundant big game species in the state of Idaho. With this being said, their numbers are still well below the carrying capacities. Like many other western states, Idaho's mule deer population peaked back in the late 1950's and early 1960's. The numbers once again declined, only to go back up and peak during the early 1990's. The winter of 1992-93 devastated the mule deer population, reducing it by 30 to 50% statewide. Since that winter, numbers have steadily declined for no apparent reason.

In 2004, the Idaho Department of Fish and Game launched what they are calling "The Mule Deer Initiative." This is a commitment from the department to provide funding and personnel that will focus on increasing the mule deer population in Idaho and the quality of deer hunting in the future. This will be done by several means such as allowing more access, protecting and improving habitat, controlling predators, getting the hunting public involved as well as keeping them informed.

Although the initiative is still in the very early stages, the IDF&G has gotten the ball rolling in the right direction. One of the first things they addressed were growing elk herds on certain critical deer habitat areas, such as the Tex Creek Zone. In order to reduce the elk numbers in this area, the elk season has been extended by three weeks, along with issuing 450 extra antlerless elk tags.

Predators are being addressed by the initiative as well. Female mountain lion quotas have either been increased or removed, in the 21 hunting units in the Southeast and Magic Valley regions.

Idaho is following suit of what Wyoming did a few years back and has standardized the opening of deer season statewide. All general deer seasons will open on October 10, in hopes of spreading out the hunting pressure. This will eliminate people from hunting one opener in one area, then hunting an opener elsewhere that opens at a later date. The October 10 opener was established from input of hunters who were complaining that earlier season openers were too hot and dry.

Other projects include: Adding acreage to the Access Yes Program (which compensates private landowners to open access to sportsmen), aspen regeneration,

working with the USFS on limiting motorized access where it may be detrimental to mule deer, and a fawn monitoring program. One other program that I am glad to see is obtaining data on harvested bucks by extracting their teeth to determine their age. The information they gather will be used to identify areas that could possibly be managed for mature bucks.

I hope that this program is continued for many years to come by the IDF&G, because it appears to me, that they are on the right track. Idaho mule deer hunting is definitely not what it used to be, but with any luck, the mule deer numbers will recover and once again, provide Idaho sportsmen with a quality hunt.

Idaho's great mule deer history covers the entire state. Out of the 44 counties, 34 of them have produced record book mulies. Adams County is at the top of the heap with 26 B&C entries. In recent history it has fallen off the map as far as trophy heads are concerned. Since 1985 it has only produced two B&C typicals and zero non-typicals. The county's largest typical was taken in 1970 by Boyd Dennis and scores 211⅞. The largest non-typical was able to elude hunters all of its life and was found dead. The buck, which was picked up back in the late 60's, scores an impressive 285⅞.

Bonneville County, which is known for its large typicals, is only two behind with 24 entries. Seventeen of the 24 entries are typicals. Since 1985, Bonneville is the top producing B&C county. As a matter of fact, the two largest typical bucks to ever come from that county have been taken in recent years. The largest buck scores 212⁶⁄₈ and was taken by J. Larry Barr during the 1996 hunting season. Although it is known for typicals, Bonneville County has also produced some good non-typical bucks, including one of Idaho's four non-typical bucks that have scored over the 300 B&C mark. It was taken by Brett J. Sauer in 1985 and scores a whopping 300⅞ B&C.

Boise County comes in third with a total of 15 B&C heads. Four of those have been in recent years. In 1970, Charles Root put his tag on the largest typical from the county that scored 209 B&C. You have to go way back to 1928 to find the largest non-typical buck. It was killed by Babe Hansen and scores 305³⁄₈ and ranks number three for Idaho and number 15 in the world.

Caribou County has made a move as of late. All-time it ranks fourth, but in recent years it is tied for second for B&C entries. Nearly half of its 14 heads have come since 1985. The largest typical from the county was taken by William Van Antwerp in 1992 and scores 203⁵⁄₈. The largest non-typical was found dead in 1948 and scores 272⅞ B&C.

Elmore County comes in tied for the number five position with 13 B&C bucks,

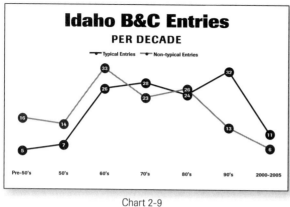

Idaho B&C Entries
PER DECADE

Typical Entries — Non-typical Entries

33

28

26 26

32

23 24

16

14

13

11

5

7

6

Pre-50's   50's   60's   70's   80's   90's   2000-2005

Chart 2-9

with half of those having been taken since 1985. The county's largest typical was picked up in 1998 and scores 199²/₈. The county's largest non-typical was taken in 1997 by Robert Arledge and scores 294⁴/₈.

Also tied for fifth with 13 entries is Franklin County. In recent years, Franklin County has slipped two notches. Franklin County has bragging rights for the 215⁵/₈ B&C state record typical. The buck was taken by Ray Talbot in 1961 and currently ranks number four in the world.

If you look at Chart 2-9, you will notice years ago, Idaho used to produce more non-typicals than typicals, but since the 1980's, the number of B&C non-typicals has steadily declined. Currently, Idaho is on pace to have 28 total entries during this decade, which means it will continue its declining pattern of B&C entries that it has had since the 1960's. Idaho definitely needs to get this downward trend reversed.

Top Producing National Forests

Idaho has a total of 16 national forests that encompass more than 20.6 million acres. That's more than any other state except Alaska. They include: Bitterroot, Boise, Cache, Caribou, Challis, Clearwater, Coeur d'Alene, Kaniksu, Kootenai, Lolo, Nez Perce, Payette, Salmon, Sawtooth, St. Joe, and Targhee.

Boise National Forest

The Boise National Forest is located in the southwestern part of the state and contains all or parts of big game hunting units 24, 25, 33, 34, 35, 39, 43. It is 2.6 million acres in size and has elevations that range from 2,600 to 9,800 feet. The major river drainages are the Boise, Payette and the South and Middle Fork drainages of the Salmon River.

Most of the hunting units in this region are managed to maintain a buck harvest above 30% for four point or better bucks. Currently the buck harvest is running at 21%, which is well below management objectives. During the 1996 season the percentage was as high as 48% but has steadily declined since then. The buck to doe ratio is at 15 bucks per 100 does, which is right at the minimum criterion set by the state.

Caribou-Targhee National Forest

The Caribou and Targhee National Forests, which are located on the eastern side of the state, were combined in the year 2000 because of budget reasons. Combined, the two forests are just over three million acres in size and they are widely known as some of Idaho's best public land mule deer country.

Idaho B&C Entries

All Years

County	Typical	Non-typical	Total
Adams	12	14	26
Bonneville	17	7	24
Unknown	10	10	20
Boise	7	8	15
Caribou	5	9	14
Elmore	6	7	13
Franklin	10	3	13
Bear Lake	9	3	12
Gem	5	7	12
Idaho	7	5	12
Blaine	4	7	11
Fremont	4	6	10
Lemhi	4	4	8
Camas	3	3	6
Cassia	1	5	6
Gooding	4	2	6
Owyhee	1	5	6
Power	2	3	5
Shoshone	2	3	5
Bannock	1	3	4
Custer	2	2	4
Madison	1	3	4
Teton	2	2	4
Twin Falls	3	1	4
Nez Perce	2	1	3
Oneida	1	2	3
Valley	2	1	3
Washington	2	1	3
Butte	2	0	2
Bingham	1	0	1
Bonner	0	1	1
Boundary	1	0	1
Clark	0	1	1
Latah	0	1	1
Lincoln	0	1	1
Totals	**133**	**131**	**264**

Table 2-5

Since 1985

County	Typical	Non-typical	Total
Bonneville	7	3	10
Caribou	3	3	6
Elmore	2	4	6
Unknown	3	3	6
Gem	4	1	5
Gooding	4	1	5
Boise	2	2	4
Franklin	4	0	4
Cassia	1	2	3
Fremont	2	1	3
Idaho	2	1	3
Shoshone	2	1	3
Twin Falls	2	1	3
Adams	2	0	2
Bear Lake	2	0	2
Camas	2	0	2
Custer	1	1	2
Oneida	1	1	2
Teton	1	1	2
Blaine	1	0	1
Boundary	1	0	1
Butte	1	0	1
Clark	0	1	1
Lincoln	0	1	1
Madison	1	0	1
Nez Perce	1	0	1
Owyhee	0	1	1
Power	0	1	1
Valley	1	0	1
Totals	**53**	**30**	**83**

Table 2-6

In order to hunt the majority of the area, you will need to possess one of the 1100 southeastern Idaho deer tags. Years ago these tags were on a first come, first serve basis and were so highly sought after that they would sell out in less than a day. Since then, the IDGF has implemented a draw system for the tags.

Nez Perce National Forest

The Nez Perce National Forest is 2.2 million acres in size and is located in the north-central part of the state and is entirely within Idaho County. The Nez Perce N.F. contains one entire wilderness area (Gospel Hump) and shares three others (Frank Church, Hells Canyon and Selway-Bitterroot) with adjoining national forests. The forest stretches all the way from the Oregon border on the west side of the state, to the Montana border on the eastern side.

Payette National Forest

The Payette National Forest is 2.3 million acres in size and is located in west-central Idaho within Adams, Idaho, Valley and Washington Counties. These four counties have a combined B&C entry total of 44 entries. The forest contains part of Hell's Canyon in Adams County, which back in the banner mule deer days, produced more than its fair share of B&C heads.

The Payette N.F. contains two wilderness areas: Frank Church–River of No Return and Selway-Bitterroot. The Frank Church is the largest single wilderness area in the lower 48 states.

Sawtooth National Forest

The Sawtooth National Forest is 2.1 million acres and is located in the south-central part of the state. Although there are some small units of the forest in southern Idaho that also run into Utah, the majority of the forest is located near Ketchum. The northern part of the forest is some of the most rugged and wild real estate in the lower 48 states. This is where you will find the Sawtooth National Recreation Area (SNRA) which is 750,000 acres in size. Within the SNRA is the Sawtooth Wilderness which has over 50 peaks that are over 10,000 feet in elevation.

Hall of Famers

By Greg Wenner
Idaho Public Land, DIY

Originally appeared in Eastmans' Hunting Journal issue 75

"Boys, if you ever want to hunt a big mule deer, you have to hunt them in Idaho," went the conversation in a cheap hotel room, somewhere in Wyoming. This was the advice given to my hunting partner and me by what I like to call a couple of "Hall of Famers." If ever there was a mule deer hunter's "Hall of Fame," then Bill and Lou would surely have been inducted years ago. I have read my whole life about the way it used to be in the "old days." Bill and Lou were the first guys I ever actually had the chance to meet in person that hunted mule deer in the 50's and 60's. And, boy, did they hunt! On that trip, we heard stories, but on later trips, we saw pictures that proved what I already knew to be true.

So, Idaho it was. Tags were applied for and plans were made to hunt with Bill and Lou again. We would camp in high country fashion and meet in town for dinners and reports in the evenings.

I shot a nice four point that year. He was a large bodied deer, high and heavy too. I was hooked on a sport that was far different from the whitetail hunting I grew up doing in Minnesota. Though hunting the two species is hard to compare and arguments will go on for years, techniques can be shard and ideas borrowed. I learned quickly that covering a lot of country gets you noticed by a lot of deer. Mike Eastman explained it best in his book, "Hunting

High Country Mule Deer," when he stated that spot and stalk might be the best method to use when hunting trophy mule deer.

The following season, while looking for new country, we came across a hunter stuck in the mud with a four-wheeler. We stopped to help and in our conversation, he told us about an area he had killed a 30-inch buck in years ago. A little luck and snow helped us find the area we would end up hunting for the rest of the week and seasons to follow. It was prime country in that it was large and open with good cover and good glassing. And, oh yes, deer! We saw deer everywhere! But we also saw quite a few hunters. This was all public land and the draw was not difficult, but it was good country and held deer.

We spotted my buck on the second morning, feeding in the shade with about 40 other deer. There were does, fawns, small bucks, and big bucks. But there was only one really big buck. I've never had buck fever before, but I can tell you with confidence, if that deer had been closer and had presented a shot, I would have had a hard time shooting. But instead, he was at a safe distance and not suspecting anything. We watched the deer for over two hours waiting for him to bed down when a pack string on the trail above us spooked every deer in the canyon. We didn't know if we should follow the deer and risk spooking the buck or wait him out and come back the following morning. We didn't have to decide because 20 minutes later, my buck stood sky-lined on the knob across from us. He returned on the same trail he had left on. Was this his escape route? He moved quickly into the shade and fed, for the most part, in the open. Having said that, I would never have spotted him without seeing him first move into the cover. Many times, I lost him in my glasses only to realize he was there in the middle of the field, just standing. He paid zero attention to the does around him and not much more than that to the smaller bucks. Only occasionally did he drop his antlers to chase one away.

Around mid-morning, he looked to be ready to bed. He looked like a dog does just before he beds down. He ended up laying down in an open area but only open to us because we were at the same elevation in the opposite canyon. Immediately, I started to look for some landmarks or anything that I could lock in on once I got above him. I figured the deer was down for a long nap and I was going to get to him. In a moment of panic, I lost the deer but soon realized he had moved about 30-40 yards and bedded again. I continued to search for landmarks and finally spotted one dead tree that I was sure could be seen from the backside. From there, I could shoot down hill at the deer.

We got off the side that we were on and got down out of sight. It took us about an hour to climb to the other side and over the top. All this time, I would check with my partner, Schmidty, to make sure the deer was still there. At the top, we rested. I paralleled below the top of the ridge and stopped below the dead tree that I had spotted from my glassing site. From there, I eased to the top of the ridge and slowly over. I could feel the air coming up from below. I took my hat off and checked my rifle and scope power. A deer stood up and I immediately recognized it as the small two-point that the big one was with. He saw me and looked right through me. I had that sickening feeling of being had and by a two-point no less. To the left, the big buck was still bedded and looking down the hill, completely oblivious to me. I think he was asleep.

I raised my rifle and put the crosshairs over him. I remember thinking about how easy it would be to miss this deer. He was about 150-yards downhill and my scope is zeroed at 250-yards. "Don't miss high," was all I could think. So I lifted the crosshairs again and lowered them right into the body, pulling the trigger as they met the ground. The bullet hit into the shoulder and down through the buck's heart and went out the opposite shoulder. The shot knocked the deer to his feet and I fired one more unnecessary shot to the lungs. He rolled out of sight and I slid most of the way down to him. Schmidty watch it all transpire through the glasses and Aaron came on the run.

By the time I shot the deer, I felt like I almost knew him personally. I had a bit of remorse as I looked at him. But what a trophy! He had it all; high, wide, heavy and lots of points. I'm not a big score guy and to this day have not had the deer measured, or any that I have ever shot for that matter. It wouldn't diminish my accomplishments if the deer didn't score well.

I must mention that I never would have shot this buck if it weren't for the help of two old timers from California named Bill and Lou. Two of the most, "Deer huntingest" guys you'll ever meet. The tip on Idaho and friends like John and Jason are the real reason I shot the deer. It's as much theirs as it is mine. I was just fortunate enough to be running the trigger.

Idaho
HALL OF FAMERS

Idaho ranks number two among the Rocky Mountain States when it comes to B&C record book entries with a total of 264. The state has 20.6 million acres of national forest which is more than any other state in the Rockies.

THE BOTTOM LINE
KEYS TO SUCCESS

Communicate With Other Hunters – Greg Wenner found this hunting area by visiting with another hunter. This is where you can obtain very important details on great hunting areas. I have found lots of good areas over the years by paying attention to what other hunters have to say.

Patience – Patience is a quality all good trophy hunters must have. When Greg's buck was spooked by the packtrain of horses, if he would have instantly took off after the buck, chances are he would have only spooked the deer off and may not have laid eyes on it again. Instead, he patiently waited and 20 minutes later, the buck was back to his regular routine.

Wait Until Buck Beds – Greg watched the buck for three hours before he bedded. A lot of people would have gotten impatient and forced the stalk before the buck bedded, which likely would result in a failed stalk.

Picking Landmarks for Your Stalk – Greg took his time and picked out a good landmark that was easily identifiable once he reached the other side of the mountain. I often pick out more than one landmark just in case I may have trouble identifying my first one.

–David Long

Montana

Montana has 56 counties of which 25 of them have been record book producers. All of the top B&C producing counties are located on the western side of the state. Montana is one of only two Rocky Mountain States that have produced more non-typical B&C heads than typicals. One interesting thing that stands out when you look at the state's records is that the top two non-typicals from the state were taken by a father and son. In 1960 Peter Zemljak harvested the best non-typical from the state with a score of 275⅛. It wasn't the best for very long though because two years later Peter's father, Peter Zemljak, Sr. exceeded that mark with a buck that scores 275⅞ which still stands as the state record. What are the odds of that?

Missoula County is at the top of the heap with 6 total entries. The best typical from the county was taken recently in 2004. It was taken by Obadiah Schulz and nets out at 195⁶⁄₈. Leland Crow took the largest non-typical back in 1952 which scores 256⅛.

Flathead County is in a four-way tie for second place. It has produced five B&C typicals with the largest being the current state record. The buck was taken in 1989 by Fran Cahoon and scores 203 B&C. Although the county has produced some good typicals, it has never produced any non-typicals that have exceeded B&C minimums.

Lincoln County has the same track record as Flathead. It has produced five B&C typicals and no non-typicals. The largest typical was harvested in 1963 by William Hubbard and is only one inch off of the state record with a score of 202 B&C. Three of the top 10 typicals from Montana have come from Lincoln County.

Madison County has produced three record book typicals and two non-typicals. The largest typical scores 200⁴⁄₈ and ranks number four for Montana. It was taken by Glenn Shelton during the 1976 hunting season. Peter Zemljak, Jr. took the largest non-typical back in 1960 which scores 275⅛ and currently ranks number two for Montana.

Rounding out the four way tie for second is Ravalli County with three typicals and two non-typicals. The top typical from the county was taken in 1973 by Sherwin Williams and ranks number three for Montana with a net score of 201⁴⁄₈. The best

Montana B&C Entries

All Years			
County	Typical	Non-typical	Total
Missoula	2	4	6
Flathead	5	0	5
Lincoln	5	0	5
Madison	3	2	5
Ravalli	3	2	5
Park	1	3	4
Sanders	1	3	4
Gallatin	0	3	3
Granite	1	2	3
Lewis & Clark	2	1	3
Powder River	2	1	3
Powell	2	1	3
Stillwater	2	1	3
Unknown	1	2	3
Petroleum	1	1	2
Pondera	1	1	2
Richland	0	2	2
Big Horn	0	1	1
Broadwater	0	1	1
Cascade	0	1	1
Dawson	0	1	1
Fergus	0	1	1
Jefferson	1	0	1
Rosebud	0	1	1
Silver Bow	0	1	1
Treasure	0	1	1
Totals	**33**	**37**	**70**

Table 2-7

Since 1985			
County	Typical	Non-typical	Total
Flathead	3	0	3
Gallatin	0	2	2
Lincoln	2	0	2
Missoula	2	0	2
Powder River	1	1	2
Petroleum	1	0	1
Pondera	1	0	1
Unknown	1	0	1
Totals	**11**	**3**	**14**

Table 2-8

non-typical was taken 10 years earlier in 1963 by Lloyd Hunter and scores $246^{2}/_{8}$.

Chart 2-10 shows that the 60's was definitely the top B&C producing decade for the state of Montana. Ever since then, the number of B&C entries has been steadily declining. Unfortunately, it looks like this decade will continue that declining trend. At the current rate, Montana will only produce five record book bucks this decade, which will make it the worst decade in the state's history.

Top Producing National Forests

Montana has 11 national forests within its boundaries. All of them, with the exception of one, are located on the western side of the state. With nearly 17,000,000 acres of national forest, it ranks second among the Rocky Mountain States. Following are the top mule deer producing forests in alphabetical order:

Bitterroot National Forest

The Bitterroot National Forest is located in Montana and Idaho, and 1.1 million acres of the forest are located in Montana. The forest has three wilderness areas which make up the largest continuous expanse of wilderness in the lower 48 states, but only two of them are within Montana – the Selway-Bitterroot (located in both Idaho and Montana) and the Anaconda Pintler.

The Bitterroot N.F. is primarily located within Ravalli County, which has produced a total of five B&C heads. There are two mountain ranges in the forest: the Bitterroot Range and the

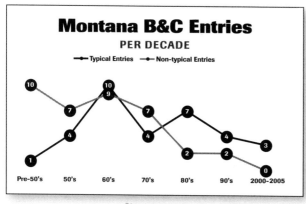

Montana B&C Entries

PER DECADE

— Typical Entries —•— Non-typical Entries

10, 7, 4, 1 / 10, 9 / 7, 4 / 7, 4, 2 / 4, 2 / 3, 0

Pre-50's   50's   60's   70's   80's   90's   2000-2005

Chart 2-10

Sapphire Range. The larger of the two, the Bitterroot Range, runs north and south along the Idaho-Montana border for 300 miles. The Sapphire Mountains are located southeast of Missoula and run north and south along the Ravalli/Granite County line. Elevations range between 7000 to 9000 feet.

Flathead National Forest

The Flathead National Forest is located in northwest Montana and extends 120 miles south from the Canada border. At 2.3 million acres, it is Montana's largest national forest. The northern part of the forest borders the western border of Glacier National Park. Nearly half of the forest is designated wilderness. The three wilderness areas include the Bob Marshall, Great Bear and Mission Mountains Wilderness.

The Flathead is primarily located within Flathead County which has produced five B&C typical bucks over the years and has been the state's top producing county since 1985. The main mountain ranges are the Flathead, Mission and Swan Ranges.

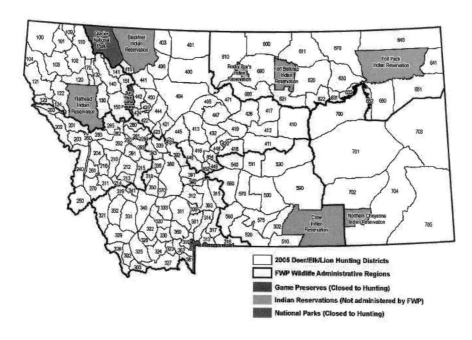

2005 Deer/Elk/Lion Hunting Districts
FWP Wildlife Administrative Regions
Game Preserves (Closed to Hunting)
Indian Reservations (Not administered by FWP)
National Parks (Closed to Hunting)

Kootenai National Forest

The Kootenai National Forest is located in the most northwest corner of Montana. The forest extends into Idaho and borders the Canadian border on the north. The Cabinet Mountains Wilderness, which has the forest's highest peak (Snowshoe Peak 8,738 feet), is the forest's only wilderness area.

The Kootenai N.F. is located in Lincoln County which has produced as many B&C typicals as anywhere in the state. Five mountain ranges, the Bitterroot, Whitefish, Purcell, Cabinet, and Salish Mountains can be found within the forest.

Lolo National Forest

Lolo National Forest, which is located in the west-central part of the state, is one of the state's largest national forests. The forest pretty much surrounds the city of Missoula. The Lolo has three small wilderness areas—the Welcome Creek, Rattlesnake and the Scapegoat, which is also shared by two other national forests. Elevations range from 2400 feet all of the way up to 9,204 at the top of Scapegoat Mountain. The main mountain range in the forest is the Bitterroot Range which makes up the western portion of the forest.

The Lolo N.F. is primarily located within Sanders, Mineral, Granite and Missoula Counties. Missoula County is the top producing Montana county with six record book entries and the other three counties have a combined total of seven entries. This region is definitely one of the state's top B&C mule deer producers.

Making the Most Out of a Great Tag

By Keith Balfourd
Montana Public Land, DIY

Originally appeared in Eastmans' Hunting Journal *issue 93*

If you've subscribed to this magazine for any length of time, it should come as no surprise that some of the best big game hunting in the West today comes from having a hot tag in your pocket. That said, this is exactly what happened for my 2005 season, plus a little extra effort and luck on my part. I learned a lot from this hunt, the most important thing being that, just holding a great tag was not enough, especially on a do-it-yourself public land hunt. Here's what else I learned that might help you if you hit big game hunting's lotto.

Today, the quality of big game in many states is at an all-time high with game managers and biologists applying the best science we've ever had. Better yet, they are following through to add the final piece to the puzzle – reducing "pressure" by backing off hunter access to allow for higher age-class bucks and bulls.

The area I drew in Montana had been managed for quality for the past eight years. It was one of those special areas that Montana Fish Wildlife and Parks, and the late Duncan Gilchrist had identified as a Game Management Unit (GMU) that could be a shining example of what proper management, genetics, cooperation from sportsmen, and Mother Nature could do together. All that was needed was to reduce the harvest by moving it to a limited entry draw. Anyone who has played the odds knows that it's still a crapshoot to draw a good tag. Once I had the tag of a lifetime in hand, my first reaction was to lock into a mindset that I would honor my good fortune and this tag with my very best effort.

I also had a good/bad situation. My tag was good for archery from September 15 - October 16, and then rifle from October 21 – November 27. That was the good news – a long season to hunt. The bad news was, things would change as I went; I would have to constantly shift my approaches and thinking as conditions, situations, and seasons unfolded.

Next on my list were maps. Since I had never set foot in this area before, I bought every USGS map that covered this 500-square-mile unit. Then, the real due diligence began. I tracked down the area game warden, the biologist for the National Forest Service, and the game manager for Montana Fish, Wildlife, and Parks assigned to this area and either called or visited them in person with notepad in hand. The consensus was B&C class bucks did exist and would be found at the highest elevations early and rutting on private land down low, late – not a big surprise.

All three of these gentlemen were extremely helpful and genuinely interested in helping any way they could. The biologist and game manager were especially helpful. This was their baby - their pet project - and they were obviously proud of what they had accomplished in turning around an average area into a true trophy mule deer destination. Plus, each of them knew what a B&C buck was, something that is not always the case when interviewing – a big buck means different things to different people. Next, I started sniffing around the local scene scouting for others who had held this tag. They, too, were helpful. Some were more helpful than others, but every piece of information would eventually play out to be useful.

From all my notes I had a head start. Ridges, drainages, peaks, saddles, anyplace someone mentioned as an early or late-season option, I located on the maps and found a way in and out of.

Next was a truckload of windshield scouting using the maps to find road access points, and more importantly what type of habitat was where. It was a big area with diverse terrain, and the mule deer habitat was what I considered "Better, Best" in different locations. In this early scouting it was just as important to rule areas out as it was to rule them in. I eventually shrunk this vast unit into three core zones.

I did locate some good bucks right out of the chute. This was early August, with summer range bachelor groups relatively easy to find. Scouting terrain and habitat is one thing, but it is always a welcome sight to see deer - bucks and does. For one, I needed to see for myself the top and middle ends of the quality spectrum in order to "give this tag my best effort." Also, if I was still going to be out there pressing in mid-November, I needed to keep tabs on does.

The velvet bucks I had seen at will early seemed to disappear when they went hard antlered – standing around to get their picture taken was off the table by the start of bow season. Then, hunting pressure began to take affect. This area was also a general season elk tag fan favorite. That shuffled the deck even more, but by the start of bow season I felt confident that I had synthesized every bit of information I collected into a pretty good game plan.

I used bow season to take long treks into as many out-of-the-way pockets as I could find. On opening day of bow season I put myself within 80 yards of a 34-inch 5x5 with two matching inline points on his G-2s; I guessed he would go 185-plus B&C. Eighty yards was all I could do, which was about 30 yards beyond my comfort zone. Later, I heard of a bow buck at the taxidermist that went 192. It was him. I wasn't the only one who had laid eyes on that buck.

Something else I noticed was the road densities could be highly variable, leaving vast tracks roadless. Once I got off the beaten trail, sign, activity, and sightings of mature bucks increased. In fact, the better bucks were taking a page out of the elk's survival book and sticking to a quarter-mile or more "buffer zone" away from roads. And so it went; I hunted hard, but saw less and less quality bucks as the season progressed, while elk hunting pressure moved the best bucks deeper into the timber.

"Good Tag" Tips

1 Determine your "no regrets" bottom end – the minimum you will be happy with

2 If B&C score is your measuring stick, learn how to score and better yet, field judge your quarry—know what you are looking at when you see it

3 To confidently answer #1 you must know the top end of what your tag/area has or can produce.

4 To answer #3, talk with everyone – past tag holders, biologists, game managers, game wardens, local taxidermists

5 Take notes. Every bit of information can be useful and can be a lot to remember

6 Next, go see for yourself. Pre-season scouting with maps is a must

7 Pay attention to what the game is doing as the season progresses—changes in weather, rut, hunting pressure, etc.

8 Be ready at all times, never give up, and stick to your guns.

—Keith Balfourd

Bow season came and went. I did see and passed on some outstanding bucks from 170 to 192 B&C. By the time rifle season started, things got tougher. Elk pressure increased and I encountered more buck tag holders. Every trip into this area brought new information, which I logged in the back of my mind.

In addition to what I had found, I got tips from friends and other tag holders. One tip was a 240-class non-typical that was seen the previous year, but not taken. He was in a hellhole and I put some time in on him, but never did lay eyes on him. Another was from a buddy who drew a sheep tag for that unit who had seen two thumpers while doing the same homework for his sheep tag – one he caught on video. I guessed him to be pushing 190 as a typical. I spent time looking for both these bucks, but no joy. Another mule deer enthusiast friend, Steve Puppe, tipped me off to a super-sized typical and agreed to take me into the area one day to look for him. We scoured the area and saw two bucks in the 170-plus range, but not the one we were looking for. The elk pressure in this drainage was over the top for what I felt a buck of this caliber would endure. I spent one other full day on him, but saw even less, so I moved on.

Finally, snow fell! Just what the doctor ordered. Unfortunately, that first dump thawed and then froze, making quiet still hunting in the deeper timber pockets just exercise. My plan had always been to stay off the beaten paths away from the roads, concentrating on thicker, out-of-the-way pockets. The crunchy snow threw this plan into a tailspin.

Research

A comprehensive gate closing on October 16, one week before rifle season opened, also changed the game dramatically. This was another part of the "quality" management plan. Putting everyone on foot or horseback ensured less road hunting and accessibility during the rut, reducing success rates.

When the rut started, finding 160 to170-class bucks was not an issue, but the big boys this area was known for and I had passed up earlier were escaping me. One evening, I pointed out a nice high-racked buck I had passed up to a gal who had never taken a mule deer buck. She was ecstatic and made a great shot at 200 yards.

I was beginning to get weary. I had logged hard miles from sunup to sundown for countless weekends in a row, plus a few weekdays. I planned to take Friday, November 18th off and hunt through that weekend as well. For this day, on a wild hair, I decided to go back into the drainage where I had looked for the big mystery typical. I hadn't been in there for a month and figured that the elk hunters would have rested the area during the week. Plus, a lot of guys had already tagged out, and with the rut in full swing, I thought that maybe this buck, if still around, would slip up with a hot doe.

What I was finding was not what I had expected now that the rut was kicking in. I was seeing multiple immature bucks tending does, which didn't seem right. In fact, nearly every doe or group of does I came across was dragging around a small buck. The big boys had seemingly not engaged yet. Of course, there was a lot of country and thick timber to contend with, but I thought I would at least see higher quality bucks popping up here and there. I did glass some long range rutting activity, but every time I closed the distance to get a better look, the best buck in the bunch had moved on. I was tempted on several occasions to end it all, but always fell back to my original mindset. It was getting to the point that, since I had passed up several nice bucks, I was thinking about eating the tag if I didn't find at least a 185 B&C buck.

I was starting to question my sanity and abilities. I had laid eyes on a number of quality 180-class bucks early, but nothing over 170 for two weeks of hard hunting. When I finally saw this buck, I was stunned. For one, I had not seen a super-quality buck in two weeks. Secondly, I wasn't ready. I was still a ways away from where I had planned to set up and glass for the morning. Lastly, he took my breath away. He had pinned me first, so he was looking straight on and all I could see was his goal-post frame. He didn't seem spooked, so I had time for a quick "honor the tag" check with my binoculars. Looking past his super frame, I could see huge fronts, but still no view of his backs. This was not a buck to wait for a better angle while still holding binoculars, so I set up for a shot and waited. Within seconds of crosshair viewing, he turned his head just enough for me to see that his backs lived up to his fronts and it was over. One shot from my 7mm mag. and he humped, bolted, staggered and dropped.

I was so focused on him that I did not see the doe he was with. When she ran out, another buck appeared out of nowhere, stood over my buck for a split second and immediately bolted after the doe. Two other bucks then appeared on the scene, slid in behind the first buck and disappeared out of sight in a cloud of snow. The whole show took about 20 seconds at 150 yards. I don't remember what the other bucks looked like, and I didn't care. I had far exceeded my highest hopes for this tag.

B&C official measurer Ryan Hatfield scored my buck at 211⁶/₈, 203⁵/₈ net typical, which is currently the number two all time for Montana and the largest taken by a hunter.

What unit you ask? This article was about doing your homework. Everything you need to know to find this exact unit is mentioned here. Best of luck.

Montana
MAKING THE MOST OUT OF A GREAT TAG

Montana is not exactly known for its B&C mule deer. Although it has the second most national forest acreage, with 70 entries, it ranks #7 among the Rocky Mountain States for record book heads. The majority of the record book heads come from the western side of the state.

The Bottom Line
KEYS TO SUCCESS

Limited Entry Tag • The odds of you drawing a quality limited entry tag are extremely low, but if you don't apply, your odds are zero! Keith beat the odds and drew a super tag for his home state of Montana and made the most of it.

Research • If you are ever lucky enough to draw a super tag, you need to do your homework and research the area to the best of your ability. You need to do as Keith did – talk to past tag holders, taxidermists, biologists, game wardens, etc. Armed with the knowledge you can get from these people, you will be able to make the most of your scouting and hunting trips.

Hunt With Multiple Weapons • If your tag allows you to hunt during the archery season, as well as the rifle season, be sure and take advantage of this. It not only extends your hunting season, but the more time you spend in the field, the better your odds of finding a monster buck.

Stick to Your Guns • Keith had a great tag and was not about to tie it on a 180-class buck. Although he started questioning himself at times, he stuck to his guns and was able to put his tag on the second largest typical to ever come from the state of Montana.

—David Long

Nevada

It is easy to see why there were so many big bucks taken in Nevada during the 1950's and 1960's when you look at the history of Nevada's mule deer population. During that time frame, there were nearly 250,000 mule deer in Nevada. That peak population didn't last long and the population steadily declined during the late 1960's and early 1970's until there were only about 100,000 mule deer in the state. Fortunately, Nevada implemented a draw system in 1975 and things took a turn for the better and by 1988 the population was back up around a quarter of a million animals.

Now the bad news: Ever since 1988, mule deer numbers have steadily declined. The major factor in the decline was the winter of 1992-93, but unfortunately, they have still been on the decline.

Out of Nevada's 17 counties, only eight of them have produced B&C mule deer. While Nevada hasn't produced a tremendous amount of book bucks, it definitely has produced some of the best bucks around. The good news is that nearly half of the book heads have came within the last 20 years.

Elko County is at the top of the all-time list by over a two to one margin over the next closest county, but it only ranks third as far as new entries are concerned. Prior to 1985, it produced more non-typicals than typicals. The largest non-typical to come from the county was taken in 1954 by Joseph W. Dooley in the Independence Mountains and scores 286¹/₈ B&C. Since then however, that has been reversed. It now produces more typicals than non-typicals by a rather wide margin. The largest typical was harvested by C.H. Wahl in 1953 and scores 203⁴/₈ B&C.

Lincoln County is in a tie for second place for all years, but has been the top producing county since 1985. Just like Elko County, it too, has produced more non-typicals than typicals. Out of the eight B&C heads from Lincoln County, seven of them have been taken since 1985, including the counties largest non-typical which was taken in the Clover Mountains by Alan Shepard in 2001 scoring 248⁴/₈. The state record typical which scores 205⁴/₈ came from this county as well. It was taken by Erich Burkhard and has stood as the state record since 1983.

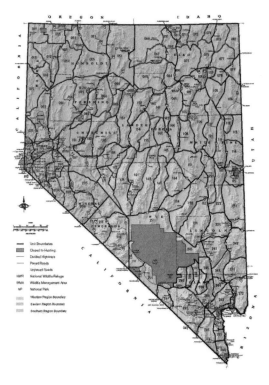

Washoe County ties for second all-time, and second for recent years as well. Prior to 1985, Washoe County only had two B&C mule deer to its credit, but now has eight to its credit. What a drastic turnaround. Seven out of the eight are typicals, with the largest coming in at 201⁶/₈ and was harvested in 1991 by Gordon Frazier. The lone non-typical harvested by Jason Langslet in 1995, just barely made the B&C all-time minimum with a score of 230.

Next on the list is Humboldt County, which prior to 1985 only had one listing in the book, but in recent years has pushed its total up to three. All three are typicals— the largest was taken by Robert Swinney in 1982 with a score of 199⁵/₈.

Eureka County comes in at number five all-time with two entries: one typical and one non-typical. The most recent was the typical taken by Michael Miller in 1995 that scored 196⁵/₈. The non-typical, which ranks number two for the state of Nevada, scores 299¹/₈ and was harvested by Dan Avery, Jr. back in 1968 while hunting the Diamond Range.

Nye County only has one official B&C entry, which normally wouldn't even be worth mentioning. But when the buck has 42 total points and is the state record non-typical scoring 325⁶/₈ B&C non-typical, I believe it is worth talking about. While hunting Stoneburger Basin back in 1955, Clifton Fauria was fortunate to put his deer tag on this incredible non-typical which still ranks number four in the world.

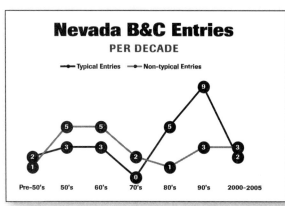

Chart 2-11

Although Nevada has produced a couple of the best non-typical trophies of all-time, a look at Chart 2-11 clearly shows that the state has never produced large amounts of B&C entries. Even during the 1960's, when so many other states were producing a lot of big bucks, Nevada only

93

produced nine B&C bucks. The state's best decade was the 90's when it produced a dozen entries. Since 2000, the state has produced 5 B&C entries. At this pace it should end up with eight total entries, which is less than one entry per year.

Top Producing National Forests

The state of Nevada only has one national forest. In 1997, the Humboldt and Toiyabe National Forests were combined and are now managed as one single forest. The forest is divided into 10 districts: Austin, Bridgeport, Carson, Ely, Jarbidge, Mountain City, Ruby Mountains, Santa Rosa, Spring Mountains Nation Recreation Area and the Tonopah Ranger Districts.

Humboldt-Toiyabe National Forest

At 6.3 million acres, Humboldt-Toiyabe National Forest is the largest forest in the lower 48 states.

The Austin Ranger District is located in the central part of the state. This part of the forest contains the rugged Toiyabe Range and the highest point is Bunker Hill at 11,474 feet. The range is located in Nye and Lander Counties and has two wilderness areas. The Arc Dome Wilderness, at just over 115,000 acres, is Nevada's largest wilderness area and is located in the southern portion of the Toiyabe Range. Table Mountain Wilderness is located in the Table Mountain Range

The Ely Ranger District is 1.1 million acres in size and spreads over three counties, Lincoln, Nye and White Pine. The district contains the Mount Moriah Wilderness which is located in the north Snake Range near the state of Utah. Mount Moriah is the highest point at 12,050 feet.

The Jarbidge Ranger District is located in the northeastern part of the state in Elko County near the Idaho border. Jarbidge is a Shoshone Indian word meaning "a weird beastly creature." Legend has it that the Shoshone braves chased this creature into a cave in Jarbidge Canyon and blocked it inside with rocks and boulders. The Jarbidge Mountains rise to an elevation of 10,839 feet at the top of Matterhorn Peak. There are a total of

Nevada B&C Entries

All Years

County	Typical	Non-typical	Total
Elko	9	11	20
Lincoln	3	5	8
Washoe	7	1	8
Humboldt	3	0	3
Eureka	1	1	2
Lander	1	0	1
Nye	0	1	1
White Pine	0	1	1
Totals	**24**	**20**	**44**

Table 2-9

Since 1985

County	Typical	Non-typical	Total
Lincoln	2	5	7
Washoe	5	1	6
Elko	2	0	2
Humboldt	2	0	2
Eureka	1	0	1
Lander	1	0	1
Totals	**13**	**6**	**19**

Table 2-10

eight peaks that rise above 10,000 feet in elevation.

The Mountain City Ranger District is located north of Elko, Nevada. Many record class mule deer have come from this district over the years. The highest point in the district is McAfee Peak at 10,439 feet in elevation.

The Ruby Mountain Ranger District is made up primarily of the East Humboldt and Ruby Mountain Ranges. The East Humboldt Range runs south from Wells, Nevada and contains the East Humboldt Wilderness which is 36,000 acres in size. The highest point in the Humboldt's is the 11,306-foot Hole in the Mountain Peak.

The Ruby Mountains are located in the northeastern part of the state and are the predominant mountain range in Elko County, which is the top producing B&C county in the state. The Rubies are well known for their spectacular high country scenery and the highest elevation in the mountain range is 11,387 feet at the top of Ruby Dome. The higher elevations of the Ruby Mountains contain 90,000 acres of designated wilderness area, as well as 10 peaks that are over 10,000 feet in elevation.

Happy Halloween

By Alan Shepherd
Nevada Public Land, DIY

Originally appeared in Eastmans' Hunting Journal *issue 69*

I have never been a real big fan of Halloween ever since my older brothers scared the daylights out of me as a kid. Halloween 2001 changed some of those feelings, because this year I got the treat instead of the trick. This year I was pleased to find out that I had drawn the best area in southern Nevada for trophy mule deer. My hunting partner Kyle and brother-in-law John also drew the same unit as did several of my friends in town. It seemed that everyone that I knew in the country had drawn this unit, so the competition was going to be tough.

As it seems with every deer tag that I have drawn, the season came in with a full moon, high temperatures and little cool weather in the forecast. This usually means that the deer are going to bed for the day within an hour of sunrise and are not coming out again until near dark. Opening morning of the hunt found us hunting an area where deer feeding in the hay fields go to spend their day. We knew that several good bucks were known to be in the area. After discussing a plan of attack, Kyle and I took off in an attempt to locate a buck and hopefully move a deer in front of John, who was hunting mule deer for the first time. Though we saw a number of deer and probably 10-15 bucks, every one was a three point or smaller so we passed. Our afternoon hunt produced no sighting of deer at all.

The next morning we decided to hunt an area in the Delamar Mountains. We hunted our way into a good spot to glass and found no deer in sight. While moving to a new location, we just about ran over a nice 22-inch 4 x 3 standing on the edge of the trail. Kyle and I both passed, but John said he was big enough for him. After digging his rifle out and getting a round loaded,

John harvested his first mule deer. He was pretty pleased with himself and the buck.

Work kept me from hunting during the week, so the second weekend found Kyle and I back in the Delamars. We decided to hike into a remote canyon that contains quite a bit of water and pretty good deer habitat. It was a nice hike, but no deer were seen. The afternoon hunt produced more of the same.

Sunday found us going to another good area within the Delamars. When we reached the top of the mountain, we found other hunters so we headed for new surroundings. While traveling to new location, I spotted two small bucks sparring on top of a ridge. We backtracked around the deer to get a better look but did not find them again. Upon reaching the road, Kyle spotted two more deer but this time on a different ridge. The larger buck was worthy of a second look so off we went again. The two little bucks we couldn't find earlier pinned us down for a few minutes in our stalk, but we were able to ease within 150 yards of the bedded bucks. Kyle asked me if I wanted to take the shot, but I declined and left it up to him. The buck turned out to be a 27 inch three-point. It is Kyle's biggest buck to date, and he was quite happy with him. The trip off the mountain made it even more exciting.

Monday morning's hunt took us back to the area we hunted opening day. We glassed a number of areas and only found two small

Data on Buck:

Location:	Lincoln Co. Nevada	
Date:	October 31, 2001	
Gross score:	$258^7/_8$	
Net score:	$247^3/_8$	
Outside Spread:	$32^5/_8$	
Antlers	**Right**	**Left**
Points	9	6
Main Beams:	$22^3/_8$	$26^3/_8$
G2:	$17^3/_8$	$17^3/_8$
G3:	$12^0/_8$	$13^2/_8$
Circumference of base:	$5^5/_8$	$5^0/_8$

bucks and several does and fawns. We rounded out the morning by taking a tour through some new areas but found no more deer.

Tuesday afternoon I decided to take my wife and two girls on an afternoon hunt as the warm weather had finally decided to break, and it gave us some scattered showers and cooler temperatures. We headed for a prescribed burn area that the BLM completed a few years ago in the Clover Mountains. The trip produced no deer but the girls got a nap out of it. A conversation with Kyle that night set the stage for the hunt on Halloween. Kyle suggested I hunt the burns in the Clovers again while I thought we should go back to the Delamars. We compromised by agreeing on the Clovers and driving to selected spots to glass from. Any other combination would have completely changed the events that were to unfold the next morning.

Maybe the rain and cooler temperatures kept him out longer than normal, or maybe it was just blind luck, but there he was. I wish that I could say that we had scouted this buck the whole summer, spent endless hours learning his hiding spots and his favorite feeding areas, and had miles of video of him, or had spotted him miles away and spent the rest of the day stalking him, but I can't. We simply got to our desired location a little later than we wanted so we headed directly to our chosen hill to glass the burn. As we eased up a jeep trail, I caught a glimpse of what appeared to be a buck standing in the burnt trees. As I prepared for a shot, if presented, Kyle was sizing up the buck through his binoculars. He informed me that its antlers were at least past its ears and appeared to be a four point. The buck was standing quartering away when I took my first shot. I watched the buck duck as I missed. I quickly shot again and saw a quick flash of white in the scope. Scared that I missed again, I was wondering where he had gone, but Kyle informed me that the deer was on the ground.

Making our way through the burnt trees, I was expecting to find a nice four-point. However, I got one of the biggest treats of my life when we got our first good look at the buck and realized it was more than just a four-point. The buck just seemed to grow and get even bigger when we rolled him over. He had nine tall tines on the left side and six on the right. His antlers were thicker than baseball bat handles and carried this weight clear to the tips. We estimated that he was at least 30 inches wide.

We couldn't wait to get him back to town to do a little bragging. I realized how big the buck was when we showed him to some friends and they got as excited as I was. I had the buck measured, and his green score was over 256 B&C non-typical and will net over 242. He is 33 inches wide and has over 20 inches of mass measurements on each side.

I would like to take the opportunity to thank my wife for putting up with my desire to hunt. She enjoys hunting and fishing, and we are able to share the outdoors with our two daughters, Amanda and Brooklin. I would like to thank my hunting partner Kyle Teel, for without him this story wouldn't have had the ending that it did.

Nevada
HAPPY HALLOWEEN

Nevada ranks #8 for B&C entries among the eight Rocky Mountain States. Although it has only produced 44 total entries, it has produced some of the biggest non-typicals in the book. The best news is that nearly half of the state's entries have come within the last 20 years.

THE BOTTOM LINE
KEYS TO SUCCESS

Apply for Quality Tags – In order to harvest quality mule deer, you must put in for quality mule deer areas. Alan was lucky enough to draw the best unit in southern Nevada. If you draw one of these premiere tags, there is no guarantee you will harvest a monster buck, but at least you will be in an area that has the potential to produce the buck of a lifetime.

Persistence – Alan was persistent during his hunt. He made numerous trips during the hunting season, often times not seeing any deer, but he never got discouraged. He was also not afraid of checking out new areas. I like to do the same. I like to hunt numerous areas during the hunting season. You can't give up on an area easily, but after hunting it hard and not finding anything, you need to start hunting other areas.

Pick a Good Vantage Point – The key to locating this buck was finding a good vantage point that offered Alan a good view of the area. Remember, you can see more game in a short amount of time from a good vantage point, than you will if you spend all day just trekking through the area. Plus, the game that you locate with your optics will be undisturbed and will not know you are even in the area.

–David Long

New Mexico

Only nine of New Mexico's 33 counties have ever produced heads large enough for the B&C record book. Rio Arriba County ranks number one out of all the counties in the Rocky Mountain States for typical entries with a whopping 88. Of those, 48 of them have been within the past 20 years. It also ranks number one for total entries of all time with 113. Don't get too excited though because the majority of these have come from the Jicarilla Indian Reservation. Since just about every entry from the state has come from the county, it should be no surprise that both the state record typical and non-typical come from the county as well. What is surprising is the fact that both of them were killed by the same hunter two years apart. In 1963 Joseph Garcia put his tag on a huge non-typical that scores 306^2/$_8$ and also ranks number 12 in the world. Two years later, he was lucky enough to punch his tag again, this time with a 211^7/$_8$ typical that ranks number 15 in the world. What an amazing accomplishment.

Coming in well behind, and I do mean well behind Rio Arriba County is Colfax County. Colfax only has four entries: two typicals and two non-typicals. The largest typical scores 195^4/$_8$ and was harvested back in 1963 by an unknown hunter. Ralph Smith took the largest non-typical in 1957 which scores 258 B&C.

Cibola County which has produced three record book heads, all since 1985, fills the third all-time slot. Two of the three heads, which are the largest typical and non-typical from the county, were both picked up. The typical was found in 1988 and scores 195^5/$_8$. The very next year, the best non-typical was picked up and scores 244^5/$_8$.

With three entries as well, San Juan County ties for third. The largest typical was taken recently in 1995. It was taken by David Brooks and scores 205^1/$_8$. The county has not produced any non-typical heads large enough to qualify for entry into the B&C records program.

The remaining five counties that have produced B&C deer—Catron, Hidalgo, San Miguel, Sandoval and Socorro—all have one entry each.

As with many other states, according to Chart 2-12, New Mexico produced the most B&C heads during the 1960's. The state definitely produces more typicals than

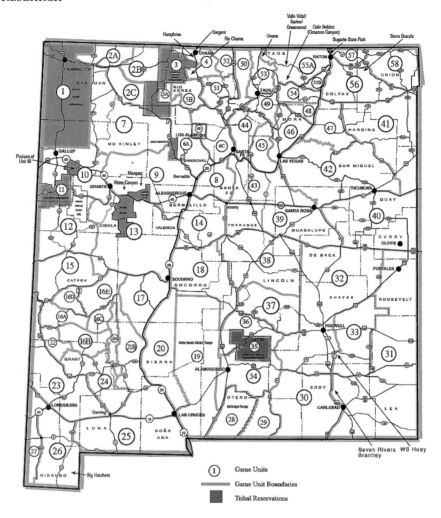

Humphries Sargent Rio Chama Uraca Valle Vidal/ Barker/ Greenwood Colin Neblett (Cimarron Canyon) Sugarite State Park Sierra Grande

① Game Units

Game Unit Boundaries

Tribal Reservations

non-typicals by a rather large margin. The state suffered a decline during the 70's and 80's, but recovered rather nicely in the 90's. The state is on pace to produce 28 entries this decade, which is down from the preceding decade, but it is still producing a fair amount of record book entries.

Top Producing National Forests

New Mexico has seven national forests which total nine million acres within its boundaries. Five of them, Carson, Cibola, Gila, Lincoln and Santa Fe are totally in the state, while the remaining two, Apache and Coronado are both shared with Arizona.

Carson National Forest

Located in the northern section of the state, Carson National Forest is the home of Wheeler Peak (13,161 feet), which is the highest point in New Mexico. The forest is

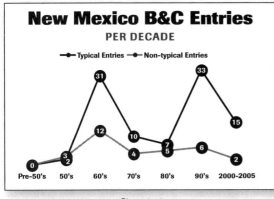

Chart 2-12

almost entirely located within Rio Arriba County which is the top B&C producing county in the state. All or parts of game management units 2B, 5B, 44/45, 49, 50, 51, 52 and 53 can be found on the forest.

The forest borders the world famous Jicarilla Apache Reservation which consistently produces B&C deer. It also has some of the states most beautiful mountains, including the Sangre de Cristos. There are four designated wilderness areas on the Carson: Wheeler Peak, Latir Peak, Cruces Basin and Pecos Wildernesses.

Santa Fe National Forest

The Sante Fe National Forest is located in the north-central part of the state. The Santa Fe N.F. has four wilderness areas: Pecos, San Pedro Parks, Chama River Canyon and Dome Wilderneses.

New Mexico B&C Entries

All Years			
County	Typical	Non-typical	Total
Rio Arriba	88	25	113
Colfax	2	2	4
Cibola	1	2	3
San Juan	3	0	3
Unknown	2	0	2
Catron	0	1	1
Hidalgo	1	0	1
San Miguel	1	0	1
Sandoval	0	1	1
Socorro	0	1	1
Totals	**98**	**32**	**130**

Table 2-11

Since 1985			
County	Typical	Non-typical	Total
Rio Arriba	48	9	57
Cibola	1	2	3
Colfax	1	1	2
San Juan	2	0	2
Hidalgo	1	0	1
Totals	**53**	**12**	**65**

Table 2-12

Satan's Hole

By Marc Smith
New Mexico Public Land, DIY

Originally appeared in Eastmans' Hunting Journal *issue 93*

This story began 10 years ago when I moved to the four corners area of New Mexico. Since 1995 my first choice on my New Mexico deer application has been 3rd rifle season in Unit 2B. New Mexicans have known for years that this is the most difficult deer tag to draw in the land of enchantment. This area of New Mexico loads up with migrating deer starting in mid October, by early November it is a big buck haven. High country mule deer migrate out of the San Juan Mountains of Colorado that border to the north and it is bordered to the East by the Jicarilla Apache Indian Reservation, known for its very high scoring B&C bucks.

In June of 2005 I was pleasantly surprised to learn that I had drawn my first choice. I was on the phone with long time friend and mule deer guru, Jeremy Dugger, of Bloomfield New Mexico as soon as I learned the good news. All summer long Jeremy and I would stay in contact, strategically developing our plan to take a magnum buck on this coveted hunt.

November finally rolled around and opening day found Jeremy and I parked at a gated forest road and hiking in to an area that has produced great deer for us in the past. I believe we saw 12 to 15 legal bucks on day one but none worth hanging a tag on. During the drive home that evening I made mention to Jeremy of the "Satan" buck he had filmed in 2000. Jeremy had been out scouting for the January bow hunt and located a giant three point that would gross near 190. We always referred to this buck as the Satan buck due to his giant body and dagger like long points. Jeremy explained to me that this area was known as Forked Horn Ridge. Jeremy's father; Leroy Dugger had taken his first archery buck there many years ago and it was a small forked horn buck, from that day on this particular area was known as Forked Horn Ridge.

On day two we were accompanied by Jeremy's brother Larry and our good friend Jimmy Hambrick. We were fueling the truck in Bloomfield and getting groceries for the day's hunt when Larry proclaimed to Jeremy that we should do a push on Forked Horn Ridge. Jeremy just kind of shrugged and said "You're the second person to mention Forked Horn Ridge. Maybe we should give it a try."

By 9:30 a.m. we had already pushed a pretty good draw and only spotted a 23-inch three point and several does. We decided to give Forked Horn Ridge a try. The plan was set; Jeremy and I were on point watching the ridge to the south. There were several escape routes to the east and west with a small canyon between us and the ridge we were watching. About 10 minutes into the drive deer began to file off the ridge to the east, they were between 250 and 300 yards away. At first there were only does and small two points, then a nice 24-inch three point with brow tines came bailing off with several does. No deer tried to escape to the west, so all of our focus was to the east. Finally Jimmy appeared on the Horizon at the east end of the ridge and soon followed Larry to the west end. Once Larry and Jimmy were in clear view Jeremy and I figured the drive was over, so we began to gather our gear and make our way over to the other guys. As I began to head down the canyon, I heard a loud "POP." I looked in the direction of the sound and a huge buck was running through the small canyon between Larry and I. The buck laid on the hillside until Jimmy bumped him and then tried to J-hook back up between Jimmy and Larry. When the buck ran into Larry he turned and headed our direction. As soon as I saw the buck I could tell he had a huge body and gigantic long sweeping beams. I told Jeremy, "I'm shooting that buck." I took off running around a point of rocks to get a view of the buck as he made his way up through the rimrock on the west end of the canyon. Jeremy was behind me trying to get his Canon XL1 focused on the deer. The buck entered a small opening in the Junipers and cedars below us and hesitated for just a brief second. I found him in the scope and touched off the shot. The buck dropped instantly. We later ranged the deer at 301 yards. Jeremy and I were stunned at how quickly everything had just unfolded. It's amazing how human instinct works. I sized that deer up, found my opportunity and dropped him at 301 yards in less than 10 seconds. Jeremy and I knew the deer was good, but it was the reaction of Larry and Jimmy that really drove the message home that we had just taken a huge buck. Larry is usually quite reserved and conservative. He was whopping and hollering so Jeremy and I put it in high gear and made our way down the canyon to the fallen brute. The buck ended up being a clean four point with no brow tines. He had 27-inch main beams and a 28-inch spread.

We knew the buck would score well, however we didn't realize just how well. We took the deer over to Brian Adair's camp. Brian is Jeremy's cousin and is also an outstanding guide and outfitter. Brian and his clients crooned over the buck for a while and then we scored it. The buck scored 191⅝ B&C and had a 26 inch neck at the ears. Amazingly Jeremy later reviewed tapes of bucks filmed in the area we hunted and has footage of this deer in 2003 when he was around 4½ years old and scored around 160 B&C. This was truly the hunt of a lifetime; 100% public land and we did it ourselves, making it so much sweeter. I waited 10 long years for this hunt and it was amazing. I appreciate the help from Jeremy, Larry and Jimmy and I hope someday I can be there when they get their chance in Satan's Hole.

New Mexico
SATAN'S HOLE

With 130 entries, New Mexico ranks #5 among the Rocky Mountain States when it comes to the number of record book mulies. Most of the state does not have record size deer, there are only a few places in the state that consistently produce B&C size mulies. In addition, the state does not produce many non-typicals. Most entries from the state are typicals.

THE BOTTOM LINE
KEYS TO SUCCESS

Migration Tag – Anytime you can hunt an area late, especially in an area bucks migrate through, you just may be in for a hell of a hunt. During this time of the year, bucks have their mind on other things and are not nearly as hard to hunt as they are earlier in the year. As can be seen, these tags are extremely hard to draw. It took Marc 10 years of applying before drawing a tag.

Hunt Known Big Buck Areas – Marc and his friends made a good choice by hunting an area that they had seen big bucks in before. There are certain areas that big bucks tend to favor, and often, you can find good bucks in these areas on a consistent basis. I have seen this many times in the past.

Conducting Drives – Drives are extremely effective for big bucks. Since I am normally hunting by myself, I personally don't do any drives, but I have seen several monster bucks taken in this fashion.

Field Judging – In trophy hunting, you need to be able to size up a buck in a matter of seconds. Marc's ability to size up the buck and touch off a shot in less than 10 seconds was very important. He may not have gotten another opportunity.

—David Long

Utah

Like several other states, Utah's deer population during the early 1900's was struggling. Deer hunting was shut down from 1908 through 1913 to help protect the state's rather small population. It was reopened in 1914 to bucks only until 1934, when a limited amount of doe tags were issued. By 1951, the mule deer population in Utah was starting to get out of control. To combat this overpopulation, the state started to allow the harvest of either sex.

During the heyday of the 1950's and 1960's, multiple permits and multiple seasons were not uncommon. In 1961, there were 132,000 deer harvested, which is the all-time peak harvest for the state. After that, deer populations were more stabilized with the increased amount of hunters and permits.

Deer numbers continued to decline and by the mid 1970's, wildlife managers began to see that it was evident that the mule deer numbers were well below the habitats carrying capacity. In order to combat the decline, the state reinstated buck only hunting. This put a lot of pressure on the bucks and led to an all-time high on the number of bucks harvested in 1983. Over the course of that hunting season, 82,552 bucks were harvested during the general season by a record 228,907 hunters.

After the 1992-93 winter (when several western states lost great amounts of mule deer), it was apparent that the mule deer harvest had to be better controlled. This led to a limit of 97,000 permits issued by over the counter sales. This was changed to a drawing process in the year 2000.

The long term goal is to bring the mule deer population up to 426,000 animals. After the 2002 season, numbers were estimated at 280,000 deer, which were well below the objective. The state has set two population objectives. The first is to reach 320,000 mule deer by the year 2008. The second is to achieve the following post-season buck to doe ratios based on a three-year average:

Area Description	Buck to Doe Ratio
General Season Public Land Units	15-20:100
General Season Private Land Units	15:100
Limited Entry Units	25-35:100
Premium Limited Entry Units*	35:100

*These units will also be managed for average age of bucks to be harvested at 5 years of age.

Utah is one of those states that has produced B&C deer from literally one end to the other. With 189 total entries, Utah ranks third all-time amongst the Rocky Mountain States. Fifty-nine of those entries have come within the past 20 years. It has turned around in recent years, and Utah has once again started producing some monster mule deer. Over the years, Utah has produced two non-typicals that break the 300-inch mark. The first one was taken back in 1943 by Alton Hunsaker in Box Elder County and ranks number three in the world with a score of 330⅛. Seven years later, Darwin Hulett took a monster that scored 302 B&C while hunting Iron County.

Kane County currently holds the top spot on both the all-time and the recent B&C listing with 25 total entries. The fact that the world famous Paunsaugunt unit falls within its boundaries may have something to do with it. The county's largest typical was picked up in 1986 and scores 207 B&C. The best non-typical was killed in 1950 by Waldon Ballard and scores 273⅞. Since 1985, one third of all of the B&C deer from Utah have come from Kane County. Sixteen of those are typicals, while the other two were non-typicals, which incidentally were both harvested in 1987.

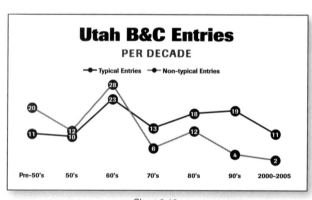

Chart 2-13

While Utah County ranks number two for Utah with 15 entries, in recent years it has fallen into a tie for eighth place. Historically it has produced nine non-typicals, but since 1985 it hasn't produced a single record book non-typical. The largest typical from the county was harvested in 1972 by Ned Losser and scores 208 B&C. The year 1950 produced the best non-typical with a score of 286⅛ and was harvested by Joe Allen.

Summit County has fallen off as well. It ranks third all-time with 13 record book heads, but has only produced two heads in recent years. The top typical scores 206 and was taken by Kendal Kiesel in 1966. Glen Holtman snagged the county's largest non-typical in 1946 with a score of 256⁴/₈.

With 12 total entries, Morgan County fills the fourth slot. With only one lone entry since 1985, it has fallen off the map in the recent year's table. K.P. Rafton punched his tag in 1973 for the best typical from the county with a score of 210⁴/₈. Jim Kilfoil managed to bag the best non-typical way back in 1938, which scores 277²/₈.

Cache County has 10 total entries which puts it in a tie for fifth place. All but one of those entries came prior to 1985. Although it hasn't been producing as of late, it has produced the number 20 typical buck in the world. It is unknown who killed the

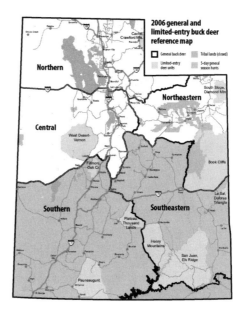

2006 general and limited-entry buck deer reference map

buck back in 1950, but it scores 211¹/₈. The largest non-typical with a score of 280 ²/₈ was taken in 1969 by someone listed in the book only as Mr. Orr.

Also in a tie for fifth place with 10 total heads is San Juan County. The good news is that half of those have been harvested in recent years. San Juan County has bragging rights for producing the state record typical. The buck, which was harvested by V.R. Rayburn in 1973, scores 212⁴/₈ and ranks number 12 in the world. The year 1966 produced the best non-typical with a score of 244⁴/₈ which was taken by Phil Acton.

Chart 2-13 shows that the 60's was definitely the decade to have been hunting in Utah. No other decade has even come close to producing as many B&C entries. The state is on pace to produce 22 B&C entries this decade, which means that it will pretty much keep the same pace producing record book heads as it did in the 90's.

Top Producing National Forests

Utah has nine national forests within its boundaries. Three are shared with Idaho. Two of them are administered by Idaho, (Caribou and Sawtooth) while a third (Cache) is combined with the Wasatch, basically leaving six national forests in Utah. With a little over 8,000,000 acres of forest, it ranks seventh among the Rocky Mountain States. Following are the top mule deer producing forests:

Dixie National Forest

At 1.8 million acres, the Dixie National Forest stretches 170 miles across southern Utah and is the state's largest national forest. Elevations range from 2,800 feet near

Utah B&C Entries

All Years			
County	Typical	Non-typical	Total
Kane	17	8	25
Utah	6	9	15
Summit	8	5	13
Morgan	7	5	12
Cache	4	6	10
San Juan	7	3	10
Garfield	6	2	8
Iron	1	7	8
Duchesne	6	1	7
Sanpete	2	5	7
Unknown	3	4	7
Washington	4	3	7
Carbon	3	3	6
Grand	3	3	6
Sevier	2	4	6
Uintah	5	1	6
Beaver	2	3	5
Rich	5	0	5
Wasatch	3	2	5
Wayne	3	2	5
Millard	1	2	3
Tooele	2	1	3
Weber	2	1	3
Box Elder	0	2	2
Davis	2	0	2
Daggett	1	0	1
Juab	0	1	1
Salt Lake	0	1	1
Totals	**105**	**84**	**189**

Table 2-13

Since 1985			
County	Typical	Non-typical	Total
Kane	16	2	18
San Juan	3	2	5
Washington	3	2	5
Uintah	4	0	4
Carbon	1	2	3
Garfield	2	1	3
Wayne	1	2	3
Iron	0	2	2
Rich	2	0	2
Summit	2	0	2
Tooele	2	0	2
Utah	2	0	2
Beaver	1	0	1
Cache	1	0	1
Duchesne	1	0	1
Grand	1	0	1
Millard	0	1	1
Morgan	1	0	1
Sanpete	0	1	1
Sevier	1	0	1
Totals	**44**	**15**	**59**

Table 2-14

the town of St. George, all the way up to 11,322 feet at the top of Blue Bell Knoll on Boulder Mountain. The Dixie has three designated wilderness areas: Ashdown Gorge, Box Death Hollow and Pine Valley Wildernesses. The forest lies within Garfield, Iron, Kane, Piute, Washington and Wayne Counties.

Dixie N.F. has a wide variety of vegetation. Desert plants can be found at the lower elevations, pinyon/juniper at the mid-elevation and aspen and conifers at the higher elevations.

A good portion of the famous Paunsaugunt Plateau, which is known for its trophy mule deer, is located on the Dixie N.F. in western Garfield County. The plateau runs north and south and is approximately 10 miles wide and 25 miles long. It rises from an elevation of 7000 feet up to 9300 feet in elevation. Spot and stalk hunting is the preferred hunting method of most people who hunt the plateau. During the archery season the bucks can be found at the highest elevations in the pines. Come rifle season, the bucks normally go into the deep canyons which are covered with pinyon/juniper, which can make hunting tough at times. There is also a late muzzleloader season which allows hunters to hunt the migration. During this time, deer are located on the south end of the plateau near their wintering grounds. Approximately 30% of the Paunsaugunt herd will migrate into Arizona to spend the winter.

Fishlake National Forest

Fishlake National Forest is Utah's second largest national forest with 1.5 million acres and spreads through eight counties in south-central Utah. The eight counties include: Beaver, Garfield, Juab, Piute, Millard, Sanpete, Sevier and Wayne Counties. Elevations range from 4800 feet up to 12,169 feet at the top of Delano Peak.

Manti-La Sal National Forest

The Manti-La Sal National Forest is located in central and southeastern Utah and is 1.2 million acres in size. The forest lies within Emery, Carbon, Grand, San Juan, Sanpete and Utah Counties.

Dark Canyon Wilderness is the forest's lone wilderness area. The wilderness is bordered on the east and south by Elk Ridge. The Elk Ridge area has produced some monster bucks throughout the years. Elk Ridge has an elevation of 8800 feet and a good portion of the higher country is covered with quaking aspen and ponderosa pines.

There are three main mountain ranges on the forest: Abajo Mountains (locally known as the Blue Mountains), La Sal Mountains and the Manti Mountains.

Uinta National Forest

The Uinta National Forest lies in central Utah and is 880,000 acres in size. The forest has three wilderness areas: Lone Peak, Mount Nebo and Mount Timpanogos Wildernesses.

The Wasatch Range is the main mountain range on the forest and contains the 11,877-foot Mount Nebo, which is the forest's highest point.

Wasatch-Cache National Forest

The Wasatch-Cache National Forest is located in northern Utah and encompasses 1.2 million acres. A small portion of the forest extends into southwestern Wyoming. The forest contains portions of seven different wilderness areas: Deseret Peak, High Uintah, Lone Peak, Mount Naomi, Mount Olympus, Twin Peak and Wellsville Wildernesses.

Mountain ranges within the forest are the Bear River, Monte Cristo, Stansbury, Uinta and Wasatch.

Just Plain Crazy!

By Gary Wilson
Utah Public Land, DIY

Originally appeared in Eastmans' Bowhunting Journal *issue 26*

My hunting partners often teased me about being crazy. Between them and my wife's continued rolling of her eyeballs, I can't help but wonder if they're right.

Raising three young boys requires my wife and I to work together in order to give each other breaks. My ridiculous passion for scouting definitely comes with a price. Luckily for me, my hunting partners are almost as crazy as I am it seems? This became vividly clear to me while saddling up llamas for our kids to ride and stuffing them into a camping trailer, just so we could check waterholes for fresh sign, only to have them pee all over the camper floor. The llamas that is. After the llama episode, I resorted to recruiting other hunters, or baby carriers. This worked well, until my 60-year-old father-in-law nearly died hauling up a 50 pound grandson on his back. Not to be defeated, I resorted to packing my four year old on my shoulders and my five year old in my backpack, which seemed like a good idea until the eye poke incident from a low hanging branch.

Most couples kiss each other goodnight. I kiss my wife good-bye about 11:00p.m. To keep hunting and scouting time in check, I often have to scout during sleeping hours. Personally, I get a great surge of adrenaline walking in the darkness and I'll tell you, scrambling up the mountain in the dark gives the term "bushwhacking" a whole new meaning.

Determined or just plain crazy…. only time would tell.

During a number of my initial scouting trips this past summer I found several good clusters of bucks ranging from seven or eight bucks to single big bucks running solo. After scouting each cluster up close on different occasions, I narrowed my options down to those that would give me the greatest likelihood of taking a buck on opening day. Once this had been accomplished I focused on trying to pattern their behavior and tendencies. After a couple more trips I felt fairly confident, but wanted to do a practice run a week before the opener.

Again, alone, at 1:30 a.m. I find myself walking nearly five miles up into a high alpine area, covering nearly 4,000 feet of elevation. At first light, I heard the sound of a critter. Squinting, I tried my binoculars and made out what seemed to be elk. Racks tell me they are elk, but the body is small like a deer. The massive dark shadows lingering above their heads make me doubt myself in disbelief.

I move on to my pre-determined position, only to find no deer. I knew I needed a second look at the "elk" behind me and proceeded back in their direction. Armed with a camcorder and digital camera, I was hoping for some excellent shots.

The sound of a deer blowing stopped me in my tracks. Busted. I held motionless. I caught movement of a small three point 80 yards in front of me. The wind was hitting my face. Smell was now their weakest defense. I suddenly caught movement out of the corner of my eye, only 22 yards in front of me, antlers were swiveling back and forth. I turned on my video camera and started to capture amazing buck footage. Deep tines, cheaters, wide rack, but my view was partially obstructed, teasing me with only parts of the rack. To my surprise, the buck walked out in front of me. After nearly 20 minutes of watching this brute, there was little doubt that I would go after this guy when the season opened in one week.

Throughout the year I had practiced shooting. I wanted to have 100 percent confidence in my shot when given an opportunity at a wallhanger. I also surprised my wife by the adoption of my very own 3-D mule deer target. I even hauled him with us on family camping trips when he wasn't set up in my unfinished basement. My shooting was coming together and groups were getting tighter.

Opening morning, I learned something—I learned that other hunters knew of this area too. I wasn't alone. Because of all the activity, no bucks were in sight. I returned to the opposite side of the hill when my hunting partner signaled to me with arm gestures that he had found a few big bucks. We monitored the wind and began our stalk forward, inching across the hillside, glassing every shaded tree. Finally, we saw antlers. Although what we had spotted was a good buck, he wasn't Lefty. We decided to wait them out until evening and see if Lefty would appear from the cover.

Rain was threatening and we had left camp uncovered intending to return before going too far. Low on water and hungry, we thought we'd have at least several hours before the bucks would get up to feed and move about. The bucks were between our camp and us. I volunteered to go all the way around the mountain on the backside of all the ridges to avoid detection of smell or sight.

This is where luck stepped in. As I topped the ridge entering into my camp, I saw velvet antlers feeding on the slope below me. I thought, "This is crazy!" I looked down the hill, through some timber, and amazingly I could see a cheater on the left side. I had just found Lefty.

I had the wind in my favor as I slowly crawled, narrowing the distance to within bow range. I thought, "Look out for other eyes." Just then I noticed a small three-point. I kept my eyes fixed on Lefty's actions. Cautiously, I drew back and held my bow at full draw. Lefty was facing directly towards me with his head down feeding. I dared not take a bad shot. I waited a few seconds and he finally turned giving me a perfect shot. As soon as he looked up, I lightly squeezed my release and my arrow was on its way.

I saw the arrow in flight and the direction it went. It sounded like hitting a large pillow. I knew I had just hit the monster buck. I remember saying to myself, "Yes! Yes! That was perfect!" I couldn't believe Lefty had moved around from the other bucks. Luck had just played a crucial part in the timing of my return to camp, but somehow my determination or craziness had helped increase the odds.

I immediately called my wife to let her share the excitement of a crazy bowhunter in the moment of taking a "Super Monster Buck." Somehow she understood my excitement and perhaps gained some clarity from all the pre-hunt madness.

I retrieved my arrow, then tried to push the bedded bucks we had been watching into him but had no luck. With all the luck having been used up with Lefty, we headed back to the shot site and began tracking. I will never forget the feeling of seeing that massive set of antlers resting on the hillside. An overwhelming sense of respect overcame me as I stared at the monster buck. I knew what I had accomplished was no everyday event on the mountain.

Call it crazy, but I could have sworn there was some ground swelling going on. An unofficial green score later estimated Lefty near 202 gross and 196 net Pope & Young. His outside spread reached an impressive 31 inches. Main beam lengths at 23⅘ inches, G2's an incredible 19 inches, G3's and G4's a monstrous 13 inches. His mass averaged nearly five inches. Undoubtedly, I had arrowed a super monster buck of a lifetime.

Utah
JUST PLAIN CRAZY!

Utah has produced 189 B&C entries which ranks it #3 among the Rocky Mountain States. Although the entire state has produced record book heads, the extreme southern counties have been producing the majority of the B&C heads over the past 20 years.

THE BOTTOM LINE   KEYS TO SUCCESS

Scouting – Gary flat worked his tail off during the preseason. He made numerous scouting trips and it paid big dividends with him locating a monster buck.

Low-Profile Camp – Keeping a low-profile camp is very important if you want to be successful at backcountry hunting. I normally position my camp so that it is well concealed and I keep all activity and noises to a minimum. Gary and his hunting partner did exactly this, and it paid off by harvesting his trophy within 65 yards of his camp.

Practice Shooting – Whether you are hunting with a bow or a rifle, you owe it to yourself and the game you are pursuing to be proficient with your weapon. This means hours and hours of practice. Gary practiced throughout the year and even took his 3D target on family camping trips. All of his time spent practicing paid off as he was able to take his once-in-a-lifetime P&Y buck with one clean shot.

—David Long

Wyoming

Wyoming has produced B&C entries from one end of the state to the other. The Cowboy State has produced 20 typical bucks over 200 B&C, but does not have any non-typicals surpassing the 300-inch B&C mark. The largest non-typical from the state scores 293⁴/₈ and was taken by J.B. Marvin in 1924. With the exception of Carbon County, all of the top producing counties are on the west side of the state.

Lincoln County is at the top with 39 entries, over double the entries of the next closest county. The largest typical ever taken from Lincoln County was taken by my good friend Victor Clark. He harvested the buck in 1992 and it scores 209³/₈ and ranks number five in Wyoming. The largest non-typical buck from Lincoln County was taken by Joe Welch in 1940 with a score of 263³/₈. Lincoln County is about 70% public land and there are three national forests within its boundaries, the Bridger-Teton National Forest, the Targhee National Forest and the Caribou National Forest.

Sublette County ranks number two with 17 total entries. The best typical from the county scores 202³/₈ and was taken by Derek Kendrick in 1992. The top non-typical was taken in 1965 by James Straley and scores 260²/₈. Over 80% of Sublette County is public land and it has one national forest within its boundaries, the Bridger-Teton N.F.

Teton County has 16 total entries which make it number three for Wyoming. Although it has not produced as many entries as the top counties, it has produced two of the top four typical bucks from Wyoming. The state record typical was taken in Teton County back in 1925 by an unknown hunter and scores 217. In 1984, Thomas Ford took the county's largest non-typical scoring 262⁷/₈.

With 13 total entries, Carbon County ranks fourth for Wyoming. The top typical from the county is also the largest typical taken in the state by a woman. It scores 205²/₈ and was taken by Shelly Risner in 1986. The finest non-typical to come from the county was taken in 1950 by Edward Vigil and scores 270⁶/₈. Carbon County has one national forest within its boundaries, the Medicine Bow National Forest.

Fremont County is tied for fifth with 10 total entries. The largest typical buck from the county was taken back in 1960 by Herb Klein and scores 207⁰/₈. The largest non-typical was taken on the Wind River Indian Reservation by Cathy Keene in

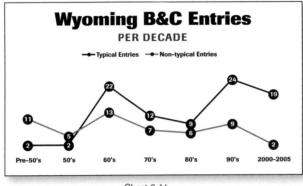

Wyoming B&C Entries
PER DECADE
—●— Typical Entries —●— Non-typical Entries

22   24
19
11   13   12
5   7   9   9
2   2   6   2

Pre-50's   50's   60's   70's   80's   90's   2000-2005

Chart 2-14

2004 and is the third largest non-typical ever taken in Wyoming with a score of 285³/₈.

Also tied for the fifth spot is Park County with 10 total entries. Over half of those entries have been taken since 1985. The Shoshoni National Forest which is 2.4 million acres in size, blankets the entire western half of the county. While antler hunting in 1995, Wes Livingston picked up a winter-killed buck near Cody that is the largest buck from the county and currently ranks number three in Wyoming. The buck scores 211⁷/₈ B&C and is proof that Park County is starting to produce some quality deer. The largest non-typical to come from the county was taken by John K. Corbett back in 1943 and scores 265⁵/₈.

A look at Chart 2-14 shows that you are definitely more likely to harvest a B&C typical than a non-typical in the state of Wyoming. Since the 1950's, the state has consistently produced more typicals than non-typicals, this is especially true since the 90's. With 21 total entries since 2000, the state is on pace for 35 entries this decade. That will exceed the total for the 90's, and will equal that of the 1960's. Wyoming is definitely holding its own right now when it comes to B&C entries.

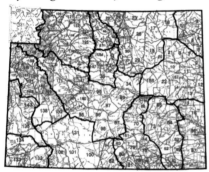

Top Producing National Forests

Wyoming has five national forests that totally fall within its boundaries as well as five others that it shares with surrounding states for a total of 8,688.844 acres of national forest.

Bighorn National Forest

The Bighorn National Forest is 1,115,073 acres in size and is located in the north-central part of the state. The forest runs from the Great Basin area of Wyoming northward into central Montana. Parts of four counties are located within its boundaries: Big Horn, Johnson, Sheridan and Washakie.

There are three highways that traverse the Bighorn Mountains: Highway 16 on the southern end and Highway 14 and 14A on the northern end. The two largest towns offering access to the forest are Sheridan and Buffalo, both of which are located to the east of the Bighorn Mountains. If you want to get off the beaten path, the Cloud Peak Wilderness offers 189,000 acres of solitude in the southern portion of the forest. This is where you can find Cloud Peak (13,187 ft), which is the highest point on the forest.

Wyoming B&C Entries

All Years

County	Typical	Non-typical	Total
Lincoln	31	8	39
Sublette	12	5	17
Teton	12	4	16
Carbon	7	6	13
Fremont	4	6	10
Park	7	3	10
Unknown	2	7	9
Sweetwater	2	4	6
Uinta	3	1	4
Albany	1	1	2
Big Horn	1	1	2
Hot Springs	1	1	2
Natrona	2	0	2
Niobrara	2	0	2
Platte	1	1	2
Sheridan	0	2	2
Campbell	0	1	1
Converse	0	1	1
Crook	1	0	1
Goshen	1	0	1
Weston	0	1	1
Total	**90**	**53**	**143**

Table 2-15

Since 1985

County	Typical	Non-typical	Total
Lincoln	20	5	25
Teton	6	2	8
Carbon	5	1	6
Park	5	1	6
Sublette	5	1	6
Fremont	2	1	3
Unknown	1	2	3
Uinta	1	1	2
Goshen	1	0	1
Platte	1	0	1
Totals	**47**	**14**	**61**

Table 2-16

Bridger-Teton National Forest

When it comes to trophy mule deer in Wyoming, the Bridger–Teton National Forest continues to produce top-notch bucks every year. The forest is made up of five mountain ranges: the Gros Ventre, Teton, Salt River, Wind River and Wyoming Ranges. At 3.4 million acres, the Bridger-Teton N.F. is one of the largest forests in the United States. A good portion of the forest is accessible by vehicle and ATVs. If that's not your style, one third of the forest is designated wilderness, which allows you to get away from all motorized vehicles. The bad news is that all nonresidents must have an outfitter or guide to hunt the wildernesses in Wyoming. However, the good news is that most of the record book heads don't come from the wilderness areas.

Three of the top record book counties fall within the forests boundaries: Lincoln, Sublette and Teton.

Medicine Bow National Forest

The Medicine Bow National Forest is 1,402,614 acres in size and is located in south-central Wyoming and northern Colorado. The highest peak in the range (Medicine Bow Peak at 12,013 ft) is located in the northern end of the range in Albany County.

The town of Saratoga acts as the gateway to the Medicine Bow Mountains which are primarily located in Carbon and Albany Counties. The section of national forest located in Carbon County has produced numerous B&C heads throughout the years and according to the following B&C entry tables, it is still producing because almost half of the entries are since 1985.

Shoshone National Forest

The Shoshone National Forest is 2,466,557 acres in size and is primarily located within two counties: Park and Fremont. It is located in the northwestern part of the state and is the oldest national forest in the United States. Yellowstone National Park borders the west side of the forest, while the state of Montana borders the northern edge. The forest consists of the Absaroka, Beartooth and Wind River mountain ranges.

There are five wilderness areas (North Absaroka, Washakie, Fitzpatrick, Popo Agie, and Absaroka-Beartooth) within the forest for a total of 1.4 million acres. With over half of the forest designated as wilderness, there are plenty of roadless areas to venture into.

Big Daddy

By Pete Foti
Wyoming Public Land, DIY

Originally appeared in Eastmans' Hunting Journal *issue 75*

My hunting partners, Earl Saucier and my brother Frank, have been hunting with me for a number of years now. Wyoming has been our choice because of its trophy potential and you still have great odds of drawing an out-of-state tag. After every season we head home feeling we've learned more about the area and will be better prepared for the next season.

This was our fifth do-it-yourself trip to Wyoming, and I couldn't help but think this was going to by my year. In past trips, Earl and Frank have taken some nice bucks, but not me. Last season, the night before we were supposed to leave, I spotted a nice four-point high on a ridge. He was a great buck, but in a spot that wouldn't allow us to stalk him. I spent the off-season thinking about how big he would be this year and couldn't wait to get back to our area.

This season, Frank and Earl set up our base camp and packed in our spike camp. Typically, we will spike out for days before returning to base camp for supplies. By the time I arrived, both camps were set up and Frank and Earl had done a little scouting.

The first morning I headed in the direction where Frank had seen a few deer. I didn't get 200 yards out of camp before spotting some. I set up the scope to get a better look, but all I could see were does. Does without a buck seemed strange this time of year.

I glassed the open countryside and spotted a 3x4 and a decent four point. I watched them feed into the dark timber, making mental notes of where the bucks disappeared. By now it was late morning and almost all the deer had bedded for the day, so I headed back to camp.

Research

I returned to the same spot that evening. I could tell by tracks in the snow the deer were using the area heavily, and after a half-hour or so a few started to feed out on the open hillside. The 3x4 and the four point joined them. The four point was a decent buck and I was tempted to stalk him, but I told myself to be patient and wait to see what else was in the area.

Just before dark, I caught some movement at the edge of the timber. I pulled up my spotting scope and there was "Big Daddy." He was feeding away and stopped to raise his head. I could tell he was a tremendous buck.

I had to make a quick decision: Should I make a quick stalk with fading light, or sit on him and try to find him in the morning? With just enough daylight left, I decided to go after him. I headed down the canyon, staying out of view of the buck, crossed the creek and headed up the other side. I was concerned that when I crested the ridge I would be too close to the buck and spook him. I went as slowly as I could, making sure to be as quiet as possible.

Now the fever was kicking in. My adrenaline started to flow and my heart was pounding. I crested the ridge slowly and scanned the area for the buck. He should have been within 100 yards of where I was, but he was nowhere to be seen. Did I spook him?

I glassed the area and about 70 yards away to my right were the 3x4 and four point. Oh no, I thought. This is a bust. I froze there until dark, then slowly backed out of the area and hiked back to camp.

Earl and Frank could tell the size of the buck by the excitement in my voice, but I couldn't help but wonder if I'd blown him out of the country.

After a sleepless night I was behind the spotting scope again. I saw several deer but no "Big Daddy." I didn't even see the 3x4 or the four point. Extremely disappointed, I returned to camp and met up with Earl. He was hunting on the backside of the ridge where I'd spotted the bucks. He'd found the four point and the 3x4, but not "Big Daddy."

Out-of-State Research

When planning an out-of-state hunt, a lot of research is required. One of the biggest questions that needs to be answered before any plans can be made is "where?" I have been a subscriber to the Eastmans' Hunting Journal for several years. It is one of my best tools for doing research. The stories and Member's Research Supplement have provided a ton of material to help me plan my self-guided hunts.

Another question you need to answer is "how?" Before we started hunting the Wyoming country, we ordered Mike Eastman's book, Hunting High Country Mule Deer. The book gave us information on spot and stalk, glassing, and how to find those trophy bucks. We also started keeping a journal of just what we encountered each day of the season.

I have learned that in Wyoming especially, optics are invaluable. The country is so vast that you need quality optics to give yourself the best chance of harvesting a trophy buck. On this hunt, I had to remind myself of the saying, "First one in, last one out." I will stay behind my spotting scope until it is absolutely too dark to see. The number of deer you'll see those last few minutes in the evening or the first light of the day is amazing.

—Pete Foti

This was good news. Maybe the buck was still in the same area. I decided on a different strategy for my afternoon hunt. I needed to be closer to the buck's bedding area so that when he started to feed, just before dark, I was close enough for a shot. Confident in my plan, I headed out again.

I set up about 1:30 and prepared to wait it out until dark. As a few deer fed out into the open, I started to wonder if they would feed right to me. I worried they would feed too close, bust me and spook out of the country, taking "Big Daddy" with them.

I glassed the country and caught a glimpse of movement in the timber. Then I spotted him. He was in the same place where I'd first laid eyes on him, traveling to an opening in the trees. I set up and in an instant, he offered me a shot.

At the sound of the rifle, the buck kicked his hind legs and sprinted into the trees. Did I hit him? Was he down?

I waited for several minutes, watching for any movement in the trees. After what seemed like an eternity, I made my way over to the trees. My heart raced, hoping to find the trophy buck. And there he was, just 15 yards from the spot where I shot.

What a buck. I'd put in five seasons on this public land do-it-yourself trophy and didn't regret a single minute. I had finally achieved my goal.

Wyoming
BIG DADDY

Wyoming has 143 B&C entries which places it #4 among the Rocky Mountain States. Although the state has literally produced good mule deer from one side to the other, the majority of the record book heads have come from the western side of the state.

THE BOTTOM LINE
KEYS TO SUCCESS

Know Your Hunting Area – When hunting out of state, it can take several years to get to know an area before you can really hunt it effectively. This was Pete's fifth year of hunting the area and he knew which areas would have bucks and how to hunt them.

Pass on Lesser Bucks – If you really want to harvest the buck of a lifetime, you have to be able to pass on lesser bucks. Pete did exactly that. He spotted a nice four-point buck on his first day of hunting, but decided it was too early in the hunt to settle for something less than what he wanted. Shortly after passing on the average four point, he spotted "Big Daddy."

Stick With an Area – If there is one point that I can't emphasize enough, it is once you locate a good buck, stick with that area. This is the buck's home and he is not going to just get up and leave the country. You might go a couple of days without seeing him, but be persistent and it could pay big dividends. After locating Big Daddy the evening of the first day, Pete returned the next morning and couldn't relocate the buck. But being persistent, he returned again that afternoon and located the buck in the exact area he had been previously.

—David Long

The Bottom  Line

This section has all of the information you need to get started in your quest for the buck of a lifetime. I recommend reading it several times before deciding on an area to apply for. Since your odds are very low in some of the more popular trophy mule deer areas, I suggest applying for several different states. I would also recommend seeking out areas that are not so well known. There are a lot of areas out there that are currently overlooked, which are producing great bucks.

There are several good resources that are currently available to use as research material. Your money would be well spent on a state record book for the state you plan to hunt. These books generally have more specific information on which regions of the state that you are more likely to find a record book class buck.

Once you have decided on an area, contact the local game and fish biologist and pick his brain. Remember, you are not the first to ever contact him regarding such information. Any details he is likely to share with you regarding the area, he has probably shared with many others. The information he gives you will get you on the right track, but you need to follow up that information with more research on the area.

One of the best tools available for research today is the Internet. There are many websites out there that have a lot of trophy mule deer information. A search of the web can turn up several good articles on mule deer as well as specific areas that are currently producing good bucks.

Once you do decide on an area, logon to that state's game and fish website and research their application process. Make sure and do this early in the year because most states have application periods several months before the hunt begins.

SECTION 3

SCOUTING

Trust Your Scouting

Your pre-season scouting paid off. You located a huge 36-inch non-typical that has eight points on either side. Over the course of the next few weeks, you make several backpack trips into the high alpine basin to watch the buck and pattern his every move. You start feeling a very special connection to the buck as you learn when and where he eats and sleeps. You feel that you know his every move and that he has become fairly predictable in his daily routine. The buck occupies your thoughts on a regular basis, whether you're at work, golfing or just laying around the house. You envision the hunt in your mind and play it over and over again. It is just a matter of time until the hunting season opens.

The day before the season, you load all of your gear into your backpack and drive to the trailhead. Unfortunately, there are other vehicles already parked there, and suddenly you get a sick feeling inside your stomach that just won't go away. You start to wonder if the other hunters know of the big non-typical and will be looking into the basin on opening morning as well. Although there are a lot of uncertainties at this point, you still have a positive attitude and begin your long, steep climb up the dry and dusty trail.

Once you set your tent up and get your camp situated, you have a couple of hours before dark, so you make your way up to the top of the ridge that overlooks the basin the buck has been living in. You begin glassing, and before you know it, a couple of the smaller bucks that he normally runs with feed their way out into the upper part of the basin. You think to yourself, "It won't be long now," but the buck never shows. As much as you try to keep a positive attitude, doubt starts to creep its way into your mind.

That evening, sleep doesn't come easy as you lay in your sleeping bag wondering what the morning will bring. Where could the buck have been? You think to yourself. Did the other hunters know where he was? Was he still in the area? Your mind at this point is a jumbled up mess trying to process all of the thoughts and questions that you have. After laying there for several hours and thinking that you may never go to sleep, the next thing you know it is time to get up.

122

Those warm comfortable boots that you took off the night before are now covered with frost and are not quite as warm as you slip them on in the early morning darkness. Dressed and ready to go, you start walking up the ridge to get to the vantage point where you wait for the sun to make its entrance over the mountains that lie to the east. You made it a point to not overdress this morning so you wouldn't heat up on the way to your vantage point and as you huddle under a pine tree, you start getting goose bumps as the temperature has not yet started to rise.

Finally, the sun starts to slowly make its way up toward the horizon and you soon forget all about being cold. Your complete attention is now focused on finding the 36-inch buck that you became so familiar with during the pre-season. Looking through the binoculars, your eyes strain to try and make out the outline of the huge non-typical buck. As the sun and the temperatures start to rise, you start to get worried. The buck is nowhere to be found. As you continue glassing the basin, you spot two other hunters on the opposite side of the basin and one making his way up the bottom. Frustrated, you continue to glass for several more hours only to spot a couple of small bucks running out over the head of the basin that were spooked by three hunters on horseback that just appeared 300 yards above and to the left of you.

After everything quiets down and your morning glassing session is done, you continue to still-hunt the area for the remainder of the day without success. Back at camp that night your spirit is down and after putting in two more hard days of hunting, you decide that the buck has left the area and you move on to your backup area, never to see the buck again.

Welcome to public land hunting. Hunting public land can be very hard to say the least. But you can't give up easy. Don't let this scenario that we just went through happen to you. All of your research and hard scouting led you to this area, so don't give up. Even if there are other hunters in the vicinity, don't leave. The worst thing that you can do is start jumping from area to area, thinking the grass is always greener on the other side.

If you do find yourself in a situation like I just mentioned, wait for everyone to clear out of the area. After the first 10 days of the season the hills are almost empty. A lot of hunters have already tagged out, and the majority of the ones that haven't are burned out and not hunting as hard as they were the first part of the season. This is when you need to be back in the area looking for your buck. Toward the end of the season the bucks have somewhat of a routine back in their lives as the mountains clear out.

I have been guilty of giving up too soon as well. One year I was camping with my family and I made an early morning hike up one of my favorite drainages and spotted five bucks in a bachelor group. I set up the spotting scope and couldn't believe my eyes when I zoomed in on the biggest buck of the group. He was only about 27 inches wide, but his velvet covered 10x8 antlers were extremely heavy and tall. I estimated his score at 220 B&C. All of his extras were in-line points and were very long. There was also a very respectable 7x8 in the group. It is not very often you get to see two bucks of this caliber together.

I watched the bucks as they continued feeding and started to make their way in the direction of their bedding area. They crossed an open east-facing slope and then crossed through a saddle onto the west-facing slope and disappeared into some scattered pines to bed. Instantly I knew where I was going to be the next morning—sitting in that saddle waiting for them.

Up well before light, I head-lamped two and a half miles to the base of the ridge I needed to climb. Another 45 minutes put me right where I wanted to be. I found a spot about 80 yards above the saddle and made myself comfortable. The day before,

the bucks passed through the saddle at 8:15 a.m. I looked at my watch and it was 7:30 a.m. If everything went as planned, I wouldn't have too long of a wait.

At 7:58 a.m., one of the small bucks appeared, and then a second. The third buck was the big guy. What an impressive sight, being within 80 yards of a buck of this caliber. I continued watching the bucks as they made their way through a couple of small openings and they entered the same patch of timber that they had disappeared into the previous day.

I now had a dilemma. I had a monster buck spotted in one area, but I had friends coming from out of state to hunt the rifle opener with me in another area. There was no way I was going to dog my buddies on the hunt we had planned, so my only option was to hunt the buck during the archery season, which opened two weeks before the rifle season.

The day before the opener, two buddies and I backpacked the 2½ miles into the drainage and pitched our tents. The next morning found me heading for the saddle that the bucks had been utilizing, while my two friends headed up the opposite side of the valley.

Just as planned, I was sitting in the saddle at 7:30 a.m. Before I knew it, it was 8:00 a.m., then 8:30 a.m. and still no action. I continued sitting there all morning, but the bucks never surfaced. After I was convinced they weren't going to show up, I started making my way farther up the ridge. When I got to where I could see the head of the basin that the bucks normally feed in, I noticed two other bowhunters standing at the top sky-lined. That explained why the bucks didn't follow their normal routine. I figured the bucks used one of their numerous escape routes out of the basin as soon as they detected the other hunters.

For the next couple of days I continued hunting from daylight to dark without laying eyes on the monster buck. I did see the 7x8 and all of the other bucks on numerous occasions, but never the big guy. The thought crossed my mind to do a stalk on the 7x8, but it is hard to go after a 200-inch non-typical when you know there is a 220-inch buck in the area.

When the rifle opener came, my buddies and I were hunting the different area, but all I could think about was that monster 10x8. After our hunt was over, I made a couple trips into the monster buck's high country home, but was never able to locate him. Looking back on it, I wish that I wouldn't have given up so easy. I should have spent the rest of the season trying to locate the buck. As you can see, I too, am guilty of giving up too easy. I still kick myself for that one. A buck of that caliber is so rare; you need to devote the entire season to hunting the buck. It doesn't make any sense to hunt anywhere else. Unfortunately, most people that are lucky enough to scout a monster during the preseason usually don't end up harvesting the buck. They give up way too easy.

There are many different forms of scouting. Scouting differs from hunting in that you can do it year round. Spring, summer, fall or winter, it doesn't matter, you can be scouting in one form or another. In this section we will discuss what type of scouting you can be doing during various times of the year.

Spring Scouting

Spring is a very good time to be in the field. Because most deer in the Rocky Mountains migrate between summer and winter ranges, watching the deer as they follow the snow line back up to their summer range, enables one to identify migration corridors that the deer use. Migration corridors are topographical features that restrict deer to a somewhat narrow passageway during migration. Mountains, canyons, creek drainages and habitat cover are some of the key factors in determining which routes the deer may utilize. This information becomes priceless if your hunting season runs into late October or early November and it snows enough to trigger a migration. The deer will utilize the same corridors on the way to the winter range as they did in the spring on the way to their summer range.

During the spring migration, weather is the key factor that determines when mule deer begin their journey every spring to their summer range. If the area has a harsh winter that carries late into spring, the deer will start their migration later in the year. When spring arrives early, this triggers the deer to begin much sooner. They seem to follow the snow line as it gradually creeps back up the mountains.

Most deer begin migrating in mid-March, but wait until the last part of April or early May before you start looking. By then, deer have reached the mountains

Mark Gocke, WGFD

Spring is a great time to identify migration routes and transitional ranges.

and you will be able to identify the migration corridors. Spend your time glassing the south- and west-facing slopes that have relatively open cover. Hillsides covered with sagebrush openings and patches of aspens are great places to check out. The vegetation on these slopes has started to grow and provides excellent food with all the nutritional requirements that the deer need for antler growth this time of year. The north-facing slopes are usually still covered with snow, which makes finding food very difficult.

Deer will use these corridors year after year, following almost the exact route during spring and fall migrations. To give you an idea of how precise their migrations are from year to year, here is an example from a deer study that was conducted in southwestern Wyoming. If you will look at Image 3-3 it shows the migration paths taken by seven GPS-collared deer that currently winter on the Pinedale Front Winter Range Complex in southwestern Wyoming. Keep in mind, this same route is utilized by literally thousands of mule deer, twice a year, once in the spring and once in the fall. As you can tell, migration routes do not vary much. These deer migrated along a very distinct corridor approximately 50 miles in distance along the Wind River Range. The well-defined path is only 0.25 miles wide in spots and very rarely exceeded one to two miles in width.

Bucks seem to start migrating first, followed by the does and fawns. Bucks will be in small bachelor groups of normally between 3 to 10 bucks. They oftentimes look pretty rough this time of year because they normally have burned all of their fat reserves to aid in their survival of the winter. The shedding of their heavy winter coat this time of year also makes them look rather mangy. Bucks will be up and feeding a large portion of the day and will be very visible on any southern exposures.

Spring is also a good time to identify transitional ranges. Transitional ranges are

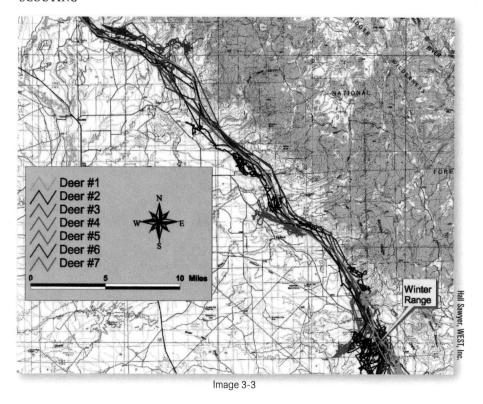

Image 3-3

areas that deer hold up in between winter and summer ranges. Transition ranges are usually lower in elevation than summer ranges and must contain three important needs for the deer. These are food, cover and water. The time period in which deer utilize theses ranges varies greatly from year to year and is solely based on the weather.

Once you identify these transition ranges during the spring migration, check them out during the latter part of the hunting season because deer will use the same transitional ranges in the fall as they do in the spring.

Jim Hamilton

Summer Scouting

Summer scouting has to be one of the most enjoyable aspects of trophy hunting. During this time of year I love going to the field because I expect to see more deer this time of year than I ever will during hunting season, and a lot less people. Very rarely do I ever run into anybody on my scouting trips.

This time of year bucks will be found in bachelor groups from the first of June through the end of September, which makes them easier to spot. While they are in their red summer coats, they really stand out when the sun hits them during the early morning and late evening hours. It's also a lot easier sizing up a buck when he has several buddies by his side. Most bachelor groups of bucks that I see during scouting contain four to five bucks, while I have seen groups as large as 17 together.

I normally begin scouting the high country around the first part of July. By then, the bucks are pretty much settled into their summer routine and I can feel pretty confident that the bucks I locate will remain in the area. Any earlier in the year and the bucks you locate will still be on the move to their summer range and may be

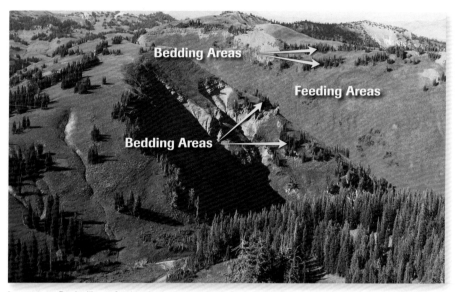

Image 3-4 • Bucks like to feed in the large openings above timberline during the summer months. They are very easy to spot when the sun hits their shiny red coats.

tough to relocate later on.

During the summer months, there is very little human presence in the high country. The bucks take advantage of this solitude by feeding in the large open spaces at timberline during the summer months with very little disturbance. This time of year the feed at this elevation is plentiful and very high in nutrients. If there is one thing that I want you to take from this book, it is this: where you find the best feed, you will often find the best bucks.

Whether it's summer, spring or fall, a good spotting scope and a lightweight tripod should always be in your pack.

Image 3-4 shows the type of high country that I like to glass during the summer. The country is relatively open and has several stringers of pines that bucks like to bed in. The place I would really expect to see bucks in the photo would be on the small finger ridge running down the middle of the basin. Bucks absolutely love these types of ridges.

Four Phase Glassing Techniques

In order to consistently spot trophy bucks, whether it be during the preseason or hunting season, you need to become proficient at glassing. Throughout this book I will be referring to Four Phase Glassing, which is a technique that I have developed over the years that I have found to be extremely effective.

During my years of pursuing trophy bucks, I have been fortunate to have taken many nice trophy mule deer, but over the course of the last two years, I have been lucky enough to harvest two bucks that have exceeded that mark, scoring $197^{2}/_{8}$ and $202^{6}/_{8}$ B&C. Lucky? You bet! But I like to think that my glassing technique which has evolved throughout my 25 years of pursuing trophy mulies may have had something to do with it. Years ago, my glassing sessions had no structure, and as a result, were very unproductive. Seeing what has worked and what hasn't worked over the years, has led to the refined Four Phase Glassing technique that I use today.

My glassing technique is basically divided into four different phases: initial glassing, secondary glassing, detailed glassing and ultra glassing. Phases I and II are normally used during prime glassing hours in the morning and evening, while Phases III and IV are mainly used during the heat of the day.

Phase I – Initial Glassing

Once I sit down and get comfortable at my vantage point, I conduct my initial glassing of the area, which has one purpose, and that is to locate any obvious deer that may be out in the open. The initial glassing is done at a fairly rapid pace covering all of the terrain in sight, especially the larger openings. Don't worry about picking the mountain apart at this stage, your main goal at this time is to cover a lot of country.

131

4-Phase Glassing

In order to consistently spot trophy bucks, you need to become proficient at glassing. In my 25 years of pursuing magnum bucks, I have developed a technique that I call 4-Phase Glassing that I feel is the most effective glassing method for record class mulies. Following is a short overview of the four phases.

Phase 1 (Initial Glassing) — Phase I glassing is done at a fairly rapid pace covering all of the terrain in sight, especially the larger openings. Don't worry about picking the mountain apart at this stage; your main goal at this time is to cover a lot of country. After you have glassed all of the surrounding terrain several times, move on to Phase II.

Phase 2 (Secondary Glassing) — Phase II differs from the Phase I in that you will glass at a much slower rate and concentrate more on the smaller openings. I will divide the mountain into sections and concentrate on one section at a time to make sure I cover all of it effectively. I will glass each section thoroughly before moving on to the next section.

Phase 3 (Detailed Glassing) — Phase III, or detailed glassing, is when you really need to start picking the mountainside apart, inch by inch. I will spend literally hour after hour picking the mountainside apart with my binoculars. I am concentrating on close up areas at this point, normally glassing everything within rifle range. You're not looking for an outline of a deer any more, now you are looking for the tips of antlers, the tip of an ear or any slight movement that could be a buck tucked away in the shadows.

Phase 4 (Ultra Glassing) — Phase IV, or ultra glassing, is when you take Phase III to the next level. This is where you dissect the terrain with your spotting scope, rather than binoculars. Not only are you picking the mountainside apart, you are literally picking every tree, bush and shrub apart.

A lot of articles you read will lead you to believe that you should start glassing the distant areas first, but I prefer to glass the closer areas. This allows me to glass any bucks that might already have me spotted and I can get a look at them before they are gone. Odds are, the deer that are a long ways off have no idea that I am even there. Once you have glassed the immediate area, start glassing the distant terrain, and I do mean distant terrain. I normally glass all mountainsides within two miles of my vantage point. I have even spotted deer at longer ranges, you can't necessarily see much detail at extreme distances, but you can definitely tell whether a buck is worth a closer look or not.

When glassing, I like to start at the top of the ridge and glass from the top to the bottom. Most of the bucks you will see will be on the upper half of the mountain. Once you spot a deer, make sure you immediately take a closer look through the spotting scope if needed. During the prime glassing hours bucks are constantly moving and can vanish from sight if you wait too long. After you have glassed all of the surrounding terrain several times, move on to Phase II.

Phase II – Secondary Glassing

After I complete my initial glassing, I settle in and move on to my secondary glassing. This phase differs from the first, in that you will glass at a much slower rate and concentrate more on the smaller openings. Many people I know like to use a grid pattern to make sure they cover the mountain thoroughly. I personally don't use this method; it takes the fun out of glassing for me. I glass more randomly, spending most of my time looking at the places that might look "bucky" to me.

Although I do not use a grid pattern, I will divide the mountain into sections and concentrate on one section at a time to make sure I cover all of it effectively. I will use things such as small finger ridges that run from the top of the mountain down to the bottom as dividers. I will glass each section thoroughly before moving on to the next section. If the section looks real bucky to me, I may glass it several times before glassing the next section. I will continue this pattern until I have glassed the entire hillside. I will then go back to the first section and repeat this process over and over. Sometimes I will do this for hours.

As you are doing your secondary glassing, make mental notes of anything that could possibly be a deer. I am not necessarily looking at every deer through the spotting scope at this time because I have already looked the majority of them over during the first phase. As you glass the country over and over, you will get to the point that you will have the mountainside memorized and it will be fairly easy to detect any new deer that may appear.

During the morning hours, I will generally use a combination of Phases I and II until everything has bedded down. This varies depending on temperature and weather conditions, but normally I will end my morning session around 9:00 a.m.

Phase III – Detailed Glassing

Phase III, or detailed glassing, is when you really need to start picking the mountainside apart, inch by inch. Most hunters have no problem with Phases I and II, but lack the patience needed for detailed glassing. I will spend literally hour after hour picking the mountainside apart with my binoculars. I am concentrating on close up areas at this point, normally glassing everything within rifle range. At this point, most of the deer have bedded down and you should be concentrating on glassing possible bedding areas. You're not looking for an outline of a deer any more, now you are looking for the tips of antlers, the tip of an ear or any slight movement that could be a buck tucked away in the shadows. The key word here is shadows. Don't waste any time glassing the areas that are in direct sunlight, concentrate all of your efforts glassing any available shade. During the morning hours this will be the northwest side of the trees and during the afternoon hours bucks will be bedded on the northeast side of cover.

Phase IV – Ultra Glassing

Phase IV, or ultra glassing, is when you take Phase III to the next level. This is where you dissect the terrain with your spotting scope, rather than binoculars. Not only are you picking the mountainside apart, you are literally picking every tree, bush and shrub apart. It is basically the same as the previous phase, except you have a

Phase four glassing requires tremendous patience, so get comfortable and pay attention to details.

lot smaller field of view and you are able to further pick the hillside apart in greater detail.

Phase Four Glassing requires a lot of patience. Each glassing session can be several hours long, but if done correctly, I guarantee you will see more game than you ever have before.

Glass Early

When scouting, it is critical that you are up and glassing well before the sun hits the mountainside, because by the time that happens, a lot of the bucks have already bedded down. Your window of opportunity to glass is pretty short because the temperature rises so quickly this time of year. I have literally watched bucks stay just ahead of the sun as it rises and starts to illuminate the hillside. The bucks will

By the time the first light hits the mountainside, a lot of the bucks have either bedded or are making their way to their bedding areas.

disappear into the trees before being touched by the sun. Normally in the heat of summer, most bucks are bedded by 7:30 a.m. You will have a few stragglers out feeding until 8:00 a.m., but even then, that's not much time to glass.

During summer scouting, I find that I locate three times as many deer in the morning than I do in the evening. This is because the temperatures are usually so hot during the day that most bucks won't get up to feed in the evening until well after the sun has gone down. With this in mind, spend most of your time glassing during the early morning hours.

Most people will call it quits after glassing the morning hours, but I like to glass all day long. After glassing from my morning vantage point, I will hike a short distance and start glassing again. This glassing is different from the morning glassing session. During the morning glassing I concentrate more on wide open basins and avalanche chutes, but during the day I will glass the timber trying to locate bucks in their beds. Pick apart all of the shadows for about an hour and then relocate and repeat this process. You will be amazed at how many deer you can see during the day glassing this way.

Make Notes

Mike Eastman making notes in his hunting journal while in the field. Making notes while scouting and hunting is very important. If you don't want to keep a journal, you should, at a bare minimum, make notes on your maps.

To me, there is no such thing as an unsuccessful scouting trip. Even if I don't find a monster buck, I still learn a lot on every trip.

Make notes on where you see bucks. Bucks will tend to use these areas year after year, especially the bedding areas. Watch where they bed and feed and how they utilize the area. I don't mean mental notes either; mark the locations on your map so you don't forget.

As you glass far and wide, don't forget to look for sign right underneath your nose.

135

I'm talking about tracks. Always be on the lookout for large sets of buck tracks. If you find a set of big and blocky tracks, make notes of where they are and the direction in which they are traveling. Remember, track size is not always a good indicator of the buck size that left them, but when you find a set that measures over three inches in length, you had better start paying very close attention and concentrate your efforts on finding the buck that made them.

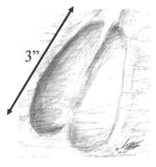

Also make notes of all water sources. This is more for your water needs, than anything else. If you sit on a water source in the high country waiting for a trophy buck to come in, you might be waiting a long, long time. While this method works well in lower, more arid country, it is not very productive in the high country. This is true for a couple of reasons. Deer can meet their water requirements several different ways, including: open water (streams, lakes, dew, etc.), preformed water (contained in their forage) and water produced during digestion/metabolism. How deer meet their water requirements depends on a number of different factors and varies seasonally. During the summer and fall, deer in the high country use open water like streams and ponds opportunistically, but they don't plan their daily routines around them. Between succulent forage, and metabolic water, and small sources like dew and seeps, it seems the high country deer have a lot of options available to them for getting enough water without visiting streams, ponds, or lakes.

This is a screenshot of the Delorme software that I use. The 3D option gives you a good feel of what the lay of the land looks like.

Scouting New Areas

Before I ever set foot into a new area, I usually feel that I know it already. I know where all of the highest points are located, as well as how all of the drainages are laid out. This is because I have already studied the area on my maps. This is very important. Don't just go wandering into an area hoping to find a good place to glass from. Be prepared, have all of that information already marked on your map before leaving the house.

I have ordered most of my topo maps from the U.S. Geological Survey. They are a scale of 1:24,000 and are better known as 7.5 minute series maps. For example, a 7.5 minute map shows an area that covers 7.5 minutes of latitude and 7.5 minutes of longitude. They show great detail and are normally 22 by 27 inches in size. These are probably the most popular topo maps sold today.

While 7.5 minute series maps are great to look at, I have a closet full of them that I don't even look at anymore. With all of the great computer mapping software available today, I just can't bring myself to dig out my old paper maps.

If you have a computer and love to look at maps like I do, then it is a must to invest in one of the many mapping programs that are available. I personally use software made by Delorme. I can't say enough about this program. With this software, you can conduct searches for certain areas, mark locations on the maps, calculate the distance of your hikes and just about anything else you would want to do. One of the best features is the 3D option. You can view a split screen that has your standard

Kyle Paxman spotted this buck in his high country hideaway during the preseason and was able to return and harvest the buck during the season.

flat map on the right, as well as a 3D image on the left. I can't emphasize enough how great this option is. You can even rotate the image in a full 360 degree view which allows you to get a bird's eye view of all of the country. And if that isn't enough, you can purchase satellite images of any particular state and overlap the image over the 3D image and you can see all of the available ground cover. You feel as if you are actually there. It doesn't get any better than this.

When scouting a new area, I normally look over maps of the area and locate the highest peak that looks like it will offer me the best vantage point to see the most country. This is important because the whole purpose of the first trip is to look over as much country as possible. Make notes of where you are seeing deer feed and bed. Also make notes of other vantage points that might be closer to any deer you may want to get a closer look at. Your second trip into the area you can utilize some of the other vantage points you located on your first trip which will allow you a closer look at some of the deer you had seen earlier, as well as see some new country as well. Normally it will take a minimum of two or three trips into a new area getting familiar with it before I feel comfortable that I can return and hunt it effectively.

If you don't have the time to scout your hunting area during the summer months, at a bare minimum, you should arrive several days before the season opens to take a look around. This is especially critical if you will be hunting an area you have never hunted before. The last thing you want to do is waste the first couple of days of the season learning new country.

Most people I know scout the same areas year after year. While I don't think that there is anything wrong with that, I try to scout at least one new area every year. I will check out a couple of my favorite spots from year to year, but I like seeing new country. Out of all the bucks I have killed over the years, I have never harvested two of them from the same area. They have all came from different locations. Maybe I would have more success if I hunted the same location from year to year, but I like variety and seeing new country.

Paul Pennie of Alpine, Utah is one of the most hardcore mule deer hunters I know. Paul owns and operates a taxidermy business and specializes in head mounts and custom pedestal mounts. He does some of the best taxidermy work I have seen. If you would like to inquire about Paul's taxidermy work, you can contact him at (801) 361-1890. Paul loves to scout and is one of those guys that don't mind hammering the same area year after year. He has had tremendous success in doing so. Over the course of the last four years, Paul has been chasing a particular buck in the high country that he named "Uno." Uno was a very predictable buck, always showing up in his favorite basins year after year.

It took four years of hammering the same area before Paul was able to harvest the buck he calls "Uno."

Uno

By Paul Pennie

I first laid eyes on the buck during the 2001 muzzleloader season. I was able to get a chance at this particular buck, but came up short. Uno won the first round, but I would be back.

The following year, a good friend, Jon Gray, and I made a mid-August three day scouting trip into the high country basins that Uno called home. We never laid eyes on Uno, but we did come across a 30-inch 3x4 with double drops. I nicknamed the buck "Double D." Over the course of the next two months, the images of Double D feeding above timberline on the open green slopes constantly occupied my mind. The season wouldn't open until mid-October and I worried that if the high country received any snow accumulations, I may never see the buck again.

Finally the time had arrived. The weather was cold and clear as Jon and I made the long horseback ride into hunting camp the day before the season opened. Later that afternoon, after getting our camp situated, we began glassing for the buck we had seen two months earlier. Just as we had hoped, Double D was still occupying the alpine basin with a couple of buddies and we watched them feed until dark. Needless to say, the combination of a full moon, adrenaline and excitement, didn't allow for much sleep that night.

Bright and early on opening morning, Jon and I put on our packs and wished each other good luck as we went our separate ways. First light found me observing the location that the bucks were feeding in the previous evening. To my surprise, the large buck's companions were there, but the big guy had disappeared. I hunted the remainder of the day but could never turn

Paul Pennie with the buck he named "Chance."

up Double D. On my way back to camp that night, I was feeling rather depressed because of the turn of events.

The night came and went and before I knew it, it was time to resume my search for the big buck. I downed a couple of Ibuprofens for breakfast and was quickly on my way.

The serenity of the alpine basin was shattered as two rifle shots rang out across the basin. Both sounded like direct hits. As it turned out, Jon had downed a nice four point. I continued glassing the basin all day long. Finally, about 3:00 p.m., I spotted two bucks feeding way down below me. It was the big guy's two companions, but once again, no Double D. I started picking all of the nearby cover apart with my binoculars, when I spotted a new buck which was 28 inches wide. He was heavy-horned and had seven points on his right and six on his left. He was bedded in a small patch of jack-pines. I couldn't help but give him the nickname of "Chance" because of the chance encounter. He was huge, definitely big enough to put Double D out of my mind for the time being. The stalk was on.

As I closed the gap to 400 yards, adrenaline raced through my body. I found a good rest and readied my rifle. I would now wait until the buck got up to feed before taking a shot. Two hours passed and he had still not moved. His two companions were now 300 yards away in the wide open feeding. I was a little unnerved to say the least as the little bit of daylight that was remaining was fading fast. Negative thoughts were now entering my mind and I expected the whole situation to blow up at any given moment.

Finally, the two smaller bucks finished their feeding and started making their way back to where Chance was bedded. One of the bucks evidently stood too close to Chance as he postured at him and then stood up. It was now or never. I pulled the trigger and the buck went down immediately. The shot was good. As I made my way down to the buck, many emotions flooded over me. I felt so privileged to pursue and take such an awesome animal in the high country.

The horseback ride out was something I will remember forever. Good company, good scenery and a 212-inch gross non-typical buck on top of my favorite pack mule. On the ride out, I was already looking forward to coming back the next hunting season to see if I could turn up the buck Uno.

The following September I was back above timberline looking for Uno, and just like clockwork, there he was in his normal routine. Unfortunately, I returned two weeks later for the hunting season, only to find an early snowstorm had pushed him out of the country. I hunted high and low but was never able to find Uno. I was now 0 and 3 against Uno.

During an August scouting trip in 2004, I was able to locate Uno on the third day of glassing the high alpine bowls. His front forks had gone downhill from the year before but his back forks were bigger than ever. His G2's were 22 inches long and his G3's were about 15 inches long. He was also a little bit wider and had grown a couple of extra in-line points. Surprised to see the old veteran, plans were once again made to go after him again. I felt a pretty special connection to the buck and decided at that point that he would be the only buck I would pursue during the hunting season.

Two weeks later I was back once again. As I had done so many times before, I was up at 4:00 a.m. making the vertical climb into Uno's favorite basin. At daybreak I instantly spotted Uno feeding out across the basin with nine other bucks about 400 yards away. There was no cover between Uno and myself so all I could do was watch as the bucks fed above timberline. Two hours passed when the group of bucks finally bedded in the only patch of jack-pines between us. I had no choice but to wait them out until they resumed feeding in the evening. Time went by slowly as I sat by a lone stand of jack-pines wondering how this might all play out. Then it happened. About 11 a.m. a group of small bucks came over the hill on the run spooked by something I could not see. They ran right into the group of bedded bucks causing all of them to stand up. After they had all stood up, they headed directly at me. My blood was pumping as 11 bucks were right on top of me coming closer and closer. Uno was the fifth buck back and I could not believe what was happening. Thankfully, I didn't have much time to think about it as the bucks came by me at 115 yards. I singled out Uno and picked a spot on his shoulder and touched off a shot from my knight muzzleloader. Uno jumped and ran straight down hill. I thought that I had missed. That thought had no more crossed my mind when he crashed in a rock slide about 100 yards below me. It all happened so fast that it was hard to believe. As I approached Uno, he was bigger than I thought. Four years after the first encounter, Uno had made his first mistake. A four-year quest had come to an end with the harvesting of this awesome high country buck. It was definitely an education which will provide me with memories that will last a lifetime.

Scouting success: Steve holding the 206⅜ B&C non-typical.

Scouting Success

By David W. Long

Steve James and Jerry Ricketts, who you will read about of couple of times in this book, were lucky enough to take a monster buck which they had scouted prior to the season. They already had a good area they normally hunt, but one summer they decided to scout a new area that Steve had glassed from a distance but had never taken the time to explore. The men left their truck at daybreak, but because there was no trail most of the way, it took longer than they had anticipated. Finally reaching their destination at 4:00 p.m., they started glassing and spotted two bucks bedded below them under a tree. One was a small 24-inch four point, but the other was the caliber of buck they had been hoping to find. He had eight points on the right side, five on the left, and 28-inch wide antlers that were covered in velvet.

By the time Steve and Jerry got back to the truck that night, both had blistered feet from the rigorous hike. However, they felt the largest hurdle of their hunt was over, having located a monster buck they could pursue on opening day.

With visions of the monster mulies in their minds, Steve and Jerry, along with Steve's son, Lincoln, began their backpack trip into the area the day before the season opened. It took half the day to reach the head of the drainage where they stopped for a break at a small spring. This was the last water source so they drank all they could and then loaded each of their packs with four quarts of water. Leaving the drainage behind, they began hiking straight up the steep mountainside. Finally, after a total of 10 hours, they reached their destination and set up camp.

On opening morning, the trio hunted the hillside where they had seen the bucks two weeks earlier. Unable to locate the deer, the hunters decided to split up. Jerry hunted back

Scouting

Lincoln James and Jerry Ricketts are all smiles.

in the direction from which they had come, while Steve and Lincoln remained on a knob and continued glassing.

Five minutes later when a shot rang out from the direction Jerry had taken, Steve and Lincoln figured their friend had killed the big buck. But what they didn't know was that there were three bucks, the big one, a 30-incher, and a two point. The 30-incher provided a perfect shot for Jerry so he took it.

Rather than walk down the rugged slope to view Jerry's deer, Steve and Lincoln decided to hunt another drainage. Finding no success, they returned to camp. A short time later, Jerry showed up with a huge, heavy-horned four point. When Steve saw Jerry's buck, the first words out of his mouth were, "That's not him!" Steve was excited knowing the big buck was still out there for the next day's hunt.

Steve and Lincoln got up early on the second day to hunt the steep hillside the big guy called home. A short ways beyond where Jerry had killed his buck, father and son split up. Lincoln hiked up to a point that protruded from the steep face, while Steve worked his way across the hillside.

Shortly after, Steve spotted a buck bedded in a small clump of trees 150 yards below him. His first thought was to go for his son, but knowing the buck might not be there when they returned, he decided to go ahead and take the buck. The buck was facing away from Steve with only one antler visible. He couldn't tell if it was the big guy or not, but by the size of the antler, Steve figured the buck was big enough.

At the report of the rifle, the buck bolted immediately from his bed and was gone. Sure enough, it was the big guy. Steve knew he had hit the buck, and hoped Lincoln would see it. His wish was answered within seconds, as Lincoln spotted the buck and put it down for good.

The buck turned out to have a record book four point typical frame scoring 191⁶/₈. With the extra points added in, the rack tallies 206³/₈ non-typical.

Later, Steve commented, "although taking two trophy bucks on the same hunt is more than anyone could ask for, it did present us with a problem. How were three guys on foot going to get all their gear, the meat, capes and antlers out of here? It was going to be brutal."

Fortunately he had told his buddy, Barry, where they were going to be hunting and to stop by and see them if he was in the area. Luckily, Barry was in the area and heard the shots and came down to investigate. The next day they packed up everything on Barry's horses and made their way off the mountain. Having Barry save the day with his horses was the end to a perfect hunt.

The Bottom Line

First and foremost, if your scouting does pay off and you locate a monster mulie, trust your scouting. Don't give up if you return to where you first saw the buck and can't relocate him. He is there. If you can't find him after a couple of trips, return toward the end of the season after almost everybody has went home and chances are, you just may find him.

In the spring, get out in the hills and locate migration routes and transition zones. This information is priceless if your hunting season runs into late October or early November because deer will utilize these same areas during the fall migration. I harvested my Wyoming droptine buck by doing this.

During the summer, try to make as many scouting trips as you can. The more time spent in the field, the better your odds of finding that once in a lifetime trophy. Bucks are in bachelor groups this time of the year which allows you to look over a lot of bucks. I normally see 20 to 30 bucks on each of my scouting trips.

How many bucks you will spot depends a lot on your glassing technique. It is essential that you develop a glassing method that suits your hunting style and stick with it. I suggest that you give my Four Phase Glassing method a try. I guarantee that you will see more game than you have in the past. It does require a lot of patience, but it has proven very effective for me over the years. When glassing, make sure to spend more time glassing the areas that look "bucky."

While on your scouting trip, make notes of any water sources you find, as well as bedding and feeding areas that the bucks are utilizing. Also, keep your eye out for large, blocky tracks.

Before setting foot into a new area, make sure you study maps of the area. Don't wander into the area blind. A lot can be learned by looking at maps or mapping software, such as water sources, lay of the land and locating the best vantage points to glass from.

SECTION 4

BACKPACKING

Being Mobile

Backpacks, dehydrated meals, small two-man tents and long hikes make up the formula that has led to my success in hunting mule deer. One of the main reasons is it allows me to be mobile. I can break camp and have it loaded in my pack and be heading down the trail in less than 25 minutes.

Since backpacking can be so physically exhausting at times, one year two hunting partners and I decided we wanted to try something a little different and comfort was very high on our priority list. The plan was to have two other friends pack us in a drop camp consisting of a 12 x 14 canvas wall tent, a wood stove and plenty of real food. We would still take all of our backpacking gear, along with MREs (meals ready to eat) in case we wanted to spike out from base camp. Sounded like a good plan, but

Our comfortable camp that we had to leave behind to increase our odds.

we soon found out that it wasn't foolproof.

The area we planned to hunt was new to all of us. It looked good on the topo maps we studied and we felt confident that we could take a good buck if we gave it an honest effort. Three days before the season, our friends Festus Krause and David Wilson loaded their horses and packed in our drop camp to a peak I had marked on the topo map. Thick fog and the area being unfamiliar to them proved to be a bad combination, as they rode for five hours and were unable to find the peak. Running out of daylight, they found a tall stand of timber located next to a small stream and set up the camp, figuring they had to be close to the predetermined site. That evening they rode back out so they could haul Victor Clark, Frank Gonzales and myself in the next morning.

We left my home in Big Piney at 4:30 a.m. and met Festus and David at the trailhead at first light. The heavy blanket of fog still obscured our view that morning as we made the 10-mile horseback ride to camp. Even though we couldn't see the beautiful scenery that surrounded us, it felt good just being in the outdoors. It was hard to believe, a year of planning was finally becoming a reality.

It wasn't long after we started riding I suspected that we weren't heading in the right direction. After arriving at the tent, I knew we were off course but I didn't know by how far. We couldn't see any distinguishable landmarks to pinpoint our position, so Victor turned on his GPS and confirmed my suspicions. We were several miles from where we wanted to be.

Since it would take too much time and work to move the camp, we decided to keep it where it was and make the best out of the situation that we possibly could and sent Festus and David on their way. Victor, trying to make something positive out of our predicament, suggested that "everything happens for a reason." I hoped he was right.

We stayed one night at the camp but decided the following day to load up all of our backpacking gear and hike another three miles on foot and set up a spike

camp closer to where we originally had planned to hunt. We hated to leave the comforts of the base camp behind, but in order to increase our odds of taking a good buck, we knew we had to camp at a higher elevation. Two hours later we had our small backpacking tents pitched and camp set up. It wasn't much compared to the camp we had just left behind, but it was the type we

Frank Gonzales, Victor Clark and I take time for a quick photo at our new spike camp.

have become well accustomed to over the years while backpacking.

We rolled out of our sleeping bags at 4:00 a.m. on opening morning and in the pre-dawn darkness hiked another mile and a half to a place that would offer us a good view to glass from. After arriving, we still had an hour before it would be light enough to glass, so we laid down on the cold ground and gazed at the collage of stars above us. While laying there, visions of past hunts came and went through my mind, as well as thoughts of what might await us this opening morning. A smile came to my face as I relived those cherished memories and I was thankful I had such good friends as Victor and Frank to share this hunt with.

As it started getting light we began to see bucks above us feeding in the grassy avalanche chutes. The largest concentration of bucks was about a half mile to the north, so I started at a pretty good pace along the base of the mountain in that direction to get a closer look at them. Victor and Frank stayed put to try and get a better look at a buck Frank had spotted directly above where we were glassing.

After hiking for about 15 minutes, I took out my binoculars and started glassing the chutes above. Seconds later, I spotted two bucks up on a bench looking to the north at some hunters that had spooked them. I pulled out my spotting scope and set it up so I could see if they were worth going after. One buck was small, but the other looked to be over 30 inches and definitely worth a closer look. I started climbing up the ravine just south of where the deer were, using the ridge between us to conceal my approach. The hillside was steep and covered with loose rock making it very difficult to climb.

Approximately halfway up the hill, I heard a rifle shot come from the direction of where I last saw the bucks and it sounded like a direct hit. I contemplated whether to continue my stalk or not, but decided I had came too far to give up and pressed on. As I was approaching the top, a buck appeared on the skyline of the ridge directly above me. I looked through my binoculars and recognized the buck as being the 30-incher's companion. I thought to myself, "You're too late, the big one is already dead." The thought had no more crossed my mind when another buck appeared on the ridge followed by another and yet another. The fourth buck over the ridge made me forget all about the 30-inch typical. When he skylined himself, I could see a lot of mass and several extra points which was all I needed to see.

The slope was steep and I knew it would be difficult to get off a good shot, so I slipped off my backpack and tried using it as a rest. I laid down with my head uphill, but just before I was ready to shoot, I slipped down the hill. After doing this several times, I managed to hold the crosshairs on him just long enough to fire a shot. At the report of the rifle I slid down the hill slightly, losing sight of the buck momentarily. When I picked the buck up in my scope again, to my surprise he was still standing motionless on the skyline. I fired two more shots as the buck stood there trying to figure out which direction the shots were coming from. He finally had enough and all the bucks disappeared over the ridge in the direction they had came from. After muttering a few choice words out loud, I figured because of the extremely steep angle, I was shooting over the buck's back.

Not giving up, I moved as quickly as I could over the ridge to try and get another chance at the buck. When I topped the crest of the ridge, I found the bucks under some cliffs above me at an elevation of 11,000 feet. They tried sneaking over the top

My 8x8 buck ended up on the cover of the Eastmans' Hunting Journal 1998 Mule Deer Issue.

of the mountain, but got rim-rocked at the top and had no place to go. There were a total of 17 bucks in the group, including the non-typical and the 30-incher.

After looking them over, I still wanted the non-typical. I removed my backpack to use as a rest again, and this time compensating for the steep angle, put the buck down with one shot to the neck. The buck started rolling down the ravine through the rocks and didn't stop until he rolled well over a hundred yards.

Visions of broken antlers were going through my mind as I made my way down to the buck. Amazingly, no tines were broke on the heavy 8x8 antlers. The antlers had deep scratches in them from the rocks and he broke his bottom jaw and his right rear leg in the fall.

The photo session was filled with mixed emotions. I was saddened that this beautiful trophy's time of roaming the high country had came to an end, but I also felt a sense of accomplishment in that all of my hard work had paid off. Giving me yet another memory to reflect back on that will, without a doubt, bring a smile to my face.

The key to harvesting this buck was having the ability to move and relocate camp and backpacking allows you to do this. I watch people with horses and it takes them several hours to break or set up a camp. I can be several miles down the trail by then. Don't get me wrong, I know of several people that hunt effectively with horses, but they just are not for me. As a matter of fact, one of my hunting partners, Scott Mansor and I tried horses for one hunting season but both of us have resorted back to backpacking.

Backpack hunting is not for everyone, but if you're into solitude, or simply just want to get away from the crowds, then you might want to give it a try. When I was young, I remember riding around with my dad and his buddies as they road hunted all day long. Simply put, we did not see much game. Even if we would have, I was the one sitting in the middle and would have been the last one out of the truck. It didn't take long and I knew that this type of hunting was not for me. I wanted to hunt the high country. Every time we would drive by some high peaks, I would stare at them wishing I was up there chasing big bucks.

After a couple of years I was hunting on my own and was marking up several maps of places I wanted to backpack into to pursue trophy bucks. These areas were too far into the backcountry to day hunt effectively, so I started looking

at backpacks and purchased an old external frame pack, a sleeping bag and a tent. I have never looked back since. Today it is still my preferred method of hunting big bucks. It allows me to hunt the backcountry effectively for several days at a time, but the biggest advantage it gives me is being mobile.

Four Keys to Backpacking Success

The key to harvesting this buck was being mobile, as well as prepared. Proper preparation and equipment is essential in backpack hunting. I often hear people talk about throwing a backpack on and heading into the backcountry for a week to do some hunting. Sounds great, but it's not as easy as it sounds. The truth is, after just a couple of days of backpack hunting, most people are tired and ready to call it quits. Many hunts that start out to be the "trip of a lifetime," turn out to be the "trip from hell." This is really unfortunate, but it is the cold hard truth.

I feel that there are four important factors that have led to my success in backpack hunting trophy bucks. In the next few pages I will hit on all four factors and offer tips in each category. Here is a list in no certain order because they are all equally important:

1. **Adequate Hydration**
2. **Ample Nutrition**
3. **Get in Shape**
4. **Proper Equipment**

1. Adequate Hydration

While backpacking is an effective way of hunting the high country, it is extremely demanding. One of the keys to enjoying your trips is to make sure you stay hydrated. This can sometimes be a problem in many places. Most of the high country that I hunt has very few water sources. I have seen many people cut their backcountry trips short because of

the shortage of water.

Unfortunately, water is extremely heavy. For every quart you pack, it adds two pounds to your pack weight. You definitely don't want to pack more than you need, but at the same time, you need to make sure that you have enough. This is usually not a problem when you are venturing into a place that you hunt on a regular basis because you already know all of the available water sources. But when you start exploring new country it is a whole different story. Just because your map shows a small stream on it, doesn't mean it will actually have water in it. Some small intermittent springs that flow one year, will not flow the next. Or worse yet, that spring you found flowing during scouting season, is dry when you return for your hunt. So if you're unsure of the availability of water, plan on taking enough to last the length of your trip.

If you will be utilizing a water source in the high country, make sure you take some sort of filter, or iodine tablets to help protect from bacteria and giardia. I personally prefer taking a filter over the tablets. There are several places which I hunt above timberline that do not have any water available for quite some distance. In such instances, I have used my stove to melt snow to get water. Some of this water from the snow can be pretty nasty looking. It usually has a film on top of it, along with pine needles, dirt and all kinds of other foreign materials and it is times like this you are glad you have a filter. Your iodine tablets wouldn't do much good to make it appear more sanitary to the eye.

This past summer I did a three day scouting trip into a new area I had never been in before and was very thankful I had my filter. During my morning glassing session I had spotted a bright reflection on some rocks approximately 250 yards below my camp which signified the presence of water. After I had finished glassing, I gathered up my water bottles and hydration bladder and headed down off the ridge toward the rocks. I had high hopes for a nice high mountain spring, but what I found was rather disappointing. It was a small seep that had filled a hole that someone had dug for their horses to water. As I approached the water hole, there were literally thousands of Mormon crickets everywhere. As they all started scattering, a bunch of them leaped into the small puddle that was to be my source of hydration. As I

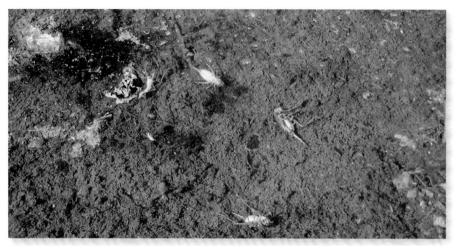

It is times like this that I am glad I always pack my water filter.

started filtering the water, I watched as several crickets drowned and there were several floating on top that had been there for several days. I had never been so thankful to have my filter with me.

Oftentimes while backpack hunting in early September, temperatures can soar to 80 degrees during mid-afternoon making it tough to stay hydrated, especially on your pack in or out. There are several things I do that I feel really help while doing longer hikes. First and foremost, you need to make sure you consume enough water. To help with this, make sure that your water is accessible and that you don't need to stop and take your pack off to get to it. If you have to take your pack off every time, I can guarantee you, you will probably not be consuming enough fluid. Sip water often. You should be taking in 4 to 6 ounces every 20 minutes or so. One mistake a lot of people make is to go long periods of time without drinking and then consuming a lot of water at once. You are much better off taking small amounts often. The best way to accomplish this is to utilize a hydration bladder. This way you don't even need to stop hiking to get a drink. If you don't have a bladder, carry a water bottle on your hipbelt, or in one of the water bottle holsters that are usually on the side of most packs. If you start suffering from a headache or dizziness, you are not taking in enough water. One of the key rules that I use is, "Drink before you get thirsty." If you wait until you are thirsty, you have waited too long.

When planning your hikes, try to do them early in the morning when possible, especially if you will be hiking in the open or on a south-facing slope. This way you can have your hike either completed, or nearly complete by the time it heats up in the afternoon. If you have no choice and have to pack in your camp during the heat of the day, make sure that you wear a hat and utilize any shade that is available. I don't stop very often when I am hiking, but when I do, I always make sure it is in the shade of a tree. I also make sure I have my hat on when in direct sunlight, but when I am in the shade I take it off to help cool down.

Once you have reached your campsite, take a rest in the shade and drink some water. Taking a breather before you start setting up your camp is always a good idea.

155

It doesn't have to be long; 5 to 10 minutes is plenty.

Throughout the day, take in water often, especially following meals or snacks and take a drink before laying down for the night. If you don't want plain water, take one of the powdered energy drink mixes that are available and mix with it if you want some flavor. There are several manufacturers that make energy drinks, such as Clif Bar, PowerBar, GU and Gatorade to mention a few. One word of caution: taste them before venturing into the backcountry. Clif Bar just sent me one of their new powdered drinks and one swallow was enough for me. It was nasty. I personally don't use the powdered mixes because they just don't satisfy my thirst like straight water does.

You should take in some fluid when you first wake up in the mornings. Coffee doesn't count because caffeine will dehydrate you. Drink water. I love drinking coffee in the morning when I am at home, but when backpacking, I only drink water. After a hard day in the mountains, you will actually lose fluid during the night through sweat and respiration so it is essential that you take in some sort of fluid as soon as you wake up in the morning.

2. Ample Nutrition

Make sure you eat throughout the day. Your appetite is suppressed when you have been hiking a lot at high elevations, so hunger is no longer a sign of when you need to take in food. Take in small amounts of food about once an hour. GU and Clif Bars are great for this because they are loaded with carbohydrates.

I have experimented with a large variety of foods over the years, and for that matter, I am always looking for something better. My meals are the same every day. It doesn't matter if I am in the hills for one day or seven days, I eat the exact same food every day. Why? First off, I feel that the food I am currently eating is providing me with the carbohydrates I need to stay fueled while backpacking. Second, I know the exact quantity of food to take so that I don't have any leftover. Years ago I would pack all kinds of food, oftentimes a lot more than I could eat. I got tired of packing all of that extra weight for nothing. Now I have a set menu and I stick to it. If you like variety, this menu is definitely not for you.

Breakfast

I like to keep my breakfast simple. The last thing I want is to be late to my vantage point for my morning glassing session. Mine is about as simple as it gets—two Pop-Tarts. Not only are they quick and easy, I can eat them while glassing and they are loaded with carbohydrates. No wasted time, I like that concept. Every now and then I switch it up a bit and take some cold cereal. I take cold cereal and powdered milk in a heavy-duty freezer bag and all you have to do is add water and you can eat it right out of the bag while you're sitting at your vantage point glassing.

Mid-Morning Snack

I like to take in a Clif Bar and a packet of GU around 10:00 a.m. to hold me over until lunch. Make sure to consume water as well. Clif Bars are one of the best tasting

energy bars I have found. But like anything, after eating a steady diet of them for a week, they get awful tough to eat. They are primarily made up of rolled oats and come in 14 different flavors. GU is a carbohydrate energy gel that the body absorbs almost immediately. They come in six different flavors, but I have found the basic flavors of chocolate and vanilla to be the best tasting.

Lunch

My lunch isn't exactly what you would call a gourmet meal. Two flour tortillas with a can of deviled ham. The flour tortillas are a great source of carbohydrates, usually around 27 grams each, while the deviled ham is a good source of fat and protein. I will also take in a packet of GU for dessert to supplement my carb intake.

Mid-Afternoon Snack

This snack is the same as my mid-morning snack–a Clif Bar and a packet of GU along with a fair amount of water.

Dinner

My dinners are the only meals that require cooking. For the last several years I have used MREs (meals ready to eat) also known as Army rations. These have advantages and disadvantages. The advantage is they are not dehydrated so you don't need to add any water, plus, they have heaters in them eliminating the need for a stove. The disadvantages are weight (they are not light), there is a lot of packaging so you end up with large of amounts of trash to pack out, but the biggest disadvantage is the preservative used in them. Since they are not dehydrated, they contain a pretty powerful preservative to keep them from going bad. After about your third meal, all you can taste is the preservative, you can't tell if you are eating a frankfurter or tuna casserole, they all taste the same. As a matter of fact, a couple of my buddies

Although I prefer dehydrated meals, MREs with heaters are a great alternative if you want to leave your stove and fuel at home.

suggested that if we kept eating them, we might start glowing in the dark because of the preservatives. The reason I have stayed away from dehydrated meals was because I didn't like packing a heavy stove, fuel and mess kit. But now that I have the new ultralight Snow Peak setup, which you will read more about in the equipment section, I have shifted back to dehydrated meals. Most dehydrated meals come in 20 oz. double servings, but if you want to cut even more weight, they do make some single serving meals that weigh only a few ounces each. The problem with most of the single serves is that they just don't fill you up.

Over the years I have tried several brands of meals made by Mountain House, AlpineAire, Richmoor and Backpacker's Pantry. They all have good tasting meals,

as well as some I am not too crazy about. Mountain House has just come out with a new dehydrated meal that they call the Pro Pak. They weigh 5 oz. each and will make a 16 oz. serving. The best thing about them is that not only are they dehydrated, but the packaging is vacuum packed. This makes them incredibly compact and you don't have all of that wasted space in your pack that you do with other meals. They also have a Ziploc type closure

The new vacuum packed Pro Pak meal (L) by Mountain House is a lot smaller and compact than the regular dinners (R).

on the top which makes them easy to seal the heat in after dumping in your hot water. These are currently my dehydrated meal of choice.

The following table shows every item I consume during each day while backpacking in the high country. I take in a total of 384 grams of carbohydrates and 2380 calories. All of this adds up to a total of 27 ounces of food for each day. I like to look at it on the bright side; my pack gets over a pound and a half lighter everyday I am hunting.

Meal	Qty	Food	Carbs	Calories	Weight
Breakfast	2	Pop-Tarts	78	440	3.6
Mid-Morning	1	Clif Bar	46	230	2.5
	1	GU	25	100	1.2
Lunch	1	Deviled Ham	0	300	5.4
	2	Flour Tortillas	54	320	4.5
	1	GU	25	100	1.2
Mid-Afternoon	1	Clif Bar	46	230	2.5
	1	GU	25	100	1.2
Dinner	1	Dehydrated Meal	85	560	5
Totals			**384**	**2380**	**27.1 oz.**

3. Get In Shape

Probably the most important factor in backpack hunting is you need to be in very good shape. You can be in the middle of the best mule deer country in the world, but if you are out of shape, you won't be able to hunt it effectively. More than likely you will have to end your trip short.

I train a minimum of two days a week, three or four days when I have the time, year round. You don't necessarily need to copy my routine, but you should come

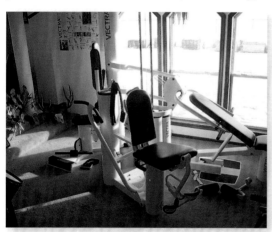

up with a routine that fits your schedule.

During the winter months, I do both cardiovascular and weight training. I train on Mondays, Wednesdays and some Fridays. I usually start with the weight training. Last year my wife and I invested in a nice home gym that makes it very easy and convenient to workout at home. It is a Vectra On-Line 1850 and we love it. It is a single stack gym with several different workout stations. I try to keep my workouts between 45 to 60 minutes. I only work

This is my workout room. Notice the antlers in the background—a little added incentive

one section of my body each workout. I will normally workout my chest on Mondays, arms on Wednesday and legs on Fridays.

After finishing my weight-training workout, I drive down to the high school and run stairs. The school has two flights of stairs above the swimming pool that I run

for 45 to 60 minutes without stopping. This really gets the sweat pouring. To switch it up every now and then, I will run laps in the hallway of the school. Six laps are just over a mile and I normally will run 3 to 7 miles. I continue these workouts all winter, until it is nice enough to start running outside. The only time I don't workout is during hunting season. I figure I will get plenty of exercise during that time as it is.

My summer months are usually so busy I don't have time for both the weight training and cardiovascular training, so I do not lift weights. If you only have time to do one, the cardio workout is definitely the most important. Rather than run the stairs at the school, I run outside. Directly

Antler hunting: the most enjoyable form of exercise I have found.

behind my house there is an amazing trail system that I can run that has a lot of elevation changes. I will normally run the trails for 45 minutes. Sometimes I will put on a loaded pack and hike up and down several of the steeper hills. Another great way of getting a good workout is to go out looking for shed antlers. I will strap a hydration pack on and literally hike for hours cross-country looking for shed antlers. Not only is it good exercise, but any antlers you may find are an added bonus.

While there are several ways of getting exercise, there is simply nothing better than hiking in the high country itself. Start with short day hikes and work up to multi-day trips. You will be amazed at how fast your legs get into shape hiking in the mountains. With all of the training I have done this past year, I have worked my way up to a point that I can hike about any distance. This summer I have a 72-mile solo backpack trip planned that I really look forward to doing.

Mix up your training so that you don't get bored with it. In 2005 I decided I wanted to take my training to a higher level by running a 26.2-mile marathon. It is something that has always intrigued me so in February, I signed up for the Salt Lake City Marathon. The marathon was six weeks away so I changed from my normal routine of running stairs, to distance running. I logged onto the Internet and researched how to train for a marathon. All of the training schedules I found said you need at least 16 to 20 weeks of distance training to be properly trained for the long run. I had six weeks. My 3-mile runs soon became six mile runs, then seven, then eight, soon I was running 10-mile runs in the evenings after work. According to the schedule I was going by, I was supposed to have several long runs of 15 to 20 miles long before the marathon, but my longest to date was 11 miles long. I was out of time. I have always had excellent stamina when it came to running and hiking, so I figured I would still do fine in the marathon.

I set two goals for the marathon. The first was to run the entire race without stopping or walking, the second, was to run it in less than 4 hours 15 minutes. I was confident that I could accomplish both.

I arrived in Salt Lake City the day before the marathon and checked into my room. I loaded up on carbohydrates by eating pasta for both lunch and dinner that day. I had also been drinking Gatorade for two days to load up on electrolytes. All of that combined with the excitement of the race, I didn't get much sleep that night.

The alarm clock went off at 5:00 a.m. and after a quick shower, I did several stretches for about 20 minutes. I ate a Clif Bar and downed a Gatorade for breakfast. I was at the starting line about 30 minutes early and did several short 100-yard jogs to warm up. It was time.

The race started off at a fairly slow pace, which can be expected with nearly 4000 entrants. I ran the first eight miles alongside of a young girl from New York. We had some great conversation and it made the first part of the race go by rather quickly. I felt so good, that I decided to pick up the pace and went on ahead of the group I had been running with.

During the next three miles I pretty much ran by myself. Occasionally I would talk with someone for a couple of minutes, but then I would move on ahead by myself. When I reached the 11 mile mark I joined up with a guy named Jon Duran from Idaho and we ran the next 10 miles together. It worked good because we kept pushing one another and our mile pace kept dropping and the mile markers seemed to be flying by. That is, until about mile marker 21. That is when Jon's previous marathons and training kicked in and he gradually started leaving me behind. I kept him in sight for the next couple of miles, but I just couldn't keep up.

Mile marker 23 is when it got really tough. At that point, I had to dig deep to find the strength to refrain from slowing down to a walk. It would have been easy to slow down, but I kept telling myself how mad and disappointed I would be with myself if I did. I kept running at the fastest pace that I was able to, which wasn't very fast. As I made the final turn, there were literally thousands of fans screaming and offering encouragement which made the last couple of hundred yards pretty enjoyable.

As I crossed the finish line, one volunteer took the timing chip off of my shoes, while another placed a finishing medallion around my neck. I must say, that is one of the coolest feelings I have ever had. I had accomplished both of my goals, I had beaten my target time by two minutes, and I had run the entire 26.2 miles without walking any of it.

I met up with Jon from Idaho. He ended up finishing six minutes in front of me. About 20 minutes later, the young girl form New York crossed the finish line. I visited with them for awhile and they asked me if I was going to run any more marathons and I told them that it was a one time thing to test myself, they told me that I would probably run more because once you run one, you get addicted. I said, "We'll see." That afternoon I drove the 200 miles home and relaxed for the rest of the day and all of the next day. And by the way, by Monday morning, less than 48 hours from finishing my first marathon, I was on the Internet looking for another one to sign up for.

161

Marathons aren't for everyone, but the main thing is to get cardiovascular training of some sort well before the hunting season and I guarantee it will make your trip a lot more enjoyable. Set fitness goals and continue to push yourself, but make sure your goals are reasonable and obtainable. All of this time dedicated to working out definitely pays dividends come hunting season. Backpack hunting has given me some of my most cherished hunting memories. It is definitely my method of choice for hunting the high country for trophy mule deer. If you will follow some of my general guidelines and suggestions, I guarantee you will leave the hills with memories you will cherish for years to come.

4. Proper Equipment

Having the proper equipment is essential when hunting the backcountry.

As I hiked up the trail, I couldn't help but look at the jagged rock peaks that were my destination. The trail I was on followed the left edge of a large creek. The trail weaved in and out of small patches of timber as the valley started to narrow. The summit was still two hours away as sweat was rolling off my forehead and into my eyes and I found myself stopping every 100 feet or so to try and catch my breath. I slid my thumbs under the shoulder straps to ease the pain in my shoulders, but it only worked temporarily. I was 12 miles into the hike but still had two more miles to go before I reached the alpine basin that would be my home for the next four days. It wasn't that I was out of shape, as a matter of fact, I was in great shape from running all winter long. It was the huge weight of my backpack. After reaching the summit, I set my pack on the ground and climbed up on a pickup sized boulder to take a break. What a view. I could see for many miles. But unfortunately, rather than enjoying the view, my mind was on my sore shoulders and feet. As I sat there eating an energy bar, it was at this moment, I decided I was going to find a way to reduce my pack weight, no matter what it took.

Since then, I have spent countless hours on the Internet and reading backpacking magazines researching lightweight gear. It didn't take long to see that all quality lightweight equipment has one thing in common—it's all very expensive. While going ultra lightweight was going to make it easy on my back, it was not going to be so easy on my wallet.

In this chapter we will take an in depth look at the equipment I am currently using, along with my reasons for using it. The key word being "currently." The reason I say this is because I am constantly trying new equipment looking for something better or lighter. We will divide the equipment into six different categories:

- · Rifle and Optics
- · Shelters
- · Sleeping System
- · Cooking System
- · Clothing
- · Other Items

One thing you will notice is that in several gear categories, I own more than one model, such as sleeping bags, tents, boots, etc. This is because different temperatures and weather conditions require different equipment to hunt effectively. I will also give you several tips that I have picked up over the years that might make your next trip into the backcountry a more enjoyable one.

A flat-shooting rifle is an essential piece of equipment when hunting bucks in the high country. My choice is a .30–378 Weatherby Magnum, which is one of the flattest-shooting rifles available.

Rifle and Optics

The rifle I use is the only piece of equipment I use that is not lightweight. It is a Weatherby Mark V Accumark .30-378 Weatherby Magnum. When hunting the high country you need a flat shooting rifle, which is why I settled on the .30-378. It is one of the flattest shooting rifles available today. The load I am currently using is a Nosler 200-grain Partition with 92 grains of IMR 7828 powder. The rifle with scope weighs in at close to 10 pounds and has a 26-inch barrel. The stock is made of Kevlar, undirectional fibers and fiberglass, making it impervious to weather changes.

My scope is a Leupold Vari-X III 6.5-20x40mm Adj. Obj. I love this scope. For the price, Leupold is hard to beat. Immediately after purchasing the scope, I sent

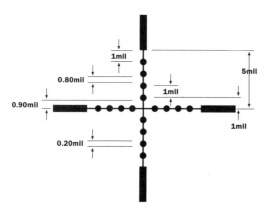

1mil

5mil

0.80mil

1mil

0.90mil

1mil

0.20mil

Leupold's Mil-Dot reticle is the best I have found for long range shooting.

it back to Leupold and had them put their Mil-Dot reticle in it. This costs around $140.00, but is well worth it if you plan on shooting long distances. The Mil-Dot reticle is a range finding reticle originally developed for military applications, such as snipers. The Mil-Dot reticle is a series of dots running vertically and horizontally. The dots are spaced exactly 1 mil apart, center to center. Although the reticle can be used to estimate the range of your target, I only use it to calculate my holdover at any given distance because I use a laser rangefinder to determine the range. I use the reticle in conjunction with a ballistic table that I have taped to the stock of my gun. In a matter of seconds, I can have my target ranged, know the amount of bullet drop and know exactly how many mils to holdover to allow for bullet drop. Leupold has a 14 page booklet on their website that discusses the Mil-Dot reticle in great detail. I suggest you log on to their site and check it out.

The most important equipment I own: my Swarovski optics. Make sure you buy the best binoculars and spotting scope you can afford.

Since I spend the bulk of my hunting time glassing, this is one place I wasn't about to skimp. I currently use a pair of Swarovski 10X42 EL's. The sharpness, contrast and resolution of these binoculars are unmatched. In addition to being

100% waterproof, they have a Polyurethane coating on the outside to help absorb shocks and noise and come with a lifetime warranty.

I use a Swarovski STS 65 HD. The image this scope provides is sharp from center to edge. It has a 20-60x zoom eyepiece and is rubber armored and totally waterproof. Don't be fooled by some scopes that claim they are water resistant, make sure the scope you buy is waterproof.

My bivy shelter is extremely compact and only weighs 2 lbs. 10 oz.

Shelters

There are basically three types of shelters: tents, bivy shelters and bivy bags. What kind of shelter you decide on is a matter of personal preference. You need to decide what is important to you, such as weight, size or certain features one model may have or doesn't have. The first thing you must decide is what size of shelter do you need. Most of the people I see, pack much larger tents than they really need. If you are going solo, or even if there are two of you, nowadays with all of the lightweight tents on the market, there is no reason to be packing any shelter over five pounds. If you do have a large tent, one way to get your tent to compress to a smaller size is to pack your poles on the outside of your pack. This gives you a lot more room inside your pack. I do this even with my small bivy.

Tents definitely give you the most choices as far as luxury and different options go. The most obvious is size. Tents give you plenty of room to stretch out and plenty of room to get dressed. They also give you a lot of room to store all of your gear inside and out of the elements. This reminds me of a trip that Victor Clark, Frank Gonzales and I made several miles back in the Gros Ventre Wilderness. We were camped at an elevation that only gave us a couple of small scrub patches of pines for shelter. Victor and Frank both had bivy bags, while I had my two-man tent. During the middle of the night, it started raining and didn't stop. We scurried around and gathered up all of their gear and put it in my tent with me to keep it dry. I almost felt guilty thinking about those guys in their bivies. The funny thing is, the day before, they stood at the trailhead deliberating on whether to pack their tent or their bivies. They were wishing they had made the other choice.

The nice thing about a full-blown tent is that they normally have better ventilation than the smaller, single wall bivy shelters. The reason for this is that tents are normally double wall. The tent can have better vents built into it because it will have a rain fly to cover the outside. The air from inside will rise through the vents and escape between the tent and the fly. This reduces condensation on the inside of the tent considerably because it builds up on the rain fly instead.

Another big advantage to having a tent is that most of them usually have a

165

vestibule of some sort. This is really a nice asset when your boots are caked with a pound of mud. It also gives you a place to store certain items such as your stove, fuel, water and other items that don't necessarily need to be in the tent with you, but you don't want them out in the rain either.

A bivy shelter is a great way to go if you want to drop a couple of pounds, but still like a little bit of room to move. In essence, they are just small, single wall tents. I use a bivy shelter on 90% of my backpack trips. The one I use is The North Face Trek Bivy, which is made of Gore-Tex and has a side entrance door. It weighs 2 lbs. 10 oz. and has two poles, one at the head and one at the foot. I really like this feature because it keeps my sleeping bag from touching the top and getting damp. I am fairly flexible and I'm sure I look like Houdini at times, but I am able to get dressed in the shelter.

Having only a single wall with no rain fly, it does tend to have condensation build up on the inside more often than my tent. It does have two vents, but they don't seem to be adequate enough to keep moisture from building up on the ceiling. One big disadvantage of the bivy shelter is that it has no vestibule. I now put my boots in a plastic trash bag to keep them dry. This works great unless it gets freezing cold outside.

A couple of years ago I backpacked deep into the Gros Ventre Wilderness during the middle of a September snowstorm. It took me seven hours to reach the high mountain pass where I wanted to camp. Although my boots are waterproof and didn't leak, the leather was totally soaked. That night the storm cleared out and the temperatures plummeted. That night my boots froze so stiff, I didn't know if I was going to get them on or not the next morning. It literally took 10 minutes to get them to finally slide on my feet. Remember, in extremely cold temperatures, keep your boots inside your tent.

If you want to cut the maximum amount of weight and go with the bare minimum, you can use a bivy bag. I love reducing my pack weight, but I have no desire to use a bivy bag. The biggest drawback to them is you have nowhere to store your gear. There have also been times during rain and snowstorms that I have had to spend full days in my shelter, and that was bad enough. I can't imagine spending all day in a bivy bag. This is one place where I will gladly pack the extra weight.

Sleeping System

The sleeping system is comprised of two components: a sleeping bag and sleeping pad. I have several sleeping bags, two of which I normally use. The first one is the Solar Flare made by The North Face. It has about nine inches of loft and is extremely comfortable in temperatures well below zero. It is a down filled bag that is rated for minus 30 degrees below zero and weighs 5 lbs. 3 oz. The only time I use this bag is when I am camping next to the road late in the hunting season. I simply don't need that much sleeping bag during the summer and early fall. Ninety percent of people I see backpacking carry way too much of a sleeping bag for the season in which they are in the field. I will often see guys packing minus 20 degree below zero bags in August scouting for deer. What's the sense in packing a huge, heavy sleeping bag that you have to sleep with the zipper open?

My second sleeping bag is the one that I use on all of my backpacking trips. It is

It is important to have more than one sleeping bag for different weather conditions and seasons. It doesn't matter if it is minus 30 or plus 30 degrees, having two sleeping bags lets me camp comfortably.

the Megalite by Western Mountaineering. It is on the opposite side of the spectrum from my North Face bag. It is a 30 degree down filled bag with four inches of loft, weighs only 1 lb. 10 oz. and compresses to the size of a football. This bag is not for everyone. If you tend to get cold at night, you will want something warmer, but for me, it is perfect. Also, if you have an ultra light sleeping bag like mine, it probably doesn't have a draft collar. If you find yourself needing one, wrapping some of your extra clothing around your neck usually does the trick.

There are a lot of good sleeping bags on the market today, but keep in mind that quality lightweight sleeping bags are expensive. Don't skimp here. Buy the best you can afford. Not only will you reduce your weight with a down bag, you will

During warm weather, I prefer my thick, uninsulated air filled sleeping pad made by Big Agnes, but when the nights start to cool down, I rely on my insulated ThermaRest pad.

167

gain room in your pack because they compress so small. The downside to these superlite bags is that they are extremely fragile. The material they are made of is so lightweight, it can't withstand a whole lot of abuse. One other tip if you purchase one of these bags, since there are only about five or six feathers in the bag for fill (ok, maybe there's a few more than that), when you have one starting to protrude, don't pull it out, stick it back in. There is one thing to remember with down-filled bags: never store them for extended periods in the small stuff sacks. Either store them in a large cotton storage bag or hang them up in the closet. If you store the bag in a compressed state for a long time, it will decrease the loft of the bag.

The second part of the sleep system is the pad. I currently have two pads I use. On scouting trips or early season hunting I will use my Big Agnes Air Core mummy sleeping pad. It is an air mattress that inflates to 2½ inches thick which makes it extremely comfortable. The downside: it has no insulation. That is why later in the year I leave it at home and take my Therm-a-Rest Prolite 3. It is a self-inflating mattress that is one inch thick and has an R 2.3 insulation value, which makes it nice on those colder nights when it gets below 30 degrees. At just over a pound, it is the lightest, most compact self-inflating mattress made.

The last couple of years I have added a new item to my sleeping system. It is a Therm-a-Rest pillow that has really helped me sleep better. It is just a small flannel like sack that I stuff my down jacket into to make a down pillow. It might sound like a luxury item, but trust me, it is a necessity. A good night's sleep is extremely important.

Cooking System

My cooking system is comprised of a stove, fuel and mess kit. When choosing a stove, there are basically two different types of stoves to choose from: liquid fuel and

My stove, fuel and mess kit combined only weigh 16 ounces.

canister stoves. The liquid fuel stoves run on a white gas and are better in extremely cold temperatures during winter than the canister stoves, but they are quite a bit heavier. Since canister stoves are considerably lighter, that is the type we will focus on. My old stove is an MSR Whisperlite liquid fuel stove. It is a great stove, but it is fairly heavy weighing in at 14 oz. The new stove I have is a Snow Peak Giga Power titanium canister stove. This ultralight 3 oz. stove is hardly even noticeable in your pack. This stove is collapsible and will burn for approx 40 minutes on a 7 oz. fuel canister. It has a built-in Piezo igniter that sends out an electric spark that ignites the flame—no matches required! (I still pack matches in case of an emergency.)

The fuel for my old stove weighed 1 lb. 4 oz., while the fuel canister for my new stove weighs 7 oz. I only cook one meal a day and that is dinner (This consists of boiling water for a dehydrated meal). I can get around 40 minutes of burn time on one mini canister which equates to about 5 or 6 dinners. One canister is plenty for five days in the backcountry.

As far as I am concerned, there is only one choice when it comes to choosing a mess kit—titanium. Titanium is light and strong. It is quite a bit more expensive than it's aluminum counterpart, but when it can cut your mess kit weight in half, it's worth every penny. Once again, Snow Peak is my choice on this one as well. They make a solo titanium cook set that weighs only 5.5 oz. It consists of a 28 oz. pot with lid (used to boil water) and a 10 oz. cup to be used for coffee, tea etc. What makes this set so slick is this: the pot nestles in the cup and the fuel canister and the stove nestle in the pot. Throw in a Snow Peak titanium spork (a combo spoon and fork) which weighs a half ounce and you have an entire kitchen that packs into 4 inches by 5 inches and weighs only 16 oz. It doesn't get much better than this.

Clothing

Clothing is one of the most important categories as far as equipment goes. It can literally make or break your hunt. Over the years my clothing system has evolved into what I think is the best layering system there is. What exactly is layering? Layering is the ability to take off, or add layers of clothing to adjust for temperature and weather changes. I have four layers of clothing for my upper body and three for my lower body.

First Layer, Top and Bottom– In the past I have always used Patagonia Capilene. Capilene has been the best selling and most widely trusted base layer in the outdoor industry for several years. It does great at wicking away moisture. This year, Under Armour supplied me with some of their camo Cold Gear base layers for a late deer hunt in Idaho and it worked great. If you don't mind an extremely tight fit, I suggest you give it a try.

Second Layer, Top and Bottom – Lightweight wool during the early season, and heavyweight wool during late season.

Third Layer, Top – Golite down jacket.

Third Layer, Bottom – Rain Gear

Fourth Layer, Top – Rain Gear

Rain Gear – Frogg Toggs Pro Action Realtree Camo suit.

Socks – Anything that has a wool/acrylic combination. The wool is for warmth and the acrylic is for comfort.

Gaiters – Outdoor Research–two pairs. Lightweight for early season and heavyweight for late season.

Gloves – Two pair. Mechanix gloves and ragg wool glommits.

If the temperature is extremely cold, I will stuff my clothing in the bottom of my sleeping bag so that it will be warm when I get dressed the next morning

Boots

I have two pairs of hunting boots–one pair for early season and the other for late season. For the early season I use a pair of Vasque Sundowner MX2's. They are probably the most comfortable boots I have ever owned. They are one-piece leather with Gore-Tex lining and are uninsulated. I use them for all of my scouting trips and normally

through September. In October, I use a pair of Danner Canadians. One of the main reasons is because of the Danner Bob soles. I firmly believe this is the best sole on the market. They are all leather and have a Gore-Tex liner. I haven't had any luck with boots that are made of cordura and leather. They always seem to split at the seams where the cordura and leather are sewn together. The Canadians are 10 inches high and have 600 grams of insulation. I literally put hundreds of miles on my boots, and normally, I will have to replace my boots every two years. By then, they are usually torn up so bad from heavy brush, jagged edged rocks and general wear and tear, I need to retire them.

Once a year, I brush on a heavy coat of SeamGrip, which is a tent seam sealer, on the seams of my boots. A 1 oz. tube only costs about five bucks, and it really helps protect the threads and seams. Also, before every trip, I brush on a waterproof coating to help deter moisture.

If there is one sure way of ruining a hunt it is getting blisters on your feet. The best way to avoid blisters is to have boots that properly fit. When purchasing boots, never buy them without trying them on first and once you find a model you like, stick with them. I have been using the same two models for years. I can now order them without trying them on because I know exactly what to expect. Before I wear them on a hunt, I will put them through a break in period. This is critical. If you do happen to get a blister, pop it and leave the blistered skin intact and either put moleskin on it or wrap it with a Band-Aid. Don't wait for it to break on its own while hiking or it may get dirt in it and only compound your problem.

Other Items

Water Filter

This is an essential item overlooked by a lot of people, but I don't go anywhere without it. The one I use is a PUR Hiker that is compact and weighs only 11 ounces. It comes with an easy fill bottle adapter, which makes it easy to fill my Nalgene

A good water filter is a necessity. The CamelBak Hydrolink Filter Adapter allows me to quickly connect my hydration bladders to my water filter.

water bottles. I also have an adapter that allows me to pump water directly into my hydration bladder without removing it from my pack. It is a quick coupler made by CamelBak that has two pieces. One piece goes into the hose on the filter side and the other goes on the hose from the bladder. You simply remove the bite valve from the bladder hose, plug in the filter and start pumping. It's that easy.

Water Bottles – Nalgene Grey Lexan

The Nalgene water bottles that I use are pretty much bullet proof. They are made out of super tough Lexan and can withstand just about any amount of abuse you may put them through. For years I have packed two 32 ounce bottles in my pack and have yet to have one leak.

During recent years, I have left the Nalgenes at home and replaced them with two 16.9 ounce bottles of Arrowhead bottled water. These bottles are extremely light and are amazingly tough. I have taken an extra cap off an old bottle and drilled a $^3/_8$ hole in the top of it to accommodate my filter hose making filling them a cinch. I just screw it on, slide my hose through the hole and start pumping. When the bottle is full, I take off the tapped cap and screw on one that isn't.

Lighting

I take two light sources when backpacking. The first is the Petzl Zipka–the smallest, lightest headlamp that Petzl makes. It has three LED bulbs and is powered by three

I pack two light sources—combined, they weigh only three ounces.

AAA batteries. It has a retractable wire strap which helps reduce weight from the conventional elastic headband. The headlamp (including batteries) weighs less than three ounces. I use the Zipka when hiking in the dark and while preparing meals at night.

The second is a Photon light that I use to illuminate my tent or bivy when I am either getting dressed or undressed or looking at maps in the evening. The Photon is an extremely small, but incredibly bright light that weighs only a little over six grams. You're really talking lightweight when you start talking grams, rather than ounces!

Digital Camera

For many years I never packed a camera only to regret it nowadays. I would love to have photos of some of my earlier trips to the high country. I can't change that, but I sure do make sure I have photos of all of my trips now. With the advent of digital cameras, photography has been taken to a whole new level. You can take and view photos instantly, and delete any unwanted images with the click of a button.

Over the past few years, digital cameras have really evolved. Canon's PowerShot line is hard to beat.

My first experience with a digital camera was when I killed my B&C typical buck in Colorado in 2003. I had an Advantix camera and my hunting partner, Scott Mansor, had a Canon 4 megapixel digital camera. We both took photos at the kill scene and later, when I got my pictures developed, there was no comparison between the two. Needless to say, I got a Canon 5 megapixel camera for my birthday five months later. I may have dropped a hint or two to my wife, Cheryl, because that is exactly the one I wanted. Imagine the odds of that. The camera has come in handy, it has taken a lot of the photos in this book, as well as the cover photo of my 2004 Wyoming buck. Do yourself a favor, take a camera with you on all of your trips.

Backpacks

I own several backpacks. In fact, the wall of my shop is lined with them. I like having a different pack for different applications. One pack simply isn't adequate for all occasions.

There are three of them that I use the most. The first one is a Gregory Z pack. It is a 3760 cubic inch pack that only weighs 3 lbs. 2 oz. It is the pack I use during summer scouting trips and some early September hunts. The pack is extremely lightweight and will pack a load of 35 to 40 pounds comfortably. Since most of my scouting trips are usually only for one or two nights, this pack works perfectly.

The second pack is a Dana Design Bombpack. It is a 3200 cubic inch pack that I normally use during all of my backpack hunts. It weighs 4 lbs. 13 oz. and is a very heavy-duty pack that incorporates the Arc Active Suspension technology and has outside load control. I can't pack any more gear in it than I can the Gregory, but with the better suspension system, I can pack loads up to 50 pounds very comfortably.

My third pack is a Dana Design Terraplane LTW. It is a 5800 cubic inch pack that weighs in at 6 lbs. 12 oz. I can pack anything and everything with this pack. Since going lightweight, I don't use this pack much any more. I just don't

need anything that big. It still comes in handy for extended trips or packing meat though. I have also integrated a CamelBak hydration system into all three packs so that I can drink on the fly. This makes it very nice because I don't like stopping when I am hiking.

Pack Selection

When choosing a pack, there are three things you must consider: size, type of frame and features of the pack. There are so many different sizes and styles of packs available today, that you shouldn't have any problem finding exactly what you are looking for. There are basically three choices when it comes to the frame of your pack – internal, external or frameless. The frameless rucksack type is best suited for short day hikes and are not very appropriate for multi-day deer hunts, so we will mainly focus on the external and internal. I have used both and currently prefer the internal frame variety. The internal packs are designed to carry the weight closer to your center of gravity, which makes the pack less likely to sway back and forth, especially on difficult or uneven terrain. However, since the pack conforms to your back, you will sweat more than with an external frame pack. One other reason I choose an internal

173

frame pack is that I can put my sleeping bag inside the pack, rather than strapping it on the outside. I like this extra protection against the elements. The only downside to internal frame packs is that they normally don't have a lot of pockets or compartments. Most of them come with one main compartment and maybe one or two small zippered pockets. To help keep gear organized in an internal frame pack, I like to use an assortment of different sized lightweight stuff

(L to R): Daypack, Weekend Pack and Expedition Pack. There are so many backpacks on the market today, no matter what features you are looking for, you shouldn't have any problem finding one that fits your needs.

sacks. You can even go one step further and use different colored stuff sacks to help identify contents without opening all of them.

The external frame packs are the workhorses. The ridgid frame helps pack the heaviest of loads and they typically have better ventilation between your back and the pack itself. Generally, they have more pockets, which make it a lot easier to keep your gear organized. No matter which style you decide on, you can't go wrong. With the advent of new tougher, lighter materials, the packs nowadays are lighter and more comfortable than ever.

The next thing to consider is what size of pack you need. Generally speaking, there are three categories of sizes: daypacks, weekend packs and weeklong packs.

Daypacks are normally 2500 cubic inches or less. The weights of the packs in this category normally range between 1 to 4 lbs. Most of these packs are good for a day hike, or maybe an overnight trip, but they just don't have enough room to pack enough gear for several days. The suspension systems on these packs will normally carry 25 to 30 lbs. of gear fairly comfortably.

The weekend pack category is my favorite. This catergory allows you to get a lightweight pack that will be good for several days, but still small and light enough to use as a daypack. They usually run from 2500 to 4000 cubic inches. The bulk of packs bought nowadays come from this category. These packs weigh in at the 3 to 4 lb. range. They have a little better suspension than the daypacks, which allows you to pack a load of 35 to 40 lbs. pretty comfortably.

Last but not least, you have the weeklong, or expedition packs. These normally range between 4000 and 6000 cubic inches and can pack more gear than I ever care to. Not only will they pack big loads, but with the amazing new suspension systems, they can do it rather comfortably. The packs themselves usually weigh between 5 and 7 lbs. Since I have gone ultralight, I rarely need to use my pack that is this size. When I am lucky enough to harvest a buck, I will use my big pack to haul it out, but that is about the only time.

Now that you have decided on the frame type and the size, the only thing left to consider is the features of the pack. This is merely a matter of personal preference. You need to decide what kind of features you like, such as a lot of pockets, less pockets, hydration compatible, etc. Personally, there are four features that I look for in a pack:

> **An outside pocket** large enough to hold my spotting scope. I don't like to have to dig through the middle of my pack if I spot something while hiking.
>
> **Straps** that allow me to strap my tripod to the side of my pack. Most packs have some form of stabilizer straps on the side that work well for this.
>
> **Some sort of pocket or sleeve** on the outside to put my rain gear. Easy and fast access is a must.
>
> **A hydration system** integrated into the pack. I like to be able to drink on the fly. I very rarely stop on my hikes.

The only thing left now is to buy your pack. I recommend that you go someplace that stocks a large inventory of packs and try several of them on. If it is any kind of store at all, they will have someone on hand that can measure you and fit you to the proper size pack. If not, you can measure yourself. You will have to measure what is called your torso length. Your torso length is the length along your spine from your C7 vertebrae, to the top of your hip bones. To locate your C7 vertebrae, bend your neck forward and it will be the bone that protrudes from the base of your neck. This measurement will tell you what frame size you need. Then go ahead and measure your waist at the top of your hipbones to find out what size of hipbelt you need. With these two measurements, you are on the right rack to getting a pack that fits. Backpacking is tough enough, much less having a pack that doesn't fit.

To help with your selection, I have included some backpack terminology and definitions that will help you in the selection process:

> **Capacity** – This is the maximum capacity of the pack, which is normally displayed in cubic inches.
>
> **Daypack Conversion** – Usually come with a removable lid that can double as a fanny pack. I have never cared about this option because I like carrying my entire pack with me while I am hunting.
>
> **External Frame** – Exactly as it implies, the frame is on the exterior of the pack.
>
> **Hybrid–Loading** – This are normally a cross between a top-loader and panel-loader, allowing you access from the top and the front.
>
> **Hydration Compatible** – This means a pack has a sleeve made especially for a hydration bladder. These sleeves are located in the interior of the pack and are not accessible once the pack is loaded. But they are located there for a reason. You want your heavier items close to your back. If you do decide to use the integrated sleeve, CamelBak makes a pretty neat quick coupler that you can install in the hose, allowing you to fill your bladder without

removing it from the pack. One side attaches to the hose on your filter, while the other attaches to the hose on the bladder. You just hook them together and start pumping. If you use a pack that doesn't have a sleeve and you don't have a CamelBak adapter, put your bladder in the lid pocket and route the hose through the zipper. This gives you easy access to refill the bladder during your hikes.

Internal Frame – The frame is on the interior of the pack.

Panel-Loading – This type of pack allows you to keep your gear very organized. They normally have a large half circle zipper on the front that gives you easy access to the main compartment. They usually have several small pockets on the sides of the pack as well. Unfortunately, they will not hold as much gear as a top-loader of the same size.

Rucksack – A frameless pack for designed for short day hikes. Some of them don't even come with hipbelts.

Shove-It – This is a large, zipperless opening on the front of the pack that was intended to be used to hold a snow shovel. Since a snow shovel isn't one of the items I like to take backpacking, I use this pocket to store my rain gear in. I don't have to dig through my pack for my rain gear and I can have it on in literally less than a minute.

Spindrift Collar – This is a short extension that extends from the top of the pack that allows you to pack more than normal.

Top-Loading – A pack that loads from the top. Usually consists of one large opening at the top of the pack that closes with a draw string. Normally has a sleeping bag compartment in the bottom of the pack. This type of pack requires some thought when it comes to loading it. Just remember, what you load first in the pack, will be the last thing out.

How to Load Your Pack

One common mistake a lot of people make is that they don't give any thought to how they load their pack. They just start cramming everything in without any rhyme or reason. Believe it or not, this can make a huge difference in how the pack rides on your back going down the trail.

First off, you want to put your lighter items at the bottom of your pack, typically your sleeping bag. That is why a lot of manufacturers put a separate compartment in the bottom of most packs. I prefer to put my bag in a stuff sack, but a lot of guys will just throw it in the bottom of the pack.

Once your bag is in, you want to load all of your heaviest items in the middle third of the pack closest to your back, such as tent, bivy, extra water, etc. This is probably the most critical step in loading your pack. Trust me, you don't want

Adjusting Your Backpack

Once your pack is loaded and on your back, there is a certain order in which you should adjust everything. The first thing that you want to do is make sure that all straps are loosened. All of those straps aren't just for looks, they all serve a particular purpose. Tighten everything in the following order:

1 Center the belt on your hips and tighten.

2 Cinch down the main shoulder straps until they are snug.

3 If your hipbelt has trim straps on the side, tighten them.

4 Tighten the shoulder stabilizer straps, which connect from the top of the shoulder straps to the top of the framesheet. You will feel the load snug up against your back.

5 Readjust the main shoulder straps

6 Buckle the sternum strap

By following this procedure every time you put your pack on, you will be getting the most out of your pack. Occasionally, you will have to readjust the hipbelt and all of the straps while you're on the trail. Heavier loads will require adjusting more frequently.

Colored stuff sacks help keep items better organized in your pack.

the heavy items too far back or too high, or it will throw off your center of gravity.

Next, you want to stuff all of your clothing and other light, bulky items around your heavier ones to keep them from shifting around in your pack. Finally, put all of the items that you might need to access on top, such as rain gear, snacks, camera, etc.

Following theses simple steps can make your pack ride significantly more comfortable than if you just cram everything in. One other thing I do to help keep my pack organized is to pack all of my smaller items in lightweight stuff sacks. These sacks are available in an assortment of sizes and colors and weigh next to nothing. I use the ones made by Golite, and by having everything in stuff sacks, it makes loading and unloading a breeze.

Pack Weight

Just about every lightweight article you read in backpacking magazines will tell you that to shave a couple of more ounces you can cut the edges off your maps, cut the end off your toothbrush or the labels off your tents etc. I take that one step further, I pluck all of the bristles, except one, out of my toothbrush to cut even more weight. Just kidding! To me, some of this crap borders on ridiculous. If you use common sense and cut weight in the right spots, the extra two ounces from all of the above items won't make any difference.

Packing light packs sure makes it easier, but there are certain times that there is no way around carrying a monster load. The heaviest pack I have ever packed was 115 lbs. That was when I packed out my buck that I named Curly in 1999. When I first put the pack on, I could only travel a short distance before I had to stop and rest. The shoulder straps were burning my shoulders and when I would sit down to rest, it was tough getting back to my feet. I was probably still seven miles from my truck back at the trailhead, but I knew of a road directly to the west that was only about five miles away. I dug out my cell phone and called my friend, Scott Mansor, and asked him if he would pick me up at the road. He agreed, which was going to save me two miles and a lot of painful hiking.

I dove off the top into a side drainage that I was going to follow down to the road. The going was slow because there wasn't much of a trail, and with a pack that weighs that much, you need to be certain of every step you take. I continued hiking until dark, but I still had a couple of miles before I reached the spot that Scott and I had agreed on meeting. Not wanting to keep him waiting too long, I took my pack off and stashed it along with the deer antlers. A couple of hours later I finally reached the road. Scott was just as relieved to see me, as I was to see the road. He had been driving up and down the road looking for me for an hour.

The next day, Scott and I hiked in and got my pack and deer antlers. We took turns hauling the load and made it out in pretty good time. After a short detour to the trailhead to pickup my truck, we headed home. We put the pack on the scale and it weighed 115 lbs. After that day, I swore I would never pack a load that heavy again.

Whenever I kill a deer, there's no way around packing a heavy load, but I have managed to lower my normal hunting pack weight considerably over the past couple of years. I have acquired a lot of new lightweight equipment and am constantly trying new gear. I will confess, I am an equipment junkie. I will have to admit that. I love

Manufacturers have a bad habit of advertising their gear as weighing less than it actually does. After purchasing gear, one of the first things I do is weigh it on a small digital scale to find out the actual weight.

knowing my equipment inside and out, including how much everything weighs. I have a spreadsheet I built in Excel on my computer that lists all of my equipment, along with its weight in ounces. All I have to do is enter the quantity of each item in the first column and the weights are automatically added and it gives me a total weight of all items at the bottom. This really works great because I can know the exact weight of my pack before I ever put a single item in my pack.

The first thing I do when I buy a new piece of equipment is weigh it and enter it into my Excel spreadsheet. I have a Pelouze digital scale that will weigh items up to five pounds in tenths of an ounce increments. You can pick one of these up for about $60.00. Never go by the manufacturer's weight, they always list everything a little bit lighter than it actually is.

Base Weight

When I'm talking base weight, I am talking about all of my standard gear that I take, minus food and water. My base weight is the same, regardless of whether I am going for one night or five nights. I still need all of this equipment regardless of how many nights I am staying. The only weight that changes is the weight of my food and water. I do not include my rifle or binoculars in my base weight. I will only include items that will be in my pack. This base weight stays the same the entire hunting season. It's a cinch figuring out how much my pack will weight for any given trip. All I have to do is add 27 oz. for each day I will be in the high country for food. With this setup, I can do a five day trip and my pack will only weigh 36 lbs. 13 oz. without water. That sure beats some of the old pack weights I used to lug around.

Before every hunt, I will print this list and as I put each item in my pack, I check it off the list. I have made this a habit because more than once I have forgotten certain items. The main thing that I usually forget to pack is silverware. By the way, if you ever forget a your spoon, the top part of the dehydrated meal that you tear off, can be bent in half and formed to make a fairly good spoon. I have had to get fairly creative at times to make do with what I had, but there's one thing you definitely don't want to forget, and that's toilet paper. There is no good substitute for this one, trust me. Now you're starting to see the importance of making a list and checking it

Loading Your Pack

One common mistake a lot of people make is that they don't give any thought to how they load their packs. They just start cramming gear in without any rhyme or reason. Here are a few pack loading tips that I have discovered throughout my years of backpacking that you might consider the next time you are loading your pack.

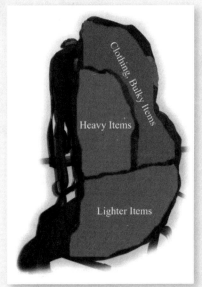

Light Items – The first thing you want to load in your pack are the light items. These items, such as your sleeping bag, sleeping pad and down jacket, need to be loaded in the very bottom of the pack.

Heavy Items – The next items you will want to load are your heaviest gear. These items are usually your tent, bivy and water. These items need to be loaded in the middle third of the pack closest to your back. This is probably the most critical loading step in order to have your pack ride snug down the trail.

Clothing and Bulky Items – Once your heavy items are loaded, place your clothing and other bulky items in the pack to secure the heavier items in place.

Small Items – Keep all of your smaller items organized in you pack with the use of lightweight stuff sacks. This is a lot better than having small items floating around in your pack.

Colored Stuff Sacks – Gear organization is a lot easier if you use different color stuff sacks. I use a different color stuff sack for each item.

Rain Gear – Keep your rain gear stored in an easily accessible location. I prefer to have mine in a mesh pocket on the outside of my pack. The last thing I want to be doing is digging through my pack for my rain gear during the middle of a downpour.

Spotting Scope & Tripod – Make sure these items are accessible as well. I secure my tripod to the side of my pack using the side compression straps. My pack also has an outside pocket for my spotting scope. In a matter of seconds, I can have my spotting scope on my tripod if needed.

Other Accessible Items – Keep items such as your water filter, camera, snacks, headlamp, map, etc. accessible at all times. The small pocket on the top of most packs is a great place to keep such items.

twice. This guarantees you will not leave anything behind.

I normally backpack alone, which means I have to pack everything on the list, but when I hunt with a partner, we divide up certain items to help lighten the loads. A couple of items you can do this on is your cooking equipment. Even if there are two or three in your hunting party, you only need one stove and mess kit. Divide those items, along with the fuel, up between all of you. Same with a water filter, you only need one. Make sure everyone compares lists so that you don't double up on anything that is not necessary. Following is a list of my gear, along with how much it weighs in ounces, that makes up my base weight:

Item	Weight	Item	Weight
Backpack	50.0	Spotting Scope	48.0
Ammunition	16.1	Tripod	40.0
Knife	8.0	Rangefinder	13.4
Zipka Headlamp	2.3	Map	2.4
Photon Light	0.3	CamelBak (empty)	7.4
Water Filter	13.1	Bivy	30.5
Therm-a-Rest Pillow	1.7	Bivy Poles	11.4
Snow Peak Stove	3.0	Sleeping Bag	26.7
Fuel Canister	7.0	Sleeping Pad	22.8
Mess Kit	5.9	Frogg Toggs Pants	8.1
Spork	0.6	Frogg Toggs Jacket	10.8
Digital Camera	9.6	GoLite Down Jacket	20.6
Under Armour Bottoms	6.2	Under Armour Shirt	7.6
Cell Phone	4.1	Bathroom Tissue	2.0
Toothbrush, paste, floss	1.5	Gaiters	10.0
Wool Gloves	4.9	Ear Warmer	1.0
Wool Pants	27.7	Wool Shirt	21.3
Alarm/Radio	7.7	Two trash bags	2.0

TOTAL BASE WEIGHT   28 lbs. 7.7 oz.

A base weight of 28½ pounds for a hunting pack isn't too bad. When I am scouting, my weight is even considerably less because I won't have any of the hunting equipment or wool clothing. But with the equipment I have listed above, it doesn't matter what weather conditions I may encounter, I am prepared for the worst.

I hope this information will help some of you in your selection of backpacking hunting equipment. The equipment that I mention is what I prefer, but that does not mean it is the only gear that works. There are several manufacturers of quality outdoor gear out there. The main thing is to do your research when shopping for equipment and remember the old saying, "You get what you pay for."

Throughout the pages of this book, you will see Victor Clark's name quite often. Victor is a very good friend and we have made several backpack trips together over the past few years. Victor is one of the most dedicated trophy mule deer hunters out there. His trophy room is evidence of that. The key to his success has been strapping on a backpack and hunting some of the most rugged, remote high country that he can find. Victor used this strategy in 1992 to harvest one of the largest B&C typical bucks to ever come from the state of Wyoming.

Victor's huge Wyoming buck nets 209⅜ B&C.

The First Shot

By L. Victor Clark

My good friend Frank Gonzales and I spent 15 long hours behind the wheel driving from Reno, Nevada to one of Frank's favorite hunting areas in western Wyoming. When we finally arrived at the trailhead it was 10:00 p.m. on the evening of September 12, 1992. Tired from the long drive we pitched the tent and laid out our bedrolls to try and get some rest. The next morning we would backpack nine miles into an area where we would begin our hunt. Over the past few years Frank had hunted this area and had harvested some exceptional bucks, one was a four point over 30 inches.

The next morning we loaded all of our gear into our backpacks and began hiking up the trail. The hillsides were colored with the yellows and reds of autumn and the excitement of this

Artist Darcy Tate's rendition of Victor Clark's huge Wyoming typical buck.

new adventure filled the air. Excitement soon turned to discouragement as we encountered several other hunters along the trail, including an outfitter who was looking for two of his horses that had wandered off. After visiting with the outfitter we learned he was hunting the general area that we had planned to hunt. Frank suggested that we climb into some less accessible country to get away from the hunting pressure. With one quart of water each, a water purifier and an assortment of freeze-dried dinners we began our ascent up into the rugged mountain range which stood before us. We climbed straight up until we ran out of daylight, making it three quarters of the way into the area we intended to hunt. The mountainside was so steep we had to dig out a spot to lay our sleeping bags on. In a full day of hiking, we had only seen three does. Discouraged and tired I drifted into a restless night's sleep.

Early the next morning we continued to the top of the mountain where we were greeted by fantastic views. These lofty vantage points had us looking into huge alpine bowls full of granite boulders and dotted with trees. I couldn't help but get my camera out and take several photos of the breathtaking scenery. As we sat down to glass, I noticed that I had lost my scope covers. I decided to backtrack a short distance and to try and locate them.

When I returned with my scope covers I found Frank watching a buck that was laying underneath a rock cliff approximately a half-mile away. Looking through the spotting scope I saw the buck of my dreams laying in his bed at the base of a pine tree. We decided to drop back behind the ridge and circle around and hopefully come out above the buck. As we neared the top of the ridge we dropped our packs and Frank said, "You take the first shot." I replied, "You take the shot, you spotted the buck." When we reached the top and peeked over, the buck was no longer in his bed. My heart sank. After a frantic search of the area with my binoculars I spotted the buck standing in front of a large stand of timber. Two steps would put him in the heavy timber and the opportunity to harvest this exceptional buck would vanish forever. I signaled to Frank who was in a rock pile 15 feet to my left. Frank acknowledged and said that he didn't have a clear shot and told me to go ahead and shoot. I squeezed the trigger, the bullet hit and the buck lunged forward. At almost the same instant Frank fired. The buck slid down a steep chute for about 150 yards before coming to rest against a boulder which kept him from cascading off a 200 foot cliff.

Once we made it down to the buck, we were relieved that the antlers were not broken during his tumble down the chute and through the boulders. Frank stared at the buck and said it was the biggest set of antlers that he had ever seen. While caping and boning the deer we found that the buck had been hit twice. After close examination we determined that either hit would have been fatal. I tagged the buck since I took the first shot. The sun had set by the time we finished caping and boning the deer. We had no choice but to dig out a place on the steep hillside to lay out our sleeping bags for the night. This spot turned out to be very uncomfortable. Unable to sleep I stared at this tremendous buck silhouetted against a full moon and relived the day's adventures.

We were unable to find a water source to replenish our canteens. It was the beginning of the third day as we finished off the last of the two quarts of water we started out with. Being short on water we were unable to eat our freeze-dried dinners. Exhausted from dehydration and lack of food we loaded up the meat, antlers and cape and started back to the main trail. Six hours later we finally reached the creek in the bottom of the canyon. We took a much needed water break. Two hours later we arrived back at the truck. After a shower, dinner and a good night's sleep we headed home. On our way home, I asked Frank, "If you had known this buck would turn out to be as tremendous as it is, would you still have told me to take the first shot?" Frank replied, "Yes, because I knew that harvesting such a great buck would mean more to you than it would to me."

This huge typical Wyoming buck gross scores 213 B&C and nets out at $209^3/_8$ B&C. The buck has an outside spread of $29^7/_8$ inches and is the fifth largest typical mule deer ever taken in Wyoming. The antlers won the prestigious First Award for the 22nd Big Game Awards of the Boone and Crockett Club.

Bill's buck is very massive and has a 34-inch outside spread.

Bucks in the Fog

By Bill Tanner

My hunting partner, Scott Mansor, and I had backpacked into one of our favorite high country areas a couple of days before deer season. We planned to spend the extra time scouting, but a combination of rain, snow and fog forced us to stay close to camp.

The sound of rain and snow pelting against our tent made it hard to crawl out of our warm sleeping bags on opening morning. We got a late start after spending some extra time getting all of our gear stowed away out of the weather. Shortly after leaving camp, we realized we would never have time to reach the place we planned to hunt before daylight. Besides that, the fog was so thick at that elevation we wouldn't have been able to see anything.

A quick decision was made to change course, so for 45 minutes we headed straight up the mountain. We really got heated up as we raced up that steep face trying to beat the morning light. I spotted a couple of different groups of deer on the way, but nothing we were interested in.

Scott spotted four bucks coming across a hill; however, we needed to gain some elevation before we could determine exactly how good they were. After climbing higher, we located the bucks several hundred yards away across the canyon on a giant rock-covered mountain. Glassing them we could tell one was a real keeper that was between 33 and 35 inches wide.

That darn fog kept dropping down over the bucks, then it would lift up so we could watch them for a while. We could tell by the way the deer were acting, they were ready to bed down. Finally the herd split up, with the big buck moving behind a tree just above some cliffs.

Scott and I moved down to the edge of the canyon and hid behind a small patch of trees. It was at least 500 yards across the bottom and we kept hoping the fog would drop down and cover our approach, but it never did. Our next best alternative was to drop way down country and come up right underneath the cliffs where the bucks had bedded. Once there, we could circle around and get above them using the cliffs for cover.

A 30-minute sneak took us up to the edge of the cliffs. We were very excited that our plan was working so well, when suddenly a shot rang out. Across the canyon from the bucks, another hunter fired nearly a dozen shots. Sitting there we wondered what in the hell they were doing…there was no way you could hit a deer from that distance!

Scott and I have always had this agreement that whoever spots a buck, has first priority. Although Scott had earned the right to the first shot at the buck, we knew we'd have a better chance if we split up. Scott was really mad at the inconsiderate hunter as he continued on around the base of those cliffs.

I decided to go straight up hoping if the deer tried to go around the top, I could cut them off. The incline was so steep I had to stop and rest after only going only 100 yards mostly on my hands and knees. Then I turned around and saw one of the neatest sights I have ever seen in the outdoors. Looking down, I could see the other hunter running up the opposite side of the canyon, while Scott worked his way around the cliffs about 500 yards away. In true big buck fashion, that deer turned back down the mountain while the others went over the top. He was sneaking along with his head low to the ground as he passed right between Scott and the other hunter.

Though the buck was only about 150 yards away, I couldn't tell for sure if it was the same one we had seen earlier. From the side I could tell he was heavy, but I really couldn't tell how wide he was until he turned and started running toward me. I thought he was going to get into some trees so I quickly fired offhand and missed the first shot. As I sat down to gain a more stable position, there was a four-foot pine tree blocking my view of the buck. When he failed to reappear, I carefully leaned over to peek around the edge of the tree. Not knowing where the shot had came from, that smart old buck had stopped in his tracks trying to pinpoint my location. When the crosshairs of the 3x9 Swarovski met his shoulder, I squeezed the trigger on my .300 Browning and watched him tumble in the snow.

"I got him!" I hollered as Scott came running up. He replied, "No way!" Neither he, nor the other hunter had seen the buck.

The Bottom  Line

Backpacking can be one of the most effective methods for hunting trophy mule deer. It allows you to penetrate and hunt the backcountry for several days at a time. The greatest advantage it gives you is mobility. In a matter of minutes, you can have your camp in your pack and heading down the trail to a new location. This mobility has led to the harvesting of many of my trophy bucks. I don't like the feeling of being limited to one area.

There are four keys to success in backpacking: staying properly hydrated, having the proper food to keep you nourished, being in shape and having the proper equipment. The quality of your backpacking experience and performance level is dependent on these four factors.

Hydration tips: make sure you drink small amounts often, rather than large amounts every now and then. Take in fluids before going to sleep and first thing in the morning. Don't consume fluids that have caffeine. *Nutrition tips*: make sure you eat throughout the day because you appetite is suppressed when you have been exerting yourself at high elevations. Take in small amounts of food even when you are not hungry.

Being in shape is probably the most important factor in how much you enjoy your backpack hunt. You can be in the middle of the best mule deer country in the world, but if you're out of shape, you won't be able to hunt it effectively. A proper fitness routine is essential to get your legs into the condition they need to be in to put on several miles everyday at high altitudes.

Make sure you have the best equipment you can afford. Not only will having the proper equipment make your trip more enjoyable, it will make your trip a lot safer. When investing in backpacking equipment, remember this, money spent on lightweight equipment is well spent. A lighter pack really does make a difference.

SECTION 5

EARLY SEASON HUNTING

It is views like this that keep me coming back to the high country

The High Country

The high country is without a doubt, my favorite place to pursue magnum mulies. There is something about looking out over a high alpine basin with views in every direction for miles and miles. It is something that you just can't get enough of. Even when the hunting is slow, the scenery is always breathtaking. I feel very fortunate to have spent as much time as I have in the backcountry. I only wish that I had more time to spend there.

The high country has given me some of my best hunting memories, but as I was writing this, there is one that came to mind that ranks as one of my favorite. In 1999 I was on a high country hunt with Victor Clark, Frank Gonzales and Doug Ayers. We had a good camp located on a high mountain bench that our friend Festus Krause packed in for us before the season. I was filming for my second video, *Magnum Mulies 2* and I had been lucky enough to be with Doug when he harvested a nice 26-inch buck early on in the hunt. Doug made an excellent 300-yard shot on the buck as he stood in a small opening directly above us. When we reached the buck, we sat down for quite some time and talked about how great it was to be on top of the world pursuing trophy mule deer bucks together.

A couple of days later, I was lucky enough to get Frank shooting a 27-inch buck on film. Victor and I were with him at the kill and it was awesome to see Frank harvest a buck. That was a pretty special moment. Festus and Doug came up and we all loaded the buck on the horses and Festus packed it out to the truck. After Festus

190

took off with the deer, Doug and I made our way over to a small spring that ran off of the extremely steep mountainside. After washing our hands, Doug and I sat there and stared out across the valley below us drinking some cold water from the spring. Doug looked at me and said, "This is probably the best hunt I have ever been on. Being in the high country with good friends hunting mule deer, it just doesn't get any better than this." That is definitely one of my favorite moments.

The early season is by far the most enjoyable time to be hunting the higher elevations. One of the best ways to do this is to archery hunt. A lot of the bucks are still in large bachelor groups and they are pretty much still in their summer routine. The mild temperatures make for a comfortable hunt, and surprisingly, there are very few hunters in the field. It is a great way to lengthen your hunting season, plus doubles as great scouting trips for the rifle season. I currently don't archery hunt, but I have made a couple of trips to the high country to pursue trophy bucks with a bow and arrow in the past. Although I never harvested a buck while archery hunting the high country, I enjoyed every moment of it. My hunting partner, Scott Mansor and I, have looked over a lot of nice bucks during the bow season.

There is one trip in particular that stands out in my mind. Scott and I had backpacked into an area that was relatively new to both of us for a three-day bowhunt. We set up camp on top of a ridge that ran from north to south and had several finger canyons that fell off the east side into a large drainage far below. By the time we got our camp situated and filtered some water, it was too late to do any glassing. We would have to wait until morning to see if there were any bucks hanging out in the basins.

Daybreak found us at the head of the first drainage that fell off to the east. Instantly, we spotted a huge buck in the upper portion of the bowl. The buck was extremely tall and had huge back forks, but his fronts were very small. Even with the small front forks, we figured he would gross 190 B&C. The buck was in an impossible spot to try a stalk, but Scott wanted to try to put one on him anyway. After a short, unsuccessful stalk, Scott met back up with me at the head of the drainage.

We climbed a short hill to the south and then dropped into a small saddle overlooking the next finger drainage. We got there just in time to see a buck that was well over 30 inches wide disappear over the ridge to the northeast. The buck was already on the move, so there was no sense in even going after him. As the sun continued higher, a lot of the animals had already begun to bed down. We continued glassing the shadows hoping to find an even better buck. I was glassing the shadows trying to find a bedded buck when a mountain lion appeared and then disappeared. I told Scott that I had just spotted a lion and pointed out the location to him. We continued glassing the ridge and soon spotted another, then another, then another. We couldn't believe our eyes, there on the ridge below us were five mountain lions walking toward a large rock outcropping where they would lie down for the day. That was truly one of the neatest sights I have ever witnessed while hunting.

We were excited; two drainages, two good bucks and five mountain lions. We couldn't wait to see what the last and final drainage would bring. A short hike and we were looking into the third drainage. As we peeked over the edge and started glassing, we located the best buck yet. He had several extra points on each side and brow tines that bent at 90 degrees facing forward. The buck was bedded down below and to the north of us. Scott wanted to attempt a stalk, so I decided to stay put, which would give me a front row seat to the show.

Scott had to follow the ridge to the south until he was out of sight before dropping down to the same level the buck was on. Once he was at the right elevation, he began closing the gap between him and the bedded buck. After quite some time, Scott was within 100 yards of the buck, which still had no idea Scott was there. I think I was just as excited as Scott was because I had such a great view of it all. Scott gradually crept closer and closer and soon was within 50 yards. Scott kept looking up at me and I kept giving him the green light signal telling him that the buck still hadn't detected him. As Scott eased a couple of yards closer, he stopped and slowly set his bow down on the ground. As soon as the bow touched the ground, the buck instantly turned and locked onto Scott's position. When Scott set his bow down, one of the limbs touched a rock which the buck's amazing ears heard. When you're within 50 yards of a buck, they can hear even the slightest sounds.

After setting his bow down, he looked up at me and I gave him the caution signal, telling him that the buck was onto him. Scott still could not see the buck from where he was, so he waited for quite some time. Finally, Scott decided to close the gap and see if he could get a shot on the buck. Unfortunately, the buck still was focused on Scott's position from when he set down his bow. As Scott eased forward, the buck bolted to his feet and ran a short distance up the ridge and then stopped and looked back. Scott stood there looking at the buck, which was now about 70 yards away standing there looking at him. Too far away for a shot, Scott watched the buck as he turned and disappeared over the ridge.

That was exciting to watch. It also goes to show you how hard it is to harvest a trophy mule deer with a bow and arrow. Although it is extremely tough to harvest a trophy mule deer with a bow, there are certain people that have became very proficient at it and consistently harvest great bucks with their bows.

Following are two archery hunting stories of successful bow hunts that took place in the high country. Both were written by Robby Denning of Idaho Falls, Idaho on a couple of successful Wyoming hunts.

Robby's 28-inch 185 Pope and Young buck

High Mountain Velvet

By Robby Denning

After four days of glassing good buck country, I'd decided to pull camp and try another area. I spent an hour packing up and was ready to load my packhorse, Missy. When I walked out in the meadow to catch her, I noticed a lone deer high on the ridgeline above, 700 yards from camp. Knowing that no self-respecting buck would be feeding within plain sight of my camp, I didn't even dig my binoculars out. As I saddled the horses, I kept glancing up at the deer. About the third time I looked, I swore I could see big antlers. I dug through an old leather saddlebag and retrieved my binoculars.

God must have a sense of humor. For four days, I'd rose before dawn and climbed the steep ridges surrounding camp and hadn't even seen a good buck. Now, right in the wide open at 11:30 a.m. was a 28-inch buck pushing 185 Pope and Young, and in full, beautiful velvet.

He fed into a small patch of timber about the size of a school bus and never came out. I didn't see any more deer so I assumed that he was alone. I pondered what to do. I'd have to cross the meadow in plain sight and climb the ridge to get above him. I finally decided that I wasn't going to be any more visible than what I already was so I climbed on my saddle horse, Rain, and rode 400 yards across the meadow with Missy in tow. It was a naked feeling riding around in the plain sight of a big buck.

When I finally reached the timber on the ridge, I tied the horses. I made a big loop to the north and came at the buck from his downwind side. An hour later, I peered over the top at

193

what looked like the same timber patch that he'd fed into. I couldn't see him laying in there so I slowly slipped down the hill. I kept thinking he must've seen me when I crossed the meadow and left once I was out of sight. Another hour had passed and I'd only moved about 10 yards when I spotted his antler tines under the heavy bows of a pine tree. I couldn't believe he was still in there. I was 60 yards from him and needed to get closer, but the ground was covered with little loose rocks and was very noisy. I didn't dare move.

Sitting there feeling helpless, I noticed that every few minutes the Mormon crickets, which had invaded the West that year, would start clicking loudly and create quite a racket. I wondered if I could time my moves with their mating calls. I waited for them to start in again and scooted down the hill a yard or so before they quieted down. It worked! The buck never turned my way.

Within an hour, I'd moved to within 40 yards. It was about 3:00 p.m. by then and I figured he'd stand up anytime and feed a little. I readied my bow and waited. Sure enough, within 20 minutes he started to get antsy and stood up. My 400-grain arrow tipped with a Rocket broadhead took him in the shoulder. I watched him pile up not 100 yards from the last bed he'd ever make. I knew God was smiling at the way He blessed me this day. I never thought I'd thank Him for crickets.

The Wait-Him-Out Buck

By Robby Denning

Almost constant rain and slushy snow had fallen for the last three days. I'd seen a good buck in the basin above camp, but the storm hadn't allowed me to see more than 100 yards since then. Since I was bowhunting, I knew my chance of blindly stalking within range of the buck was worse than winning the big Powerball jackpot. So there I sat in camp for nearly the third day. The only reading I had was a small Bible my wife had tucked away in my gear before I left. I read a month's worth of church in those three days. I had to leave the next afternoon and I finally came to terms with the fact I may not get to hunt the buck I'd seen.

Sometime during the night, I felt the temperature drop sharply in my little tent. I smiled as I snuggled deeper into my bag, knowing that outside the fog and clouds that had hugged the mountain were retreating. When the alarm went off at 4:30, I poked my head out of the tent. Sure enough, Orion the Hunter was shimmering down from a clear black sky.

After picking my way up the mountain in the dark, I reached my vantage point at first light. Immediately I spotted five bucks feeding on the same hillside where I'd seen the good buck. Looking through the spotting scope, I found that he was with them. He looked to be at least 28 inches wide with long main beams and enough extra points to put him easily in the book. The bucks were in the wide open feeding toward a dense stand of spruce.

I really don't know why I didn't wait for them to bed before starting my stalk as I usually do. Maybe I knew they'd make the timber before I could close the 1000-yard gap between us. Nearly an hour later, as I stuck my head over a rocky rim above the bucks, I saw that indeed they were almost to the timber. The shooter was about 80 yards out on the extremely steep 45-degree slope. Several of the smaller bucks had already bedded at the timber's edge 40 yards below me. He was feeding their way. I pushed my body into the shade of a big boulder and waited.

At about 65 yards out, he suddenly turned broadside toward the timber. I knew instantly that he wasn't going to bed near the other bucks and he was now only a few steps from disappearing into the spruce. I quickly drew and held my 60-yard pin on his front knee and then let 'er fly. The hit looked good as he bolted for the timber.

Robby with his high mountain non-typical

I waited an hour after I saw the other four bucks trot out of the basin without their leader. Slipping down the steep hillside, I found that he had only gone about 20 yards before piling up and sliding a good ways down the mountain. As I snapped some pictures, I thanked the good Lord for making deer hunting.

Spot & Stalk Hunting

There are several different hunting methods that can be used during early season hunting, but the most effective hunting method I have found for the high country, whether you are bow hunting or rifle hunting, is spot and stalk. Which is exactly as the name implies, you spot an animal, then put a stalk on it. All three bucks in the previous stories were harvested using spot and stalk techniques. The high country is very susceptible to this type of hunting method. It is my preferred method and the majority of the bucks I have taken have been harvested by utilizing this method in one form or another.

I used the spot and stalk method in September, 2003 in the high country of Wyoming to harvest a 190-class buck. I was just about ready to release my third video, *Magnum Mulies 3* and really wanted to get a good kill scene on video. This wasn't going to be an easy task considering I was by myself. Not only was I going to be the hunter, I was also going to have to play the role of cameraman as well.

It was two weeks into the deer season and the trail had been beat to dust by numerous horse pack trains since opening day. It was late afternoon and I was working my way up the rather open trail, which offered very little relief from the sun. The temperature was 10 degrees above normal and in the mid-70's, not exactly prime deer hunting weather, but I was going to give it my all during the next five days and hope for the best.

Just before I reached camp, I noticed a buck feeding in a ravine approximately 250 yards below me. I took my pack off and put my spotting scope on the buck. He had a mid 180 typical frame with a long hook cheater on his left side coming off his G3. A good buck, but it was too early in the hunt to pull the trigger. I had several days to hunt and felt confident that I could find something bigger.

Ten minutes later I arrived at the small patch of trees I would call home for the next few days. I set up my bivy shelter and arranged my camp the way I wanted it. I only had one hour before dark, but rather than glass for deer, I had to make a water run because I had just ran out moments before reaching camp. I grabbed my filter, CamelBak and water bottles and dropped off the ridge to the north to a spring that was located on the trail coming from the opposite direction that I had just came in from. Darkness found me returning to camp with a gallon of water and after cooking a dehydrated meal, I nestled into my bivy and called it a night.

The next couple of days I saw several small bucks along with a few average four points, but nothing that got me too excited. There was quite a bit of hunting pressure in the drainages I had been hunting, so the third day I decided to move my camp three miles to the west to an area that wasn't receiving any pressure.

Once I had my new camp situated, I glassed the large basin to the east until dark.

On the third day of the hunt, I moved my bivy camp three miles to the west.

There was definitely less hunting pressure in this new area, but there were definitely less deer as well. I was still excited though because I hadn't even glassed the basin to the west of my camp yet. That would be the plan for the next morning.

First light of the fourth morning found me looking into the new basin. The first hour of glassing was rather disappointing. A group of does midway down the drainage was all I could find. I kept picking the mountainside apart, piece by piece, when I finally glassed a buck working his way toward the top of the steep face on the opposite side of the canyon. I put the spotting scope on him only to find out that he was a very small buck. I continued to glass other country, but kept finding myself going back and glassing the small buck to make sure he wasn't alone. Sure enough, he wasn't. Now there were three bucks. The spotting scope confirmed what I thought—the middle buck was a good one. I figured he had a typical frame that would score 180 along with several small extras. The bucks were directly across the drainage from me at about the same elevation. I continued to watch the bucks work their way up the extremely steep slope toward a couple of small scrub pines. Once they reached the pines, the large buck bedded immediately, while the two smaller bucks fed for a few more minutes and then bedded about 50 yards to the right of the bigger buck.

The stalk would be a tough one. It would require dropping off to the north of the ridge I was on and sidehill for quite some distance, dropping down through a saddle

198

and a steep climb up to another small saddle which I figured would put me within 300 yards of the buck. One and a half hours and two miles later I found myself approaching the small saddle that I had set out for. Twenty yards from the top I took my pack off and dug my rangefinder out. I belly-crawled up to the top and glassed the scrub pines. The buck hadn't moved, he was still in his bed. I put the rangefinder on him and got a reading of 306 yards. I eased back down to my pack and grabbed my video camera. Once back on top, I set the video camera up on a tripod and started recording the buck there in his bed. I crawled back down and grabbed my rifle, chambered a round and returned to the top. After making sure the buck was still centered in the viewfinder of the camera, I laid my rifle across a large rock and eased the safety off. I took a deep breath and pulled the trigger. The bullet hit its mark. It went through the lungs and exited through the left shoulder. Dead on his feet, the buck bolted from his bed and disappeared over the ridge. A large dust cloud kept rising from the other side of the ridge as the buck tumbled down the other side. I had no idea what was on the other side, but

The buck slid 150 yards down a rockslide before stopping.

judging by the amount of dust coming over the rise, I figured it wasn't good.

I loaded up all of my camera gear and started making my way across the extremely steep sidehill where the buck had been bedded. Once I reached the top of the ridge, I was surprised to see how far the buck had rolled. He had tumbled 150 yards down a steep rock chute and if he hadn't of stopped where he did, he would have rolled another hundred yards. Luckily, the only casualty during the fall was a half inch off the small cheater on his left antler. The buck's typical frame scored 182 B&C and he had 8⅝ inches of extra points for a gross score of 190⅝ B&C. His outside spread was 27½ inches.

It was 10:00 a.m. and warming up fast so I made the photo session a short one. I dressed and quartered the buck and put him in the shade of one of the few trees that provided any amount of shade. I had ran out of water and was getting pretty dehydrated so that only left me with one option. I needed to drop down into the bottom of the drainage to get some water out of a spring I had noticed while doing my stalk. This added several hours to my hike and I didn't arrive back at camp until 3:00 p.m. I packed up my gear and started my long hike to the trailhead. I arrived at the truck at 6:00 p.m.

The next day it took me nine hours to pack the buck out. Tired and sore, I just kept putting one foot in front of the other. As I got closer to the truck, the pack

The body on this buck was huge. It took me nine hours to pack him out.

seemed to get lighter and lighter and a smile came to my face that would not leave. This was probably one of the most physically demanding hunts I have been on, but definitely one of the most satisfying.

Most people would probably be bored to death hunting the way I do, spending hour after hour looking through my binoculars. Spot and stalk hunting does require a tremendous amount of patience and the majority of your time will need to be spent sitting stationary looking through optics, but when done right, it is the most effective method I have found for trophy mulies. Using this method gives you several advantages; the most obvious is that you can cover a lot of country. While glassing, you can literally look over miles of great mule deer country in no time at all. The other advantage you have is normally the deer that you spot while glassing, have no idea that you're there. To me, this is a huge advantage. It allows you to formulate a plan, and put on a stalk, which with any luck at all, will be successful.

The last part of August and the first week of September, the bucks will be losing their red summer coats, which made them so visible during the summer. They will now be turning gray in color, which makes them blend in a little better with their surroundings. The older, more mature bucks seem to turn colors first, followed by the younger bucks. I have seen this year after year. So when you are glassing a bachelor group of bucks, make sure you look at the grayest ones first.

Bucks will also be shedding their velvet this time of the year. Normally they do this the first two weeks of September. Once a buck decides it is time, he will have the velvet off in short order. Usually in one or two days the majority of the velvet is gone. When glassing this time of year, pay particular attention to areas that have a lot of small saplings. Bucks prefer to use these to rid of their velvet, rather than larger trees. They will be up and rubbing their antlers for extended periods of time.

Early Season Glassing

In order to be successful using the spot and stalk method, you need to become proficient at glassing. Over the years I have learned when and where to glass to observe the most game. This knowledge, combined with my Four Phase Glassing method has worked very well for me on my high country hunts.

First and foremost, you must be able to glass effectively. Although the temperatures warm up quick this time of the year, it can be fairly cold at daybreak and dusk and if you're not properly dressed, you will not doing much good if you're shivering and shaking while trying to glass. Be sure and dress warm for these times. Make sure to have an extra layer of clothing for when you sit down to glass. Sometimes I will attach my binoculars to my tripod which totally eliminates any movement. Nowadays, you can buy adapters to mount just about any set of binos to a tripod, but years ago, there weren't any, so I had to make my own. I made a bracket out of lightweight aluminum, which is tapped with a $3/8$ hole, so that I can attach it to a quick release. It is then attached to my binoculars via a one-inch-wide strap. I also have a quick release on my spotting scope so that I can switch back and forth very quickly. This system works very effectively. No matter how much I am shivering because of the cold, my binoculars remain perfectly still. Trust me, it does make a difference. Also, a tip from experience, set up your spotting scope before you begin. I can't count the times in which I have spotted a buck in the distance and by the time I managed to get my scope out of my pack and set up, the buck was out of view.

Quick Release Setup

If I had to pick only one tip that would help the average hunter improve their glassing skills, it would be to mount their binoculars on a tripod when glassing. The first time I tried it I was amazed at the difference that it made. I was able to hold my binoculars perfectly steady. Even when I found myself shivering from the cold while glassing during the early morning, or late evening, my binoculars remained motionless. I can't emphasize enough how important it is to have your optics stable while glassing.

Years ago, there weren't any adapters being manufactured, so I had to make my own. I made a bracket out of lightweight aluminum, which is tapped with a $3/8$ hole so that I could attach it to a quick release. I then attached it to my binoculars via a one-inch wide strap. Nowadays, you can buy adapters to mount just about any set of binos to a tripod.

If you do decide to try mounting your binoculars to your tripod for stability, it is absolutely essential that you use a tripod that has a quick release mounting system. This is a plate that can be removed from the tripod head by the slide of a lever in only seconds. When removed, the plate remains attached to the optics, not the tripod. Most tripods only come with one plate, but you will want to order an extra one from the manufacturer so that you have one for your binoculars and another for your spotting scope. This way, you can switch back and forth between your binoculars and spotting scope in a matter of seconds.

Save yourself the frustration.

I normally have the vantage point that I will be glassing from during the morning picked out ahead of time. That way I will know approximately how long it will take me to get there and I can be set up before daybreak. Once situated, I set up my spotting scope and begin glassing with my binos as soon as it gets light enough. It is essential you are ready to go at sun up because the temperatures rise so fast this time of year that the bucks won't be up for very long.

The first places that I glass in the mornings are feeding areas. These are normally fairly wide open areas and are located relatively close to the bedding areas. Even if I don't spot anything immediately, I keep glassing. Bucks constantly move while they are feeding, and while they might be hidden when I glass an area the first time, I might catch them in the open on my next pass with the binos. I only use Phase I and II glassing methods during this time. I am not concerned about bedded bucks at this point, I am only glassing for bucks that are either feeding or are on their way to their bedding area.

If the area I am glassing has any cliffs at all, I will glass below these first. Normally bucks like to feed under these cliffs and they will continue to travel along them until they fade out and then they gradually angle up the hill toward their bedding areas. Once I have glassed below all of the cliffs, I will glass above them. Normally there are small patches of timber that the deer like bedding in along with a lot of smaller openings where the bucks like to feed.

Image 5-9

Take a look at Image 5-9. This is an area where I spotted several bucks this year, including one that would score right around 180 B&C. This country is the classic type of mule deer country that I like to be glassing at daybreak. I started glassing the basin first thing in the morning. Guess where I found the bucks feeding? You

Image 5-10

guessed it, right underneath the cliffs. The bucks fed along the bottom of the cliffs and the first break in the cliffs, the bucks angled up the hill to their bedding area.

This hillside is identical to the one I spotted a 38-inch non-typical on several years back. The 38-inch buck, along with his two buddies had the exact same routine. They would feed along the base of the cliffs to a point where the cliffs faded out and then they angled up close to the top of the ridge to some scattered pines where they bedded for the day.

Image 5-10 is some of the best high country deer habitat I've seen. I have spotted many bucks on this hillside over the years. Why do the bucks like it? That's simple. It has a lot of feeding and bedding areas, as well as a lot of terrain variation offering the bucks many escape routes. Although you could pretty much find a good buck anywhere in this country, there are a couple of spots that the bucks tend to favor.

I have marked two feeding locations on the photo where I have consistently seen the most bucks feeding, along with where they normally bed down for the day. The primary reason the bucks utilize these two areas is because there is good feed at both locations. There are several other areas in the photo that have just as good of feed, but the bucks tend to favor these two because there is a lot of cover nearby. In a matter of seconds they can be out of sight. The only time you will see bucks utilizing the more open feeding areas will be during the scouting season or archery season. Once that first rifle shot has been fired, the bucks will use the smaller openings.

When I see bucks using feeding Area A, they normally bed down in bedding Area A. They normally bed right on the edge of the rim, which allows them to see in a couple of different directions. Sometimes they elect to travel past bedding Area A and will continue farther on up the hill to bedding Area B. Bucks feeding in Area B will always use bedding Area B. Most of the time, the bucks bed just underneath the small saddle at the top of the bedding area.

203

The one common denominator that both of these bedding areas have in common is they offer more than one escape route. It doesn't matter what direction a hunter may approach from, the bucks always have a direction that offers them a way to escape.

When glassing this type of country, you will want to look for feeding and bedding areas that are close to one another. This minimizes the buck's exposure when they are traveling from one to another. Another thing that is important is that the bedding area is always higher in elevation than the feeding area. This seems to always be the case. Almost every buck I see when done feeding will travel uphill to his bedding area. Very rarely do you see the opposite. Mule deer like to have a good view from their beds during the day.

Image 5-11 is one of my favorite areas to hunt. There are not very many deer in this area, but when you do see one, he's normally a good one. Plus, I just love being in this type of country. It's beautiful. The mountain in this photo has two features

(Top) Image 5-11 (Bottom) Image 5-12

that big bucks love: benches and saddles.

Bucks love benches for several reasons. First and foremost, they normally have a lot of feed. This particular bench has a lot of it that attracts both mule deer and bighorn sheep. I have probably seen just as many bighorns feeding on the bench as I have mule deer. It is also out of the way and doesn't receive much hunting pressure at all. It is a nine mile hike to get to it and in all of the years I have hunted it, I have never seen another hunter climb up on the bench. They all ride right by it on the main trail in the bottom. From the bottom the bench doesn't look like much, but as you can see in photo 5-12, the bench is a lot bigger than it appears.

The deer normally use the two small timber patches on the right to bed during the day. With all of the cliffs, you can only access the bench from the left side, or on the extreme right. The bucks can normally see you coming well in advance and are extremely tough to hunt when they are bedded in these areas.

This brings us to the second feature that bucks like—saddles. The large saddle in the middle of the photo offers a superb escape route for bucks that bed anywhere on the bench. Depending on the direction of approaching hunters, the deer have several options as far as escape routes go. They can go either cross the bench to the left, or go around the point on the right, or over and through the saddle.

After glassing these types of areas during my morning session with Phase I and II glassing methods, I have to change my glassing technique once everything has bedded down. I no longer glass the hillsides at a distance. I am now concentrating on closer areas. This is when I will incorporate Phase III into the mix. I will move along the top of a basin, just below the skyline, glassing down into the bedding areas. I will move at a very slow pace, stopping to glass often. See Image 5-13. Every time I stop, I glass all terrain within rifle range with my binoculars, concentrating on the shaded areas where I might spot a bedded buck.

Image 5-13   Bucks love to bed on the uphill side of trees. Spend a lot of time glassing any shade on the north side of any available trees.

When glassing bucks in their beds, the main thing to remember is that most deer beds are located on the uphill side of a tree. They usually have a large depression that has been dug out, and once bedded in it, deer are rather tough to see. In most cases, it is almost impossible to glass them from below. The only way to glass bucks in their beds is to be at the same elevation or higher. I prefer to be slightly higher and at an angle to the hillside that I am glassing. That gives me the best possible angle to glass from.

When you spot a buck in its bed, spend a lot of time picking all of the surrounding cover apart. This time of year they are usually not alone. Make yourself comfortable and glass for a long time. Once you feel you have covered all of the surrounding trees, move a short distance and pick it apart again. Don't get in any hurry. You need to be extremely patient at this point.

Beds are located on all facing slopes, east, west, south, and north. But weather and the time of day will determine which beds they will be using. Generally, during the hot summer months after bucks get done feeding in the morning, they will bed on the cooler, north or northeast facing slopes for the day. After their evening feeding session, they will bed on the south or southwest facing slopes for the night.

After covering two or three basins, I like to drop down in elevation and reverse my direction. (Image 5-14) The route I take will depend on the topographic features of the hillside. As you can see by the photo, I like to follow the contour of the land. I will hunt it the exact same way that I hunted when I was on top. I will stop and glass often, and when I reach any elevated locations that offer good views, I will glass for a minimum of a half hour. By dropping down in elevation on the mountain, I am able to glass all new country that was out of view when I was on top. I spend a lot of time glassing the edges of the avalanche chutes on the lower part of the hill. I still glass uphill at the area I was glassing from above because I am looking at it from a different angle, but my time is better spent glassing the terrain below me.

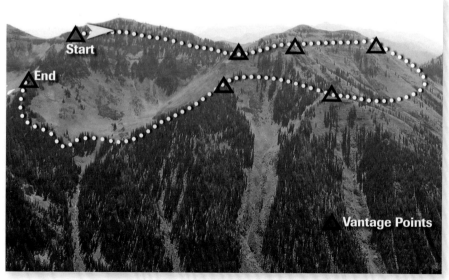

Image 5-14

Some of the most common bedding locations for big bucks in high alpine basins include any small finger ridges that run down the middle of the basins. Bucks love to bed down at the upper end of the small timber patches that dot the top of the ridges. These patches are absolute buck magnets for two reasons. The first is that they offer a commanding view of the surrounding area, which allows them to spot any approaching danger. Second, when bedded on top of a ridge, it gives them two escape routes. In literally only a step or two, they can be off the opposite side of the ridge and out of sight in a matter of seconds.

Another spot where bucks like to bed is in the small patches of timber located at the head of the basin. In Image 5-15 I have highlighted one such timber patch. The key to locating bedded bucks in these patches is to glass them from different angles. If you were to glass this basin only from one angle, you probably wouldn't have much luck locating any bucks. What I like to do is work my way around the basin, trying to use any available cover to stay concealed, and glass into the trees from different angles using Phase III and IV glassing. I will spend at least 30 minutes glassing at each one of the vantage points that I have marked. I will also stop several times in between the vantage points to glass, but I won't spend as much time glassing at those locations as I will at the vantage points. If I glass patiently, odds are if there are any bucks bedded in the patch of timber, I will find them. Glassing from that many angles is very effective. As new basins come into view, I will glass them as well. It's amazing how many bedded bucks you are able to find when you're looking under every tree with a 20-60X spotting scope.

One thing worth noting is that as the position of the sun changes, deer beds that were in the shade will be exposed to the sun and the deer will get up to change their beds. Usually this occurs about 10:00 a.m. in the morning and 3:00 p.m. in the afternoon. So make sure you're glassing around these times. Don't spend much

Image 5-15

time glassing large openings, spend your time glassing the smaller ones. Bucks like to bed on the edge of these clearings, where they're only a quick jump from the heavy timber. I have seen this time and time again, so make sure to concentrate the majority of your glassing near the edges of any heavy timber patches in view.

I will continue using this hunting method of glassing bedding areas until about 3:00 p.m. At that time I like to be set up at a good vantage point to where I can look at a lot of country using Phases I and II until dark. My evening glassing session is the same as my morning session is, with one exception. During the morning session I glass around the feeding areas first, where in the evening, I am paying more attention glassing in the vicinity of the bedding areas first.

Stalking

Now the real fun begins. Your glassing has finally paid off and you have located a huge buck on the opposite side of the drainage feeding about a half mile away. What do you do? The outcome of your hunt will depend on the next couple of decisions you will have to make. During the stalk there are going to be times that you must be very patient, while other moments require you not to lollygag around and cover some ground.

When I spot a trophy mule deer, the first thing I do is determine if he is within rifle range or not. If he is within range it is very simple, there will be no stalk. If he is out of range, it is crucial that I make the right decisions. If the buck is bedded down, I will immediately start planning my stalk, but if he is up moving or feeding, that requires another decision. If the buck is relatively close and I feel that I can get within rifle range before the buck disappears, I will begin my stalk immediately. But if the buck is a long ways off and will require a lengthy stalk, then I need to be patient. It is absolutely critical that I watch the buck until he beds down. Otherwise, by the time I get to where I initially spotted the moving buck, I won't have any idea where he would be. So make sure you watch the buck until he beds.

Once the buck is bedded, you can start planning your stalk. The first thing I look for is the place I want my stalk to end, which will hopefully be the spot I will be able to set up and shoot the buck from. This is normally at or above the elevation the buck is bedded at. If you pick a spot below the buck, odds are, you won't be able to spot him in his bed.

Once I have that spot picked out, I need to decide on the best way to get to that point. To make the stalk faster and more effective, I like to find ridges that I can drop behind, out of the buck's sight, allowing me to cover a lot of ground in a hurry. Make sure you look over several options and then decide on the best one.

After deciding on the route I want to take, I look over the surrounding country around the buck so that I have a couple of landmarks to help locate the buck once I arrive at my predetermined point. These landmarks can be several different things such as boulders, dead trees, small patches of trees, rock slides, etc. This is absolutely critical, and when overlooked, can cause a stalk to fail. If I get in a hurry and don't pick out a good landmark before doing my stalk, it will be very difficult to locate the buck. I will then have to do a lot of moving around to try and locate him and instantly that puts me at a disadvantage.

Even with good landmarks it can be hard to locate your buck at times. There

Image 5-16

have been several times I have had good landmarks picked out only to arrive at my designated point and have everything look totally different than what I had expected. Make sure you take your time and pick your landmarks wisely.

While doing my stalk, if I am out of the buck's sight, such as behind a ridge, I move as fast as I can. There is no reason to be dragging my feet at this point. When hunting public land, anything can happen, so I need to close the gap at a fairly rapid pace if the terrain allows.

Image 5-16 shows the mountainside where I killed my 1998 high country Wyoming buck. As you can see, it has several small finger ridges that run down from the top to the bottom. I used these to my advantage during my stalk on the buck. If I would have came up from directly below the bucks, I wouldn't have had a chance. Not only that, I would have had to have moved at an extremely slow pace to keep from being spotted by the deer. Instead, I hiked up the draw to the south of the bucks, using the ridge between us to conceal my approach. I was also able to move at a very rapid pace and didn't have to worry about the bucks seeing me.

Ideally you will arrive at your predetermined point as planned and the buck is right where you expected him to be. Unfortunately, it doesn't always happen this way. If you can't locate the buck during your initial observation, this is where you need to be extremely patient. Every move you make at this point is very important because you are at a relatively short distance from the buck, and his sight, sense of smell and hearing are absolutely amazing at this range. If you have to do a lot of moving around, chances are that you are going to blow your stalk.

First off, make sure that the wind is in your favor because if it's not, it doesn't matter how slow you move, you don't have a chance. Pick all of the terrain apart with your binoculars. Once you're satisfied that you have seen everything, very slowly move a short distance and repeat the process. If you still can't locate the buck, back off and try locating him from a distance with your binoculars. Don't keep trudging around his bedding area, you will only blow him out of there and never see him again. It is better to back off and try again.

A Buck's Core Area

A buck's core area during late summer and hunting season is about two square miles. This seems like a rather small area when looking at a map, but when you're in the high country, sometimes it seems like an impossible task to locate a deer in that much country. Deer will occasionally leave their core area, but they will always return. Images 5-18 and 5-19 are good examples of how deer remain in their core areas throughout the summer and early fall. They show the locations and movements of two different deer throughout an entire summer and fall. They also show how the deer may drift out of the core area occasionally, but they always return.

The longer you hunt the area, the better chances you have of locating the best buck in the area. Radio collar studies have proved that hunting pressure does not

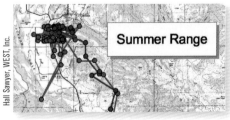

Image 5-18

Image 5-19

cause a buck to leave his home range; it only makes him use it differently.

Deer use several means other than distance to get away from hunting pressure including using steeper slopes, heavier cover and they also utilize north-facing slopes early in the hunting season. Under hunting pressure, some bucks move to dense patches of cover, while others move to more open terrain. You might think that moving to more open terrain would increase the chance of being harvested, but most hunters would walk right by this kind of terrain, thinking there is no way a buck would inhabit such a place during hunting season, so spend time glassing those open areas above timberline, you might be pleasantly surprised.

While some deer choose heavy cover and others open country, they all become more nocturnal in their habits. The main point here is a buck doesn't change his home when hunting season begins, but he will change his habits and the way he uses it, leading you to believe he has left the country.

Seeing that a buck won't leave his home turf has been reinforced to me on several occasions, but my 2002 hunting season really stands out in my mind. I had heard stories of a nice buck that had been spotted in a small drainage before the season. My brothers and several other hunters were in the area on opening morning and saw the buck, but nobody managed to get a shot. After opening day nobody saw the buck again and everyone figured he had left the area. Toward the end of the season, after everybody cleared out of the area, I made a trip into the area to see if I could locate the buck.

I took my time on the way in, glassing all of the surrounding hillsides, but couldn't locate the buck. Once on top, I immediately glassed three bucks making their way toward some dark timber on a north-facing slope where they would bed down for the day. The buck in the rear was the buck everyone had been talking about. He was about 28 inches wide and had several extra points. I knew I wouldn't be able to get within range before they made it to the timber, so I just sat and watched as they disappeared over the ridge. I didn't like my odds of going into the thick timber after them, so I figured I would wait them out until they fed back out that evening. It was 9:00 a.m., so I knew I had a long wait.

As I laid there and soaked up the sun, I stretched out and made myself comfortable. I pulled my hat down over my eyes and the next thing I knew, I was waking up from a 45-minute siesta. The good news was that I was wide-awake now. The bad news was I still had about seven hours before I would likely see some action. I couldn't help but reminisce about old hunts and wonder what my future hunts might have in store. All I could think about was life doesn't get any better than this.

That evening, I heard a bull elk bugling 500 yards below me in the dark timber. The bugling kept getting closer and closer, and finally a large five point elk and his harem fed out into a small saddle only fifty yards away from me. The bull had obviously defended his harem numerous times before, which was evident by looking at his antlers. His entire right antler was broken off about midway up and his left antler had several tines snapped off. As he stood there and bugled again, this time only forty yards away, the hair stood up on the back of my neck. It was exciting being that close to the bull when he had no idea I was there. There was no cover between me and the elk, so I had to remain motionless for about 30 minutes until the elk finally fed far enough away that I could at least move.

For a short time, I forgot all about the task at hand. But as soon as the smallest buck of the three appeared, I totally forgot about the bull and shifted gears back to mule deer. The small buck slowly fed in and out of the trees directly to my right. As I watched him, I felt confident that the big one wouldn't be too far behind. As the sun was setting, the small buck disappeared into the timber and did not return. I waited until it was to dark to see, but the other two bucks never appeared. An eight hour wait all for not.

During the hike out that night, I had a positive attitude because it had been a very enjoyable day. While head-lamping it out, I was already making plans for round two with the buck the next morning.

I got an early start the next morning and had already covered the 2½ miles that put me near the top of the ridge I wanted to glass from by the time it started getting light. I was traveling at a pretty good pace so that I could reach the top and start glassing when I looked up ahead and saw the buck go over the top. I blew it. I had been so worried about reaching my vantage point that I forgot to pay attention and look for deer. I continued hunting the area all day but never saw the buck again. I was 0 for 2 and only had one more chance – the next day was the last trip I would be able to make into the area.

As usual, I was leaving the trailhead about an hour and a half before daylight. Once I got close to the area where I had jumped the buck the previous day, I reduced my pace and started to hunt very slowly along the ridge hoping to locate the buck before he spotted me. I reached the top at 8:00 a.m. and still had not spotted the buck. The snow and wind had formed a cornice, which I eased out on as far as I dared and peeked into the basin the buck was in the day before. Directly below, the buck was feeding toward a patch of pine trees. It was an extremely steep angle and I wasn't real sure about being that far out on the cornice. I backed off and took my pack off to use as a rest and eased back onto the cornice. I laid the pack down and rested my rifle over it. I wanted to range the buck, but he was only a step away from the trees so I felt rushed. I took a deep breath and fired. The buck lit out of there and disappeared into the trees and around the far ridge. I had shot over the buck's back. I went down and looked for blood, but there was none. I followed the buck's tracks and he led me in a circle and several hours later I tracked him back to the basin where I had shot at him. I watched the basin until dark, but never saw the buck again.

The whole point behind this story is a buck will usually hang tight in his core home area during the entire hunting season. Even after being shot at, this buck returned to the basin he called home. I always hear stories of people locating bucks while scouting but never being able to locate the bucks during the hunting season. After not being able to locate the buck once or twice, they give up and assume the buck is gone. Remember, bucks normally don't leave their high country home until mid to late October. The only exception to the rule is if the high country receives a major snowfall, which will cause them to exit earlier than normal.

Not only do bucks use the same core area all fall, they utilize the same area year after year. On several occasions, I have spotted bucks utilizing the same basins year after year. One particular buck, I spotted three years in a row on the same ridge. The main point here is, don't give up. Even if you find a buck and don't harvest him during the hunting season, return the next year for a rematch.

Dave Siegfried with his opening morning 38-inch 10x10 high country buck.

Weather

Weather plays the biggest factor in where you will locate a buck in his core area. Without any change in the weather, a buck will remain very consistent in his daily routine. But throw in a big change in the weather, and things change.

An early snowstorm during the 1996 season cost me a huge buck that year. Several weeks before the opener, I was scouting a new area in the rugged Salt River Range in western Wyoming. I had a knob picked out that I wanted to glass from that would give me a good 360 degree view of two drainages that ran parallel to one another.

Once on top of the ridge, it was tough finding a place good enough to pitch my tent. The ridgetop was narrow and covered with sharp edged rocks. Thirty minutes of digging out rocks and leveling the ground as best I could, finally gave me a place to put my two-man tent. After a couple of bent tent stakes and putting the finishing touches on my camp, I grabbed my spotting scope and headed to a nearby rock outcropping which was about 100 yards east of my camp.

After just a couple of minutes, I located three bucks feeding easterly underneath some small rim cliffs midway up the opposing ridge. Through the binoculars I could see what looked like extra points on one of the bucks. I rushed to get my spotting scope set up so I could find out exactly how good he was. Once I had him in my scope, I couldn't believe my eyes. He had points going everywhere. After calming down, I counted 10 points on each side and guessed his outside spread at 38 inches wide.

I would not get much sleep over the next couple of weeks waiting for the season to open. I made two more trips into the area and watched the buck on both occasions. He was pretty predictable. At first light the bucks would be feeding easterly under the rim cliffs just as they were the first time I laid eyes on them. They would continue feeding across the face of the ridge until they came to some scattered pines and then they would angle toward the top of the ridge and bed approximately 75 yards from the top. In the evenings, they would work their way back down under the cliffs to eat again. I felt my chances of taking this buck were excellent. It was just a matter of waiting until the opener. I considered bow hunting the buck, but I hadn't been shooting my bow very much, so I figured I would wait and pursue him during the rifle season.

The day before the season, I was at the trailhead at first light ready to go. I was excited because there wasn't any sign of any other hunters, so I figured I might be lucky enough to have the drainage to myself. It was midday before I reached my campsite and had everything set up. That afternoon I glassed, but the bucks weren't there. I could only locate one lone buck. He was a 7x6 that had an outside spread of 34 inches, but not the buck I had come for. Walking back to camp that night, I was worried about what my plan would be the next morning. I decided that my best chances were to go with my first plan and be glassing the rim cliffs at first light.

It started snowing that night and came down pretty hard. Several times during the night I had to hit the walls of my tent to knock the snow off so that the top of my tent would quit sagging. It must have taken several hours to go to sleep that night. Every possible scenario was going through my head. Where was the buck? Would he be there in the morning? Had he moved into another drainage?

I awoke before the alarm even sounded. I was excited and ready to see what the day would bring. Once dressed, I slipped on my cold boots, threw on my pack and started making my way toward a spot that would put me within three hundred yards of the ribbon cliffs where the bucks normally fed. Twenty minutes later I was tucked underneath a large tree where I would sit and wait for daylight.

I started glassing as soon as the light allowed, but didn't see anything at first. Ten minutes later I located the 34-incher feeding in a small patch of scrub pines in the avalanche chute directly above me. As I sat and watched the buck, I heard a rifle shot about 300 yards down the ridge. Instantly, I got a sick feeling to my stomach. I feared that my 38-inch buck might be dead. Rather than panic though, I decided to stay put and see what happened. A few minutes later, the 34-inch buck bedded down in the scrub pines. I glanced over my left shoulder and spotted another hunter coming directly toward me. So much for having the mountain to myself!

We talked for a couple of seconds and introduced ourselves. His name was Rich Kolmetz from New York and I told him I had a 34-inch buck spotted and was watching it. He told me that he had two other hunting partners in the area of where the rifle shot came from. I noticed that he had a two way radio, so I asked him if he would call his partners to see if he could get a description of the buck they had just shot. He got his hunting partner, Dave Siegfried on the radio and Dave told him that he had just made a four hundred yard shot on a feeding buck but they hadn't made it up to the buck yet to see what he looked like. He said he would call us back shortly to let us know what the buck looked like. Deep down in, I knew my buck was dead, but I hoped for the best. About five minutes later we got a call from Dave, confirming that the buck was indeed the 38-inch 10x10. I was devastated.

As Rich and I sat there talking, the 34-inch buck got up to feed again. Normally, I would be pumped to see such a buck but under the circumstances, I was not. I told Rich that I did not want to shoot the buck and that he could if he wanted. He wanted the buck and made a fine three hundred yard shot on him. I went up and helped Rich take care of his buck and then we went to find Dave and his buck.

A short while later, we found Dave admiring his tremendous buck. A close-up observation of the buck confirmed what I thought. He was indeed 38 inches wide and had 10 matching points on each side. What a buck.

After eating lunch with Dave and Rich, I loaded up my camp and headed home. In one morning, I had missed out on a 38-inch buck and had passed on a 34-inch buck. I was happy for Dave and Rich though because they backpack hunt and they hunt hard. You won't have many days like that. I never did shoot a buck that year.

My scouting didn't get me that buck that year, but I feel if it hadn't snowed, I would have killed that buck. I had the buck's routine figured out and knew exactly where he was feeding and bedding every day, but the several inches of snow caused the bucks to move a little lower in elevation down the ridge.

Camp Placement

When hunting the high country, one of the most overlooked things I see is camp placement. Placement of your camp is very important and can make the difference between a successful or unsuccessful hunt. Although I often put my camp very close to where I want to glass the next morning, it is always well concealed from the area I am hunting. Oftentimes I am hunting at such high elevations that there simply aren't any trees, or there are not enough to hide my camp, I still have it hidden from the country I plan on hunting. Just this past hunting season, I ran into several guys from Nebraska while on an early season backpack hunt. They were nearly out of water and were talking about cutting their elk hunt short because of it. After a short conversation, I told them of a spring located about five hundred yards below us, which made their day. They asked where I was camped and I told them that they had just walked within 40 yards of my camp without noticing it. The funny thing is, on their way out they walked by it once again, this time looking for it, and still didn't see it. My point is, conceal your camp. Don't put it right out in the open smack dab in the middle of the area you intend to hunt Use some common sense when considering your camp placement.

Image 5-21 shows my favorite type of camping spot. I love camping at the highest possible elevation that I can in a small patch of timber. The small patch of trees is all I need to conceal my camp and I am able to camp very close to where I am hunting. This eliminates a long hike in the morning.

Once you find a small spot tucked away in the trees, the next thing you will need

Image 5-21

to do is to make it suitable for staking out your tent. I start by moving any loose debris, such as rocks and dead branches, until I have the area relatively clean. I level any high spots in the soil with my feet by kicking in a forward motion and then smoothing it out. Never, and I do mean never, drag your foot sideways to level it or you just may end up tearing something in your knees. Trust me, I have just about done it. Some of the higher elevations that I camp at, also requires excavation of some larger rocks. I normally use a flat, small rock to dig out any larger rocks that need to be removed.

Once leveled, roll out your tent and make sure it fits the area you have cleared. Make sure you give yourself plenty of room to get in and out of your tent and that there are no leaves or branches touching the outside of your tent. This can make the difference in whether you get any sleep or not. When the wind blows during the night, any vegetation touching the tent will make all kinds of noise which is greatly magnified by the nylon tent material. If you do have a hard time going to sleep at night because of noises, one thing you might try is taking a pair of small foam earplugs to help you block out any sounds that may prevent falling asleep.

One other thing to remember is make sure your head is uphill. This may sound easy enough, but sometimes the lay of the ground can be deceiving. After setting up your tent, lay down in it and give it a trial run, so to speak. The last thing you want to do is get up during the night and re-pitch your tent because your head is below

Camp Placement

6 things to take into consideration when considering your camp placement.

1. First and foremost, you must conceal your camp from the area you will be hunting. If you ignore this rule, then there is no sense in reading any further, plain and simple.

2. Place you camp within a reasonable distance of where you will be hunting. If you have to make a long hike every morning, after several days of hunting, it gets harder and harder to get out of bed.

3. Seek out topographical features such as high mountain saddles. These make great camp sites. They are normally at very high elevations and you are usually only a short distance from a good glassing vantage point.

4. Keep your camp within reasonable distance of water. The number one reason I see people cut their backpack hunts short is because they run out of drinking water after only a couple of days.

5. Avoid standing dead timber. This is something that you definitely don't want to overlook. At high elevations, the wind can often be very ferocious. Over the years, I have weathered many wind storms in the backcountry and have seen first hand that dead trees are very susceptible to being blown over.

6. Last, but certainly not least, always keep lightning in mind. Never, and I do mean *never*, set up your tent near large, solitary trees near the top of the mountain. I normally place my camp in patches of medium sized trees just below the top.

your feet. Or worse yet, sleep with it that way and be totally miserable all night long. It only takes a couple of minutes, so make sure it is right.

When setting up my bivy, I like to stake it out first, then insert the poles. This ensures me that the bivy will be stretched tight. After my tent is up and ready, before I do anything else, I blow my mattress up and place it in the tent and lay out my sleeping bag on it. I like to get my sleeping bag out of the stuff sack as soon as possible, allowing it the maximum time to reach full loft. I take all of the empty stuff sacks from the bivy, mattress, sleeping bag and any others and stuff them all into one. This really helps keep things organized and eliminates time looking for stuff sacks come time to pack up your camp. Once this is done I proceed to set up the rest of my camp.

When you see clouds starting to stack up and the sky turning this color, you had better seek shelter.

Safety in the High Country

Safety while in the high country should not be taken lightly because medical assistance can be a long ways out. It doesn't mean that you have to be paranoid, but there are several safety issues that everyone who treks into the backcountry should keep in mind.

Let someone know your plans

Even though I mainly spend most of my time in the backcountry on my own, I never leave without letting my wife know exactly where I will be hunting. I also pack a cell phone with me on every trip. To me, the cell phone is one of the most important items I have in my pack. I normally call home every night to check in and make sure everything is ok. Cell service is pretty hit and miss in the high country, but at the elevations I normally camp, I can usually reach out.

First aid kit

You don't need anything elaborate as far as a first aid kit goes. A couple of Band-Aids and a few aspirin will work for the bare minimum. Since hiking in the high country is not easy on the feet, it's not a bad idea to pack some moleskin or something similar just in case your feet get blisters while hiking.

Water Purification

This is something that most people tend to overlook. Giardia is the main thing you need to worry about in the Rocky Mountains. Giardia attaches itself to the walls of your intestines, where it steadily reproduces. I for one, have never had Giardia, and never intend to. My filter goes with me everywhere. The symptoms of Giardia include: diarrhea, bloating, stomach cramps, fatigue and weight loss. I go by the old rule "better safe, than sorry."

Standing Dead Timber

About five years ago I was backpack hunting high up in the Wyoming Range in western Wyoming. After a long day of hunting, I was sitting on a log next to my tent eating a dehydrated meal planning my hunt for the next morning. I was camped on the edge of a large opening and the wind was blowing as hard as I have ever seen it blow. Suddenly, I heard a large "snap" to my right, as I turned and looked, I watched as a tree fell and landed within a couple feet of my tent. If that tree had been 10 feet taller it would have taken out my tent. I casually finished my dinner and then proceeded to move my tent a safe distance away from that stand of timber. That was a perfectly healthy tree that had just been snapped like a twig. Just think if there had been any standing dead trees in the vicinity.

This is something I never used to think about a whole lot. Nowadays, when I am looking for a location to set up my tent, I scan all trees and look for any possible candidates that might be likely to come crashing down. Definitely stay clear of any standing dead timber, as well as trees that have large dead branches on them that could come down at any given moment.

Lightning

To me, there is nothing like being in the high country on top of the world. It is simply a beautiful place to be. Unfortunately, this beautiful place can turn ugly fast. I can't count the times that I have been caught in the middle of a lightning storm hunkered under a tree, hoping that it is not my unlucky day.

During the summer months and early fall, you can count on thunder and lightning storms happening on a regular basis in the afternoon. What may start out being a superb weather day can often turn bad in a short amount of time. The temperature of the ground rises to a maximum during the mid-afternoon, warming overlying air parcels and causing them to become unstable enough to rise, generating scattered thunderstorms, normally between the hours of 2:00 p.m. and 5:00 p.m. I remember one scouting trip in particular that I had to weather a long lightning storm. I was above timberline and it had been a relatively beautiful day. It was nearing the "witching hour" of 2:00 p.m. and the clouds were starting to stack up to the west. I had been glassing several alpine basins and had one more that I wanted to look into. To get to the basin, I had to traverse up and across a large open ridge at an elevation of a little over 10,000 feet. I had made it about midway to the basin when I heard the first faint rumble of thunder miles away. I knew I was taking a chance continuing to the basin because there was no way I would make it back to cover before the afternoon storm would be on top of me. But my desire to see what was in the basin outweighed my common sense to drop back down off the top of the mountain.

Twenty minutes later I was glassing the basin and located a bachelor group of five bucks bedded on the opposite side near the head of the drainage. One buck definitely stood out as being the biggest. As I was setting up my spotting scope, I was thinking to myself, "You just found Mister Big." Once I finally settled the spotting scope in on him, excitement soon turned to disappointment. The buck had huge back forks, but didn't fork in the front. What a bummer! While I was watching the bucks, as well as scouring the basin for any other bucks, I had totally forgotten about the fast approaching storm until I heard a loud blast of thunder that made me suddenly realize I was in a spot that I did not care to be in. I crammed my scope in my pack and began making exceptional time down across the bare ridge as lightning was now snapping all around. To my relief, I finally made it to a very small stand of timber without incident. I set my pack down and crouched as low as I could get on the balls of my feet at the base of one of the trees. The next 45 minutes seemed like an eternity as I watched several lightning strikes hit nearby. I did not feel very safe in the small patch of 10 to 12 trees.

Thankfully the storm was gone just as fast as it had arrived. Anymore, I have a lot of respect for lightning and try to do everything I can to keep myself from getting struck. Not everyone has been so lucky. Following are a couple of stories of people who were unfortunate enough to have been victims of a lightning strike while hunting mule deer in the high country.

Tim Mazac

When Lightning Strikes

By David W. Long

Murphy's Law – What can go wrong will go wrong. Sometimes it seems there is no escaping it, and no matter how hard you try, things just don't go the way you would like. Two days before the 1997 Wyoming deer hunting season, Tracy Tolbert and his son, Brian, suddenly came down with the flu. That night they didn't get much rest, and before they knew it, the alarm clock sounded and it was time to get up and drive the 200 miles to Wyoming for their long-awaited hunt. Tracy's cousin, Rudy Tolbert, and his son, Ryan, who were also fortunate enough to have drawn the highly coveted deer tags, joined them on the trip. Tracy's father, Stan, accompanied the group to help with camp and wrangle the horses.

On the pack in, Stan rode horseback and led two pack horses with all the camping gear, while the remaining four men hiked to base camp. About halfway in, Tracy and Brian, who were still ailing from the flu, couldn't keep up and told their companions to go ahead and they would meet them at camp.

Four hours later, Stan, Rudy and Ryan had camp set up in a stand of tall pines located next to a small spring. Tracy, Rudy and their wives had found the spot two weeks earlier while scouting and Rudy had killed a nice 26-inch buck in the area one year earlier. Just after dark, Tracy and Brian arrived, tired and weak, but in good spirits.

Tracy and Rudy with Tracy's buck and the lightning damaged water bottle that was hanging on the saddle horn of his horse.

Early the next morning, Stan remained in camp while the other four men started their ascent of the mountain toward a vantage point they wanted to reach by first light. Their glassing spot was located about one mile up through the basin and across a ridge overlooking the next drainage. The sun was just starting to make its way over the eastern horizon when Tracy, who was still suffering from the flu, told the others to go ahead and he would meet them at the lookout point.

Thirty minutes later, Tracy was about 100 yards below the summit when he heard five or six rifle shots coming from the direction of Rudy and the two boys. Tracy still didn't know which direction the deer would be traveling until he heard a shot ricochet over the top of his head! He knew then the deer were coming straight at him. Anticipating some action, he got set up and waited. Seconds later, a large buck came running through the saddle 200 yards away. When the buck reached the top, he stopped to look back. Thanks to a mild case of buck fever, Tracy's bullet missed its target and the buck disappeared into a steep ravine on the other side of a small ridge.

Tracy, knowing he had just blown the chance of a lifetime, was amazed to see the buck reappear from the ravine a little over 300 yards away. Making use of his bipod, Tracy dropped the buck instantly with one shot from his .300 Weatherby Magnum. The hillside was so rugged and steep that the buck slid approximately 200 yards before coming to rest with its antlers tangled in a small patch of scrub pine.

Rudy came running over the hill and told Tracy that while glassing, he and the boys spotted

Tracy's two horses were killed immediately by the lightning strike.

a group of seven bucks. Five took off in one direction, while the two largest headed in another. When Rudy started shooting at the larger of those two bucks, they split up with the bigger one running through the saddle where Tracy spotted him.

When they reached the buck, the hunters were elated. Tracy had finally taken a buck large enough to hang on the wall. With good mass and an outside spread of 30 inches, his buck gross scored 186 B&C typical. After dressing the deer, Rudy went to check on the boys, while Tracy headed back to camp for Stan and a couple of horses to pack out the buck.

When Tracy and his dad returned to the basin, they joined Rudy and watched as Ryan and Brian put a stalk on the other group of bucks. A short time later the boys got a shot at one of the bucks but missed.

The young hunters then hiked back to the basin and met up with the rest of their party. It was about 1:45 p.m. and the sky was beginning to cloud over as the group started across a large treeless basin toward Tracy's deer. Rudy and Ryan were up the ridge about 100 yards, while Tracy, Brian and Stan led the two horses through the bottom of the basin.

Fifteen minutes later rain was pouring, so the hunters stopped to retrieve their rain ponchos from the saddlebags. Stan grabbed the first poncho and handed it to Tracy. As he leaned against the horse to get the second raincoat, it was as if a bomb went off.

Suddenly, everything seemed to be moving in slow motion, as Tracy found himself rolling down the hill, coming to rest about 30 yards away. Due to the intense light and loud explosion, it took Tracy a minute to regain his senses. Realizing they had just been hit by lightning, Tracy looked back up the hill and saw his dad, his son, and the horses all laying motionless on the ground. Tracy tried to get up, but couldn't. He had no feeling in his right arm and leg.

Meanwhile, Rudy and Ryan turned and saw what looked like a war zone. Tracy was trying to crawl up the hill, Brian was rolling on the ground moaning, and Stan lay motionless, draped over one of the horses' legs.

Rudy and Ryan dropped everything and ran down to Stan, who finally regained consciousness but told Rudy he couldn't feel anything from his neck down. Rudy then helped Tracy up the hill to where Stan and Brian lay. Both horses were killed instantly and Tracy had a hole burned in his pants where his pocketknife had been. He also had a one-inch hole blown in his right boot where the lightning exited. Stan's lips were blue and he was as pale as a ghost. Fearing Stan was near death, everyone said prayers and hoped for the best possible outcome.

By then, it was raining heavily and the men were at the mercy of Mother Nature, trapped out in the wide open basin. Rudy unsaddled the dead horses and removed the saddle blankets, using them to cover Stan.

Rudy knew of another hunting party in the area, so he took off running in the direction of their camp. Luckily, he found the camp and told them of the situation. One of the men told Rudy that he had a cell phone in his truck parked near the trailhead at the bottom of the mountain. He handed over the keys to the truck and Rudy took off on a dead run.

Not knowing how long it would take Rudy to return with help, Tracy sent Ryan back toward their camp, where he knew another party was camped. Within the next two hours both of the hunting parties arrived with blankets to cover all the injured men. The storm steadily worsened, pelting the group with rain and hail. With lightning flashing in every direction, the hunters felt helpless. All they could do was sit and wait for Rudy to return with medical help.

Finally, around 6:00 p.m., a medical helicopter dispatched out of Jackson Hole arrived on the scene. Because of Stan's condition, the crew loaded him first and transported the injured man down the mountain to where an ambulance was waiting.

Moments later, the helicopter returned and picked up Tracy and Brian. Ryan chose to remain on the mountain in case his father returned. Ryan ended up weathering the storm by himself that night because Rudy went to the hospital and did not return to the mountain.

Tracy and Stan both regained all the feeling in their bodies but had to remain in the hospital overnight for observation. Because of the tremendous electrical shock, the doctors wanted to make sure there were no internal injuries to either of them. Brian was not required to spend the night in the hospital. The next day, Tracy's two brothers arrived and went in with Rudy to get Ryan, Tracy's deer and the camping equipment.

One year after the accident, both Tracy and Stan said that all the joints in their bodies still ache from the lightning strike. All three also suffer from insomnia.

Incident on the Mountain

By Steve James

On this particular hunt, my good friend, Jerry Ricketts, decided to bring his horse along which would make it a lot easier to pack in our camp. In the past, we had always backpacked the extremely steep six mile trip. But this year was going to be different. With the horse, we could pack all of the comforts of home and we could just enjoy the scenery on the trip in. Well, it didn't turn out that way. We practically ended up dragging that horse up the mountain. We had to stash part of our gear halfway up the trail and I ended up carrying my fully loaded pack up the last part of the mountain. It took all day, but we made it.

I pioneered this camp in 1992. It is located right on top of a ridge which makes it very susceptible to high winds. We've spent some nights up there where your tent about beats you to death. The camp is also susceptible to something else—something I had never even considered. Lightning!

Once we had camp situated, we dropped off the backside of the ridge to water the horse. On our way back to camp, we were surprised when some good friends from Wyoming, Barry Coster, Laree, and Tiger came riding down the ridge to water their horses as well. It was good to see them. I've known Barry and Tiger for years and have had some good times in the backcountry with both. They had set up their tents 50 yards from our camp which meant that we would have a little more hunting pressure, but I didn't mind.

Clear blue skies greeted us on opening morning and almost immediately, Tiger and I spotted three bucks. We tried to put a stalk on the bucks, but could never get close enough to take a shot. The bucks disappeared over the ridge and were gone. Of course, I had to hike all the way down there to make sure they were gone. I should know better by now. Did I think they would be right over the ridge waiting for me? Never happens, but hey, you gotta try. It was a long three hour hike back to camp.

In the meantime, Jerry had bailed off the mountain looking for his horse. It had escaped the night before when it broke this super high-tech carabineer climbing cable apparatus. I had warned Jerry that it looked pretty cheesy, but he assured me that it was real strong. Anyway, Jerry spent half the day looking for his horse. A couple of guys riding in had found it and tied it up along the trail.

We both got back to camp around noon. Up until this time it had been clear, calm and warm. Little did we know that within 2 hours we'd be caught in a 30 hour El-Nino lightning storm from hell.

It came in fast. It was big. It was black. It was powerful and totally infested with lightning. We spent several hours in our tents enduring the first wave of hail and lightning. It was kind of neat being warm and dry in the apparent safety of my tent with all the chaos going on outside.

Over the next day and a half the storm came in waves; several hours of intense rain and lightning followed by brief periods of clearing. During a break that afternoon, Jerry and I decided to hike 150 yards up to the top of a nearby peak to take a look around. We were almost to the top when literally out of nowhere a helicopter appeared right in front of us. It was weird because we didn't even hear it until it was right in front of us. They were hovering 40

Steve hiked in a year later and took this photo of the lightning struck tree.

yards away looking right at us. The pilots had on helmets with visors covering their faces. We didn't know what was up, so we just stood there. They hovered a few more seconds and then quickly flew away. Strange! We found out later that they were looking for the Tolbert's (people I knew) who had been hit by lightning earlier in the day.

I hunted alone the rest of the day in the basin behind camp. The storm returned and at one point, I didn't know whether to seek shelter from the rain under a tree or take my chances standing in the open. Lightning was hitting everywhere. It was scary. It rained the rest of the day and all night.

The next morning Jerry and I tried to hike to the top of the peak again. We stopped about 30 yards from the top and stood behind a tree. With all the wind, rain and lightning, we didn't feel safe getting right on top. We waited about 45 minutes for it to clear a little bit before hiking to the top. I remember telling Jerry we should try to stay low and lay our guns down. Oh! The power of the mule deer pursuit!

Twenty minutes later we were back in our tents for another round of excitement. I can only stay in a tent for so long, so Jerry and I decided if we could get a fire going we'd rather stand in the rain. After getting out of our tents, Jerry was tending to the fire and I was walking over to give the horse an apple when it hit. BOOM! I jumped about two feet and the horse reared back and jumped about three.

"That was real close!" I said. Both of us were looking the other way so neither of us

Steve holding the 12' splinter which landed next to the tent.

saw where it hit. After a couple of moments Tiger came running down to us. "Barry and Laree just got hit by lightning!" he screamed. I just stood there stunned. I couldn't believe what I had just heard. "They got hit in their tent!" he said as he started to run back.

In their camp we saw pine needles, bark and branches everywhere. A chunk of wood about 12' long lay right next to their tent. The lightning had hit a tree about 6' from their tent and it was blown into three pieces. The top third luckily fell away from the tent and landed in some scrubby pines. The center section had fallen straight down and was sticking in the ground next to the trunk. It was a disaster zone.

We knew that we needed to get a rescue helicopter fast so I volunteered to head off the mountain to summon medical help. Not feeling comfortable on a horse and anticipating horrible trail conditions, I decided the safest and fastest way was to walk out on foot for help. Three hours later, I arrived at Jerry's pickup and drove to a nearby gas station where I called 911. It wasn't long until the local sheriff and ambulance arrived. I showed them on a map where our camp was situated and they relayed the information to the helicopter crew which had been dispatched out of Jackson Hole. A short time later, the helicopter arrived with Laree. According to the weather report, there was another storm fast approaching so we all decided it would be best if I flew back up to help break camp before its arrival.

The helicopter ride was spectacular. Flying over those high alpine basins was very exciting. I felt like slapping the pilot in the back of the head and saying, "Slow down, I'm looking for deer." In less than five minutes we were landing at camp. Once Barry was loaded and the helicopter had taken off, the task of breaking camp and loading the horses was at hand. We had to hurry, the next wave of the storm was fast approaching. It was a black wall as high as you could see and it went all of the way down into the valley below. It was ugly and it looked like we had about 15 minutes. We were frantically saddling horses and ripping down tents.

The plan to get off the mountain was that Tiger was going to ride his rental horse and lead one of Barry's horses. Jerry would lead his own horse and I'd lead Barry's other one. We were in such a hurry we did a lousy packing job. Anyone who has ever loaded up a pack horse knows that you have to get each side weighted exactly equal. Well, I didn't have my scales with me so it was just tie that thing on there.

228

We didn't beat the storm out of camp. Oh good, some more 40 mph winds and of course plenty of lightning and don't forget the hail and rain. We hadn't got out of camp more than 200 yards before we had the first re-tie in about the worst place you could imagine. My horse's load completely shifted off to one side. We were on a steep muddy sidehill. The wind was blowing so hard up the canyon that it was raining up. Instead of untying everything and starting over, Jerry helped me push the bag back on the saddle and we added some more rope.

Walking down that ridge, leading a horse in another lightning storm is something I'll never forget. Thinking that five people I knew had just been hit by lightning in two days gave me the creeps. At times I felt like just dropping the lead rope. I really didn't want to be anywhere near that horse. I often thought about my family and the fact that they had no idea what was happening to us right now.

Once we were about halfway down, off of the steep ridges, I felt much safer. We stopped and picked up the stash we had left on our initial trip in. Because I had done such a professional packing job, Jerry and I had to stop every 20 minutes and adjust and balance my horse's load. Instead of taking the whole thing apart and repacking it the right way, we just kept throwing more rope at the problem. By this time, it probably would have taken us at least a half an hour to just untie the thing. Actually, I think that we had created something quite special. You won't find these types of knots and lashing techniques in any Boy Scout handbook. We finally got it all balanced and tied down good when we were about 15 minutes from the truck.

Once back at the truck I called Barry to see what the doctor had said. The doctor had informed him there could possibly be heart or kidney damage. Barry and Laree would have to spend the night in the hospital for further observation. I finished talking to Barry and assured him his horses were in good hands and we'd visit him at the hospital in the morning. Then I called home. I was emotionally drained and extremely tired.

Barry and Laree were both released from the hospital the following day. One year later I returned to our campsite and took pictures of the tree that the lightning bolt had reduced to splinters. As I took the photos, the memories and emotions from the previous year came rushing back.

Lightning Tips

To help ensure your safety in the high country, here are a couple of guidelines you should follow: Rule #1 You should never allow yourself to get caught out in the open in the high country during a lightning storm. However, if you should ignore Rule #1 and you just happen to find yourself out in the open during a storm, stay away from tall, exposed objects such as solitary trees or away from open areas such as lakes, ponds or above timberline in the mountains, etc. The safest position to be in is crouched down on the balls of your feet, which is the position I always use when I get caught in a storm. Do not allow your hands to touch the ground, and keep your feet as close to one another as possible. This is very important because when lightning strikes an object, the electricity of the lightning discharge does not necessarily go straight down into the ground. Sometimes it will travel along the surface of the ground for quite some distance. This is known as a "side flash." Many people who are "struck" by lightning are not necessarily hit directly by the lightning, but they are affected by the side flash as it travels along the ground, especially when the

Early Season Hunting

The early season is undoubtedly my favorite time of the year to pursue monster mulies. The weather is usually very moderate and the bucks are still hanging out in their high country hideouts. There is truly no other place as peaceful and beautiful as the high country. Following are a few things to remember while pursuing bucks at timberline in the early season.

THE BOTTOM LINE • KEYS TO SUCCESS

Archery – If possible, take up archery hunting. Archery success rates are extremely low, but the lack of archery hunters in the backcountry normally makes for a quality hunt. If nothing else, your archery hunts will double as scouting trips for the rifle season.

Spot & Stalk – Spot & Stalk hunting is by far the most effective hunting method I have found for bucks that are near timberline. Optics are the biggest advantage we have over the mule deer, it only makes sense to put them to work for you. Remember, glassing from a good vantage point allows you to cover large tracts of mule deer country without moving. Not only are you stationary, but you are not spooking the deer either.

A Buck's Core Area – Remember, a buck's core area in late summer and fall is about two square miles. If you know a good buck is in the area, don't give up. This is the buck's home. He is not going to leave. You may go several days without seeing him, but he is still there.

Lightning – Always respect lightning when hunting the high country. As can be seen by several stories in this book, it can be devastating. When it comes to lightning, always abide by the 30/30 Rule.

ground is wet. Whatever you do, make sure that you don't lie down because keeping the surface area of your body touching the ground to a minimum can reduce the threat of the electricity traveling across the ground from affecting you.

The "30/30" Lightning Safety Rule

There are two things to remember about lightning safety. First, how close should you let the lightning get to you before making tracks to a safe place, and second, how much time should pass before resuming outdoor activities? The combination of steps 1 and 2 below is known as the 30/30 Lightning Rule and should be used when in the high country.

1 To estimate the distance between you and a lightning flash, use the "Flash to Bang" method: If you observe lightning, count the number of seconds until you hear thunder. Divide the number of seconds by 5 to get the distance (in miles) the lightning is away from you.

If Thunder is heard...	The Lightning is...
5 seconds after a Flash	1 mile away
10 seconds after a Flash	2 miles away
15 seconds after a Flash	3 miles away
20 seconds after a Flash	4 miles away
25 seconds after a Flash	5 miles away
30 seconds after a Flash	**6 miles away**
35 seconds after a Flash	7 miles away
40 seconds after a Flash	8 miles away

Example: If you see lightning and it takes 10 seconds before you hear the thunder, then the lightning is two miles away from you (10 divided by 5 = 2 miles).
It is recommended that you should begin to seek shelter if the time between the lightning flash and the rumble of thunder is 30 seconds or less.

2 You should not resume activities until after 30 minutes after the last audible thunder. This is especially important considering the fact that the majority of the lightning is normally at the beginning and the tail end of the storm.

Backcountry Safety Tips

1. Let someone know your plans, especially if you are going on a solo trip. At a bare minimum, make sure they know where you will be camped and when you plan to return.

2. Take a cell phone with you. I take mine along on every backpack trip I make. Cell service is usually pretty hit and miss in the high country, but at the elevations I normally camp at, I can usually reach out.

3. Filter your water.

4. Camp Placement. Always consider the possibility of a lightning strike, or the possibility of dead timber being blown down when placing your camp.

The Bottom  Line

Taking up archery hunting can extend your amount of time in the high country pursuing mule deer. There are very few people in the mountains this time of year, and normally, you will see three times the deer archery hunting than you will during the rifle season. The bucks are still in bachelor groups and are very easy to spot when out feeding in the high alpine bowls. Even if you don't harvest a buck with your bow, your hunt doubles as a scouting trip for the rifle season.

Spot and stalk hunting is by far the most effective hunting method I have found while hunting the high country. But in order to be effective, you need to be proficient at glassing. How do you become proficient at glassing? Spend countless hours looking through your optics. Simply put, the more you glass, the better you will get at spotting game. Develop a glassing technique that suits your hunting style and stick with it. I suggest you try my Four Phase Glassing technique and I guarantee you will start seeing more game. But remember, Four Phase Glassing requires patience—a lot of patience.

A buck's core area during late summer and fall is about two square miles in size. Although they may occasionally drift out of this area, they will always return. Several factors such as hunting pressure and weather determine how deer will utilize this area at different times of the year. Deer will use several means other than distance to get away from hunting pressure, such as utilizing steeper slopes and heavier cover.

Always take every safety precaution you can while hunting the high country. This is no place to be careless because medical attention can be a long ways out. Pitch you tent clear of standing dead timber and don't ever get caught out in the open in the high country during a lightning storm, but if you do, remember the 30/30 Rule.

SECTION 6

MID-SEASON
HUNTING

Secondary Ridges

The snooze button was all I could think about when the alarm sounded at the dreadful hour of 3:30 a.m. I was tired and wanted to go back to sleep, but I knew I would kick myself if I was to sleep any longer, so I forced myself to get out of bed. This was my 13th day of mule deer hunting during the 1999 Wyoming season. As with the first 12, I hoped this would be my lucky day. I grabbed a cup of coffee and hit the road, reaching the trailhead by 5:30 a.m. I threw my backpack on and headed up the trail at a brisk pace hoping to make it to the head of the drainage by daybreak.

As planned, I was there at first light and glassed the steep walls of the canyon but was only able to find one small buck in an hour of glassing. I continued still-hunting to the north until I came to a fork in the trail. There were fresh horse tracks going to the right, so I took the left fork hoping to get away from most of the hunting pressure. By 10:00 a.m. I still hadn't seen much and the thousands of domestic sheep tracks blanketing the ground pretty much told me why. The sheep had been grazing in the drainage forcing all the deer into the surrounding, more rugged terrain. Seeing this, I left the main trail and climbed straight up the east-facing slope, which put me in position to glass several avalanche chutes I figured a few bucks would be held up in.

On top of the ridge there was a game trail running north and south above the avalanche chutes. To the north there was a bald knob with a few scattered pines near the top, which looked like it would offer me a good vantage point to glass from. I worked my way up the trail and nestled underneath a pine tree and began glassing.

The bald knob, which I later named "Curly Knob," fell off into a huge rockslide that was surrounded by timber in all directions. The area looked very "bucky" to me. Instantly I spotted a heavy 27-inch four point directly below me about 200 yards away feeding on the edge of the trees bordering the south side of the slide. I watched him for about 20 minutes until he bedded down under a lone scrub pine. I decided I would stay there the remainder of the day glassing, figuring I would eventually see

Curly Knob is what I named my vantage point that I glassed "Curly" from.

more deer feed out.

Approximately 30 minutes later, I caught a buck moving out of the corner of my eye on the opposite side of the slide. I put the binoculars on him and could see that he wasn't very wide, but it looked as if he might have numerous extra points. I put my spotting scope on the tripod and could count nine points on the right, and seven points on the left antler. What a pretty buck. I watched the buck feed along the rockslide for about 20 minutes until he bedded down next to a pickup sized boulder. I mounted my video camera on the tripod and got some video footage of him and then continued glassing, hoping to find something bigger.

A short time later, after picking apart every clump of trees, I found an extremely tall, 26-inch four-point buck bedded in some scattered pines at the bottom of the rockslide. He had good back forks, but was weak in the front and lacked the mass I was looking for. Approximately a half a mile away on the opposite side of the basin, there was a nice 27- to 28-inch four point that had a cheater on his left side. He kept appearing and disappearing as he fed his way through a patch of scattered pines. Although a nice typical buck, I kept focusing my attention back on the non-typical that was still bedded near the large boulder.

For the next two hours I watched the buck, trying to decide whether or not to harvest him. Finally he got up and started feeding toward the thick timber. I knew it was now or never. I only had three days of hunting left and I figured I would be hard-pressed to find a better buck in that amount of time, so I elected to take him. After ranging him with my rangefinder, I found a solid rest on an old pine snag jutting out of the side of the hill and fired. The buck jumped and disappeared into the pine

Curly was aged at 9½ years. He was a veteran of many hunting seasons.

trees. I was unsure if I had hit him or not, so I loaded all my gear in my pack and started working my way over to where I last saw him.

Once there, I looked for signs of blood, but found none. Figuring he would be watching his back trail, I went about 50 yards above where he went into the trees and started hunting across the hill, keeping a close eye down below. I hadn't made it 75 yards into the trees when I spotted the buck down below me, laying there. I could tell he was hit, and as I chambered a round, he stood up and looked directly at me. I squeezed the trigger, dropping him instantly.

The buck was very old and hardly had any teeth left. They were worn all the way down to his gum line and he probably wouldn't have survived another year. He had a total of 16 measurable points over an inch long, matching that of the deer I harvested in 1998.

One interesting note about this buck is this was not the first time that I had crossed paths with him. Five years earlier, Mike Eastman and I were out filming deer on the winter range when we came across this buck. He hadn't changed much over the course of five years. His antler configuration is pretty much exactly the same as it was then. Who would have thought that we would meet again, only this time in his high country hideout. What are the odds of that?

While bucks utilize the high alpine bowls during the summer months, most bucks of any size have moved down in elevation before or shortly after the hunt begins. By the middle of the season, the bowls that had a lot of deer only a couple of weeks ago, will be totally empty except for maybe a few smaller bucks. Granted, there will always be a few bucks that stay at the timberline level, but most likely the more mature bucks will drop off onto what I call secondary ridges. These ridges have a lot of cover which offer deer the needed protection that is required in order

Mark McCord

Mark McCord took this amazing photo of Popeye in the high country of Wyoming while on a scouting trip. While Popeye spent the summers in the high alpine basins, he disappeared down onto the lower, secondary ridges just before the season opened.

to survive the hunting season.

I have heard countless stories of guys spotting bucks in the days prior to opening morning in the high country, only to never see the buck during the hunting season. They continue glassing the bowl for a few days but the buck is no where to be found. That is because more than likely, the buck has dropped off onto a secondary ridge. Can you blame a buck for wanting to head down into the timber? There is so much activity in the days prior to opening day and the first week of the season that the bucks bail off onto these lower ridges. That is the only way they can survive. There is one thing that a high country buck won't tolerate and that is a lot of activity.

A good example of this is the famous buck known as Popeye that lived in Wyoming during the 1990's. How did Popeye survive? I believe there were two reasons for it. Number one was that with the influx of all the hunters and all of the activity, Popeye ducked into the timber where he spent the remainder of the hunting season. Second, I think that the hunters suffered from tunnel vision as we talked earlier. I honestly believe too much time was spent watching the exact hillside that Popeye was spotted on and not enough time was spent hunting the lower, secondary ridges. Think about it, if Popeye had remained above timberline, there is absolutely no way he would have survived. His only means of survival was to seek out cover and to get away from the hunting pressure. So the next time you spot the buck of your dreams while scouting, spend more time hunting the lower ridges rather that the high alpine basin that the buck inhabited during the summer.

Secondary ridges are usually at elevations between 8500 to 9500 feet. The north sides are usually covered with pines, while the south sides are relatively open with small to medium sized patches of timber. A lot of the ridges also have small ribbon cliffs located halfway to three quarters of the way up the ridge. Make sure and spend time glassing under these cliffs early in the morning, bucks tend to utilize the trails at their base on the way back to their bedding areas. If the weather is hot, I will spend most of my time glassing the north or easterly facing slopes. In cooler weather I normally have better luck glassing the south- or west-facing slopes.

Once the bucks move to this lower elevation their entire daily routine changes. They no longer have the large bowls to feed in. Instead they feed more in the small avalanche chutes that dissect the dark timber on the north facing slopes. The best way I have found to hunt this type of terrain is to be set up on a good vantage point and glass all ridges within view. I don't limit myself to nearby country either. I will glass openings that are several miles away as well. If you spot a buck a couple of miles away, you might not be able to tell a lot of detail about his antlers, but with a quality spotting scope you can definitely tell whether he merits a closer look. Pay particular attention to the avalanche chutes. They are great places to catch bucks out feeding. Make sure you are glassing these areas early because by the time the sunlight hits the hillside, most of the bucks will already be in the trees.

Continue to glass the ridge for two to three hours after the sun is up. Even though the hillsides appear to be covered with dark timber, you'll be amazed at what you can see through the gaps and small openings in the timber. This is exactly how I harvested my 1999 Wyoming buck.

Jim Hamilton

Mid-Season Glassing Tips

Hunting the mid-season can be very frustrating at times. I believe it is the toughest time to harvest a trophy buck. This is because of several reasons. First off, the bucks have had to alter their normal routine because of all of the human presence in the mountains during the first couple of weeks of the season. They have been disturbed while feeding, pushed from their beds and shot at. They have been forced to become nocturnal in their habits in order to survive. This makes for some pretty tough hunting conditions.

To be successful at hunting the mid-season, you need to change your glassing technique from what you do during the early season. I don't glass the large open areas that I glassed in the early season, now I will spend most of my time glassing the small openings located on the lower secondary ridges. These ridges normally run parallel to one another which make them very susceptible to glassing. You can set up on one ridge, and glass another ridge in either direction.

The first and last hours of daylight are still the most important times to be glassing during the mid-season. When glassing secondary ridges, don't spend much

Image 6-4

time glassing the bottom of the ridge, concentrate your efforts on the upper half of the hillside. I mainly see does and fawns occupying the lower portion of the ridges, while the bucks are typically located close to the top. See Image 6-4.

Since food is very sparse in the pines, bucks will have to utilize the small openings and avalanche chutes to find enough food. Spend your time glassing these areas utilizing Phase I and II glassing. Make sure you keep repeating the process over and over. The openings you are glassing are very small, so it is important to glass them several times to better your odds of catching a buck moving through one of them. While feeding this time of year, bucks will only cover a very small area. Rather than feeding their way continuously along a hillside like they do in the early season, the bucks will only feed a small distance before reversing their direction. The nice thing is that during this time of the season, the temperatures have started to cool down. This, combined with the lighter hunting pressure, causes the bucks to remain up feeding a little bit longer in the mornings. I will continue to utilize Phase I and II glassing until everything beds down.

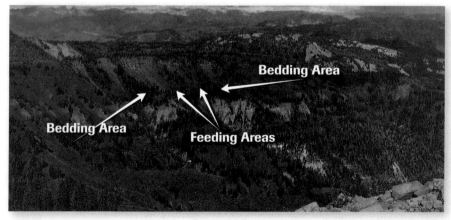

Image 6-5

My hunting technique during the day is a lot like it was during the early season, with one exception. I don't move as much. While I might glass from as many as 12 different vantage points during the early season, I will only glass from two or three this time of year. Normally I will glass from my morning vantage point, move to another point and glass until mid afternoon and then move to another and glass until dark. Sometimes I will remain on the same vantage point from daylight to dark. I will switch back and forth between all four phases of glassing while on my vantage points.

The reason I like to be fairly stationary and glassing, rather than moving this time of the year is that bucks are starting to feel a little more secure. With all of the cover that the secondary ridges offer, and the lighter hunting pressure, bucks will start to feel a little bit safer and will actually get up several times during the day to feed. They will only feed for a couple of minutes, but they will feed more often. I like to take advantage of this by being set up and glassing.

Image 6-5 is a secondary ridge that I can always locate bucks on. I spotted a nice non-typical on it a few years back, but decided to pass on the buck. The buck had a lot of small extra points and I figured he would be a real wallhanger if he had another year to grow. He was with two other bucks and they utilized the feeding areas that I have marked. I looked for him the following year but was never able to locate the buck.

One thing that doesn't change is that bucks still seek out the higher elevation bedding areas. Bucks absolutely love to bed on the small finger ridges that dissect the mountainside. When glassing during midday, spend a lot of times glassing these ridges. On ridges such as in image 6-5, where the feeding and bedding areas run vertical, bucks don't seem to travel very far while feeding. They will reverse directions often, while normally staying in one or two of the avalanche chutes.

Image 6-6 shows another type of secondary ridge that bucks love. This ridge

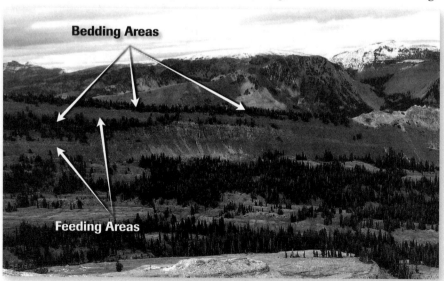

Image 6-6

differs from the previous one in that the feeding and bedding areas run horizontal, rather than vertical. Bucks are more apt to cover more distance while feeding on this type of ridge. They will feed in the long horizontal clearings, often traveling from one end to the other. After feeding, they will bed in the long, horizontal patches of timber.

During my evening session I will go back to using only Phase I and II glassing. Start glassing the areas closest to the bedding areas. This is where the bucks are going to appear first. Normally, this will be the small finger ridges that run from top to bottom. Later in the glassing session, start concentrating on the feeding areas. Remember, don't glass the large openings, concentrate on the smaller ones.

Glass Areas That Look "Bucky"

In order to maximize your glassing success, you need to be able to read deer country. Earlier I stated that I like to glass areas that look "bucky" to me. I feel this

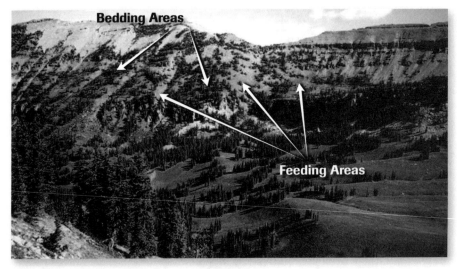

Image 6-7

increases my odds of locating a monster mulie. Learning to identify which parts of a mountainside will most likely hold bucks and spending the majority of your time glassing these areas will greatly increase your chances of finding bucks.

First of all, all mountains are not created equal. While one mountain might normally hold bucks near the top, another may hold them in the middle, or even the lower section. This is normally dictated by the available feed and the amount of cover. The three previous images are of ridges where I would expect to find bucks near the top of the mountain. Image 6-7 shows a mountain that has a different makeup than the previous image. You won't find many bucks near the top of this mountain. Your time would be better spent glassing the middle third, rather than the top third. Why?

That is where the best feeding and bedding areas are located. The top of the mountain lacks in both of those departments. Remember, all mountainsides are different. But once you can identify "bucky" areas and concentrate your glassing efforts on those areas, you will be amazed at how many more bucks you will start seeing.

Glassing "bucky" looking terrain paid big dividends for me in 2004. The morning began like so many other mornings as I sat and glassed the large mountainside in front of me. The magical first hour of glassing was over, but it was overcast with a slight drizzle so I continued glassing the smaller openings in hopes of finding a buck still feeding. The light rain persisted and eventually forced me to take a break from glassing to put my rain gear on. I had glassed several bucks on this morning but it was always the same result after putting the spotting scope on them – not big enough! After continuing to scour the west-facing slope, I spotted one lone deer that was a good distance from all of the other deer I had seen. The deer was 1½ to 2 miles away, so I put my scope on it to see if it was a buck or not. As I was focusing the scope on 20 power, the first thing I noticed was that the deer had a huge body. As I zoomed it up to 60X and focused it, I saw that it could very well be a good deer. As the buck made his way through the timber feeding, I tried to make out as much detail as possible. The most noticeable thing was his deep forks. It didn't take long to realize I was looking at a buck that had a Boone and Crockett typical frame. I could make out one non-typical point and guessed the buck to be 30 inches wide. I wanted

to take off and go after him instantly, but I forced myself to stay there and watch the buck until he bedded. Five minutes later, the buck bedded on the uphill side of an old dead tree.

The buck was on the opposite side of the drainage about midway up. There was a group of pine trees slightly above the midway point of the mountain and I figured once I reached that point I would be slightly above the buck and about three hundred yards to his left. He bedded down about 40 yards to the right of a small stunted quakie patch. The patch of trees would be my landmark to locate the buck once I reached the other side. I gathered up my gear and threw it in my pack and headed back down the hill toward the bottom of the drainage. It didn't take long to reach the bottom, but that was the easy

I backed off because I didn't want to risk a stalk in the fog. Luckily, the fog lifted 10 minutes later.

243

With a score of 233⁴/₈ B&C, my buck was the highest gross scoring non-typical taken on public land in Wyoming during the 2004 deer season.

part. Now I had a little over an hour of straight uphill, and I mean straight uphill.

About halfway up I was wishing I would have taken my rain gear off. I was climbing as fast as I could and I was sweating profusely. Every few steps I would have to wipe the sweat off to keep it from running into my eyes. At his point, I didn't want to stop to take the rain gear off because the fog was starting to drop down the side of the mountain and visibility was deteriorating fast.

Once I reached the small patch of pines I eased over the ridgetop and looked for the small patch of quakies he had bedded near. The slope had a convex shape to it so I could only see the very tips of the yellow quakies. So much for having an easy 300-yard shot. At his time I felt like I had two options. Wait for several hours in hopes the buck would get up and feed in my direction or go in after him. I didn't like the idea of waiting because if the buck got up and traveled in any direction other than toward me, I would never see him. The decision was made. I would go in after him.

I left my pack on the ridgetop, chambered a round and started down the slope. I told myself that I would probably only have one chance at this buck so I moved slower than I ever had before. I would take two steps then glass for several minutes and then repeat this. I knew if I took my time and glassed effectively, I would be able to spot him before he did me. I had only covered about 25 yards when the fog moved in and visibility shrunk to only about 50 yards. I backed off and walked back to my pack. I didn't want to risk the stalk in the fog. Luckily, the fog lifted 10 minutes later. Once again I started down the steep hillside picking apart every clump of brush with my binoculars. It took 30 minutes to cover the first 100 yards and I still hadn't seen the buck. I could now see the bottoms of the quakies and the vicinity in which I figured the buck was bedded. I was really nervous now because I knew that something could happen at any moment so I slowed to an even slower pace. As I scanned the brush near the quakies with my binoculars, I spotted the tips of his antlers protruding above the green shrubs. I couldn't see the body of the buck, only the antler tips sticking up. I ranged the tree the buck was bedded near at 158 yards. It was impossible to get any closer so I would have to wait the buck out until he got

Mid-Season Hunting

Hunting the mid-season can be very frustrating at times. I believe it is the toughest time to harvest a trophy buck. First off, the bucks have had to alter their normal routine because of all of the human presence in the mountains during the first couple weeks of the season. They have been disturbed while feeding, pushed from their beds and shot at for days. They have been forced to become nocturnal in their habits in order to survive. This makes for pretty tough hunting conditions.

THE BOTTOM LINE
KEYS TO SUCCESS

Secondary Ridges – During the mid-season, concentrate more on the lower secondary ridges rather than the higher alpine basins. After the opener, most of the mature bucks will drop off onto these ridges which offer them the much needed cover they need in order to survive. These ridges are normally at elevations between 8500 and 9500 feet.

Glass Smaller Openings – During the mid-season you need to concentrate most of your glassing efforts on the smaller openings in the timber, rather than the larger ones. Bucks will still get up and feed several times during the day, but they won't travel very far. They will usually only travel a few yards and will utilize the very small openings in the timber when feeding.

Glass "Bucky" Areas – Glassing is very effective, but in order to make the most of your glassing sessions, you need to be concentrating on areas that look "bucky." "Bucky" areas are those areas of the mountain that contain features that bucks are attracted to such as rim cliffs, stringers of pines, avalanche chutes and benches.

up from his bed.

I couldn't sit down because the shrubs blocked my view and the buck could leave without me knowing. I had no option other than stand and wait. Thankfully there was a small branch on the tree I was standing next to that I could rest my rifle on. I looked at my watch. It was 10:33 a.m. I took the safety off, put my finger on the trigger and watched the antlers through the scope hoping the buck would stand up. Every time the antlers would move I would think to myself, "This is it," but the buck remained bedded every time. By now an hour had passed and I was getting impatient. The angle I was standing at was very awkward and my legs were starting to cramp up. But there was nothing I could do other than wait. As I stood there watching the antlers move back and forth I had plenty of time to judge them. He definitely had a 200-inch typical frame and I figured his width around 30 inches. He also had more extra points than I had thought. The wait was getting intense.

Another hour had gone by. I now had stood there looking at those amazing antlers for two hours. At his point I found myself praying for the buck to get up to put this standoff to an end. Finally, after what seemed like eternity, the buck started to get to his feet. He didn't even get his legs stretched out when I touched the shot off. The buck instantly fell back in his bed. It was over. I looked at my watch and it was 1:10 p.m. For 2 hours and 37 minutes, I had stood there waiting. I made my way down to the buck and the antlers were even more impressive up close. I knew I had just taken the best buck of my life and what a way to do it.

The buck had nine points on each side and was 31 inches wide. He later officially gross scored 233⁴/₈ B&C which made him the highest gross scoring buck killed on public land that year in the state of Wyoming. His typical frame was huge, gross scoring 202⁶/₈ B&C.

Evaluate Your Hunts

One thing I like to do, and I think it is a very valuable process, is to sit down and evaluate my hunts. When hunting, you are required to make many decisions that will affect the outcome of your hunt. One wrong move and all of your hard work can be lost. I like to look at the things I feel I did right, as well as the things I did wrong, and learn from it. To show you what I mean, let's take a look at my thought process and decisions I made during my 2004 Wyoming hunt because I would like to point out several things that I think were critical in harvesting the buck.

First of all, I was out hunting when it was wet and raining. Hunting in inclement weather can be very good at times. I saw two other camps that day and no one in the camps was hunting. Instead, they were laying around camp waiting for it to clear up. Rain, sleet, or snow, it doesn't matter, I hunt in all of them. The only thing I don't like is when the wind is blowing, but I will still be out hunting.

Second, I forgot all about the high alpine bowls and started concentrating on hunting the lower, secondary ridges. There is no way you are going to find a buck of this caliber hanging out in an open basin above timberline during the middle of the season. You need to concentrate all of your efforts glassing the timbered ridges. Don't waste your time glassing the huge openings; spend your time studying the smaller ones.

Next, I kept glassing after the magical first hour of glassing was over with. If I had stopped glassing when it appeared everything had bedded down, I never would have even laid eyes on the buck. Remember, time spent glassing is time well spent.

The next thing that I did was one of the most critical decisions I made that led to harvesting the buck. Once I spotted the buck feeding, I waited for him to bed down. If I had taken off immediately, I would not have known the exact whereabouts of the buck when I reached the ridge he was on. By putting the buck to bed, so to speak, I knew exactly where he was which was critical.

Once the buck was bedded, I began to plan the stalk. The very first thing I did was picked out the spot I want to end up at. Once that was decided on, I looked over the terrain and studied all possible routes to take during the stalk. During this process, make sure you look at all options. This is no time to limit yourself. After I decided on the route, I picked out a good landmark near the buck. In this case it was the small patch of yellow-leafed quakies. You might want to pick out several because, trust me, it doesn't always look the same once you arrive at your destination.

After deciding on which route to take and what landmark to use, I needed to make it to the other ridge as fast as I could. There are times to be patient, but this isn't one of them. This is public land hunting and you never know when other hunters will enter the picture and blow your stalk. I had several miles to cover and I wanted to cover them as fast as possible. There is no reason to go slow when you are miles away. The route I had chosen allowed me to travel as fast as I could until I reached a spot approximately 300 yards from the buck. Of course this will not always be possible, so travel only as fast as the terrain and available cover lets you.

When I reached the spot I had picked out, this is when it really got exciting. I knew that one wrong decision and it would be over in a hurry. Patience was the name of the game now. Little did I know how much patience would be required before it was all over with.

Once I started my stalk, and the fog came in, I had to decide on whether to continue my stalk, or back off. I decided to back off and retreat to where I had taken off my backpack. I felt if I had continued with the decreased visibility, the buck may have detected me before I spotted him. With visibility of only 50 yards, I would have had to have gotten closer to the buck than I wanted to.

When the fog lifted and I was able to begin my stalk, I forced myself to go slower than I ever had before. This was tough. I am so used to traveling at a fairly fast pace, that I had to keep telling myself to go slower. Once I could see the tops of the quakies that I knew the buck was bedded next to, every step was slow and deliberate. If I would have been going at my regular pace, I never would have spotted the buck before he spotted me.

Not only was I moving slowly, but I was using my binoculars after every step. If you are going to spot a buck bedded in the timber, it is an absolute must that you use your optics. I wasn't looking for an entire deer body. I was looking for things such as the tip of an ear, the deer's muzzle or the tips of antlers. This proved to be very important because as I picked the brush apart, I located only the very tips of the antlers protruding out of the green shrubbery.

During the next hours, my patience was tested like never before. Never have I had to stand there and stare at a set of antlers of that caliber for so long. I had made a lot of good decisions up to this point and definitely didn't want to jeopardize all of that by trying to get closer to the buck. I was only 158 yards from the buck so there was no sense in moving any more. All I could do was sit and wait. In the end, I had enough patience to wait out the buck and made one good shot.

Any time you have a hunt, whether it is successful or not, you need to dissect it and learn from it. I do that with all of my hunts. I have blown a lot of stalks in the past, but by evaluating my decision process, I can learn from them. I can identify good decisions made, as well as bad ones that may have cost me a big buck.

Pursuing mulies above 12,000 feet can be very interesting, to say the least.

Weather

The weather while hunting the high country during the mid-season can vary greatly. You will need to be prepared for all different type conditions. It can be extremely hot one day, and you just might have several inches of snow the next. A good example of this is a hunt in Colorado a few years back where a friend and I experienced one extreme to another.

When we arrived, the skies were clear and we made camp at the end of a high mountain road that was at 11,000 feet. The country we would be hunting was a short hike south and then up thorough a pass to the summit which was over 12,000 feet. We hunted the first day without much success, but as we went to bed that night, the snow was beginning to accumulate outside which I thought might just change our luck. During the night, the snow kept piling up and it wasn't long before one of the tent poles gave out. The weight of the snow snapped it in two. This was more snow than I had hoped for.

The next morning we shoveled our way out of the tent in the pre-dawn darkness and began to make our way across the extremely steep slope toward the summit. The snow was extremely deep and it took us a lot longer to reach the top than we had hoped it would. Once on top, our efforts were greeted with an amazing view of a gorgeous alpine basin. We found a good vantage point to glass from and began picking the basin apart.

I spent most of my time glassing for tracks and found several sets, but there was only one problem. They were all heading out of the country. During the night after the storm had let up, all of the deer that were in the basin had migrated out to lower elevations. We were the only ones stupid enough to be up there above 12,000'.

249

Our tent (middle of picture) was totally buried in snow. It snowed so much that night that it snapped one of the tent poles like it was a toothpick.

After spending all day glassing the high basins without locating any deer, we dropped down a few thousand feet in elevation and found where the deer were held up. I passed on a couple 27- to 28-inch bucks, but never did pull the trigger. During the mid-season, you have to be prepared for all weather conditions as well as be prepared to change your plans. One day you may be hunting at 12,000' and the next you may have to be hunting at 9000'. Be willing to change your plans as dictated by weather conditions.

Being persistent paid off for Danny with a 32½-inch wide non-typical.

Perseverance

By Danny Adams

I always look forward to the first week of August because that is when I normally make my first scouting trip into the high country to glass for bucks. My first trip during August of 2002 found me glassing some of my favorite high mountain basins that I like to check out every year. I had backpacked in on Saturday morning and after getting my camp situated, I began glassing all of the basins where I have seen deer in the past. I continued glassing all day and evening, but couldn't turn up anything good. I still had a couple of areas that I had not glassed yet, so the plan was to be looking them over at sunup.

As planned, I had a good vantage point and was picking the mountainside apart at daybreak but could only locate a couple of small bucks. I continued working my way along the ridge glassing new country and at 9:00 a.m. spotted a bachelor group of bucks out feeding about a half mile away in a large opening that was dotted with scrub pines. As I glassed with the binoculars, I counted 11 bucks. I put the spotting scope on them and noticed two of them looked really good. There was a good typical that would gross score close to 190 B&C, but he wasn't the buck that had my attention. The one that caught my eye was over 30 inches wide and had a lot of extra points.

Curiosity was getting the best of me and I wanted to get a closer look at the bucks. I threw on my pack and began making my way over to a spot that would offer me a good look approximately 200 yards from the bucks. I hurried every chance I could and when I finally arrived and peeked over the ridge, the bucks were still up and feeding. They were feeding on

251

a north-facing slope which was providing them with a good amount of shade which allowed them to remain feeding for so long. I watched them feed until 11:00 a.m. before they decided to bed down for the day. Once they were bedded, I backed off and started making my way off the mountain toward the trailhead.

The next weekend found me making my way up the trail once again in the early morning darkness. I arrived at the top of the ridge where I had last glassed the bucks from and just like clockwork, the bucks were up feeding less than 300 yards from where they were a week earlier. There were only four of them this time. The seven smaller bucks were nowhere to be seen, while the four largest were in their regular routine of feeding along the hillside and then bedding in the scrub pines at the top of their feeding area. On the hike out that afternoon I was very excited knowing that they were still in the area.

The following weekend I hiked into a couple of other hidey holes to see what I might turn up. As I spent the weekend glassing a lot of average bucks, my mind kept drifting back to the big non-typical. I was almost wishing that I had gone back in to look at him again. It was then that I told myself that I needed to forget about finding something else. I needed to focus all of my efforts on patterning the habits of the big non-typical.

Other than one other missed weekend, I checked on the buck every weekend before the season. On the last weekend before the opener, the bucks moved about a quarter of a mile, but were still in the same canyon that they had frequented all summer. The two smaller bucks had shed their velvet, but the two larger bucks were still in full velvet.

The day before the season I hiked into the area and set up a good comfortable camp. That evening I glassed until dark, but there was no sign of the bucks. I wasn't too concerned because I only glassed from one spot. I didn't want to do to much moving around before the season opened. I figured it wouldn't be too hard locating them the next morning.

Opening morning excitement soon turned into disappointment. As I glassed all of the surrounding ridges, I glassed no less than 20 other hunters in the same general area. Every time I would hear a rifle shot, I would think to myself that someone probably just killed my buck. I forced myself to keep glassing, but all I could turn up was five small bucks the remainder of the day.

After glassing the second morning and still not locating the bucks, I figured it was time to get a little more aggressive. I began making small one-man drives through some of the patches of pines. I continued doing this all day without any success until it was time to glass for the evening.

I was very disappointed when I couldn't locate the buck that evening, or the next morning. I had hunted hard for 2½ days but did not see neither hide nor hair of the bucks that I thought had became so predictable in their habits during the preseason. It's amazing how everything changes once there is an increase of human presence in the backcountry.

My next trip into the area produced the same results: nothing! On my third trip I ran into one of my good friends, Rick Miller, who owns an outfitting business. He had a hunter with him and they had been trying to locate the non-typical as well. Rick had seen the buck during the preseason just as I had, but neither one of us had seen him during the season. We wished each other good luck and went our separate ways.

The remainder of the trip I continued to see bucks in the 24-inch range, but still couldn't turn up the big bucks. On the trip out, I contemplated on whether to return again or not. The whole way out I tossed it back and forth trying to decide what to do. Since I hadn't heard of any good bucks coming out of the area, I was still convinced the buck was alive and had to be there somewhere. I had made up my mind. I would return the next weekend.

The fourth trip was more of the same. I kept asking myself "Where is that damn buck? Is he dead?" I was driving myself crazy running question after question through my mind. After two more days of hard hunting I had had enough. I was out of food and surrendered. The buck won. I grabbed my pack and headed home.

When I got home I was starved. I put down several slices of pizza and was looking forward to laying around the house and resting the remainder of the evening. That's when my buddy Mark called and said that he wanted to go hunting. I told him that I was tired and had just eaten nearly a whole pizza and didn't know if I was up to doing another hike. But I told him if I was going to go hunting again, I would have to look for the non-typical one more time. We talked about it for a while and before you knew it, we had our packs loaded and were headed for the trailhead.

It was 6:00 p.m. and dark when we pulled up to the end of the road. We grabbed our packs and flashlights and began making our way back into the basin I had become so familiar with. Normally the trip doesn't take too long, but because I had a full stomach of pizza, we didn't arrive at our camp spot until 1:00 a.m. After setting the tent up Mark and I visited and had a few laughs before hitting the sleeping bags.

The alarm sounded at 6:00 a.m. and we broke camp so that we wouldn't have to return. Since we had camp on our backs, we could just hunt our way out. We had only covered a short distance when I noticed the white rump of a deer moving through the trees ahead of us. I could see there was more than one deer so I quickly ranged the distance at 312 yards just in case one of the deer happened to be a good one. I recognized the first buck that busted out across the basin as the large typical. The adrenaline started flowing because I knew the non-typical would be close. That though had no sooner crossed my mind when the second buck that came out of the trees was him. I couldn't believe it. There he was, followed by a smaller buck. By the time I got set up to shoot, the bucks were 350 yards out and moving to my right. As I squeezed the trigger, the buck instantly dropped and started rolling down the steep sidehill. The other two bucks stopped momentarily and watched the buck roll as if they were trying to figure out what had happed to their buddy before disappearing over the ridge. Mark and I were whooping and hollering as we made our way over to the buck.

I couldn't believe it, I had hunted this buck all season long without any luck and finally, on the last day of the season, he reappeared. What an experience it had been. The buck turned out to be 32½ inches wide with eight points per side. My persistence had paid off. And to top everything off, I felt very fortunate to have a friend like Mark by my side to share this amazing experience with.

Kyle's public land Nevada buck scores 180 B&C typical.

Is it Worth It?

By Kyle Paxman

What doesn't kill you will make you want to do it again, right? Going into the application period for Nevada in 2005, I envisioned a semi-comfortable horseback hunt deep in the pristine wilderness with one of my good buddies. That vision was snuffed out as the drawing results arrived and he did not draw a tag and I did. So much for the ponies I had planned on carrying me and all my stuff!

Although the unit is not known for producing a lot of giant deer, I figured I could find a respectable buck if I did some homework and hunted hard. The only problem was that 2005 was turning out to be an extremely busy year. My dad had finally drawn a coveted elk tag after applying for 15 years. I knew this elk hunt was where all my energies needed to be focused even though I had two out-of-state permits myself along with the tags my brother and friends had drawn.

I spoke to the biologist of the area several times about regions I had deemed as "bucky" on the map. He confirmed my thoughts that in order to find a buck of the caliber I would consider shooting I would need to get as far from the beaten path as possible. In between elk scouting trips I did squeeze in a two day scouting trip. We tried to hike in the first night in the dark but ended up getting lost and spending the night on a 45 degree angle. Only when we woke up did we realize we were trying to scale the highest mountain in the unit. We had missed the correct trailhead by about three miles! After a nap we hiked into my second choice area to spend that night and the following morning glassing bucks. I had found a buck haven and they were everywhere! Only problem was they were all the same age class—two to three years old. The best buck was a 3x4 frame with three stair step cheaters off his three-point side. Even though I did not think the buck would get to the predetermined goal of 175 B&C, I figured that if he was all that showed up during the hunt I would take him.

After chasing bugling bulls in Utah the entire month of September, it was finally time to load the backpack and head for Nevada. My brothers Keldon and Kirk had volunteered to tag along as my substitute pack mules. We packed in a day early to try and find a shooter buck or at least the cheater buck. The weather was nice and warm and the forecast was for more of the same. In the day before the hunt we probably glassed up eighty different bucks, none of which would break the 165-inch mark. From our primitive camp we had a great vantage point of the entire head of the basin. The view from our tent doors was a high country hunter's dream.

Opening morning came and all of the same bucks could be seen feeding in the basin below our perch. Several other groups of hunters popped into my secluded honey hole, one of which put a stalk on the biggest buck in the bunch and bumped him right past us. As the 26-inch-wide, 160 buck passed by at a mere 40 yards we had to take cover as hunters I had not seen above us in the basin started shooting. Several of them raced down the ridge after the dozen or so bucks that had nearly caused my death stopping long enough to apologize for making us scramble for shelter.

That night we headed far down the basin, descending several thousand feet for some brushy rimrock country. After the mornings fireworks I figured if there was an older buck around, this is where he would be. After jumping some more does and smaller bucks we entered some very steep rocky chutes. It was about an hour before dark when I got my chance on a wide heavy buck at an extreme distance. I wasn't able to connect on the long range shooting and if it wasn't for another group of more mature bucks being sighted, I would have figured I had blown my chance at my goal.

The long hike back to camp in the dark was a tough one as I continually replayed the shots in my head. We awoke the next morning and glassed the head of the basin. Where there had been dozens of bucks the day before, only a few does and a couple small bucks were visible. There was a definite change in the temperature that morning and clouds could be seen forming way off on the western horizon. Not exactly what you like to see when you are backpacked five miles in and sitting at close to 11,000 feet.

Despite the changing weather I knew we needed to return to the rough country from the night before to have any hope of sizing up the group of bucks we had seen. The clouds on the horizon continued to darken; so much for weathermen ever getting things right. It was obvious this was not a summer rainstorm and that fall was definitely upon us. As we sat and waited for the group of bucks to appear, a drizzling, make you miserable, kind of rain began. As we turned our glance up the basin toward camp, snow could be seen below the socked-in clouds. The group of does (the ones bucks were with) finally appeared feeding their way through the brush. We waited until dark but the bucks never joined them in the miserable conditions.

The two mile, 2,500 foot ascent back to camp was not a pleasant one. The temperature had dropped and it was not long till we reached the snow line. The snow was accumulating extremely quickly and the wind was blowing just enough to ruin whatever visibility we did have. Luckily my GPS had acquired our now half tent/half snow cave home. It was close to midnight when we exhaustingly tried to resurrect the tent my brothers were hoping to sleep in. There was already 10 inches of snow as we hunkered in to wait out the storm. I pulled socks over my hands and huddled into my bag trying to fight the chill.

Three hours later I awoke with a sick feeling. My bomb proof Walrus tent was struggling under the weight of the snow and was only inches from my face. My brother's tent was not capable of handling this much Mother Nature and I worried they were in trouble. I pulled on my hydro-fleece and stumbled into the 18 inches of snow. The other tent wasn't even recognizable and I feared the worst. I started frantically scooping snow off as muffled voices inside finally confirmed they were alright. Knocking as much snow as I could from my own tent I climbed back inside my soggy home.

It was still snowing two hours later when I heard the other two hunters in the basin climb past our camp and make their way out of the basin. I began to wonder if we should be considering the same idea as somehow I drifted back to sleep. About 7:30 that morning I heard my brothers stirring and realized the sounds of the snow had stopped. I unzipped the tent just in time to see Keldon take a face plant into two feet of snow. Luckily I had brought my cold weather gear with the exception of my boots. My brothers weren't so fortunate. After multiple attempts we finally got a fire going by using my stove as a torch. Everything we had was soaked. We huddled around the fire and planned our exit strategy. We started defrosting packs, coats, and other paraphernalia around our best imitation of the infamous "white-man" fire.

About 9:30 the hunter in me took over and I couldn't resist glassing as the clouds began to lift. Other than the foggy binos, glassing conditions where beyond ideal. I actually spotted the buck with my own eyes moving through an opening at over a mile while trying to let the Leicas dry. I knew we had a decision to make as I could immediately tell the buck had potential. I walked back over to the fire and told my brothers I had found a shooter buck. I could tell they thought I was crazy for even letting the thought cross my mind. The spotting scope confirmed the buck would surpass my goal. The only problem was that we were not in any condition to go after him let alone get him out if the stalk was successful.

The more I looked at the buck the more I wanted him, probably not fully comprehending what it would take. Finally, after about an hour of going back and forth, my brother Kirk stepped forward and said that we were here to kill a big buck so let's go get him. The mile long descent to the basin floor was planned and off Kirk and I went. The downhill travel through the immense amount of snow was relatively easy going and we covered the distance quickly. Kirk stayed back in the trees to be less noticeable for the last leg of the stalk. I saw movement ahead at about 600 yards as the buck fed through a clearing and out of sight. Angling around another group of deer I popped out of the trees in perfect position and caught the buck's antlers move at a little over 200 yards bedded down in a small willow patch.

The buck was a little below me and faced straight away nibbling on some willow leaves. He was totally oblivious as I made a nest in the snow and prepared for the shot. The Nosler AccuBond struck the buck right between the shoulder blades breaking his back and penetrating his lungs. A quick insurance shot guaranteed he was mine. The sky was a color of blue I don't think I have ever seen as I stood admiring the gorgeous four point. Kirk arrived and we went to work taking pictures and processing the buck for the long uphill climb.

We reached Keldon at camp and relived the stalk from his point of view through the spotting scope. After a quick freeze-dried meal we started the journey through the deep snow toward the trailhead. The hike out in the dark through the drifted, crusty snow was spent falling, slipping, and battling to remain in one piece. With 100 pounds of gear and deer on my 160 pound body and similar loads on my brothers, the end of the road could not have been a prettier sight. However, since then the 180-inch antlers and the memories of

Kyle's pack weighed in at 100 pounds.

the adventure have made me forget the pain and anguish and already thinking about a return trip. Was it worth it? It always is and always will be!

The Bottom Line

Spend more time hunting secondary ridges than the open alpine bowls above them. While some bucks will remain above timberline after the opener, most mature bucks of any size will be utilizing the lower secondary ridges below.

Secondary ridges are located at elevations between 8500 and 9500 feet. During hot weather, bucks will normally utilize the north-facing slopes to bed down for the day. When the weather starts to cool down, bucks will utilize the more open, southern exposures.

Spend most of your time glassing the upper sections of the ridges. This is the section of the mountain where you will find the bucks most of the time. Especially areas that have ribbon cliffs that run horizontally across the mountain. Bucks love to feed along the base of these cliffs and bed in the small patches of timber above them. Concentrate on the smaller openings, rather than the larger ones. Spend a lot of time glassing the stringers of pines that are located on the top of small finger ridges that run vertically on the mountain because bucks love to bed in these patches. It gives them several different escape route options.

One important thing that I like to do is evaluate my hunts. After I get home, I will think about the hunt and will decide what I feel I did right, as well as what I think I should have done differently. I feel this is a very valuable process and makes me a better and more knowledgeable hunter because of it.

The weather in the high country can vary greatly during the mid-season. Temperatures can range from anywhere between 30 and 70 degrees. You need to be prepared for the worst. You must also be able to change your hunting technique as the weather changes. A hunting method that works when it is extremely cold, doesn't necessarily work that great when it is 70 degrees.

SECTION 7

LATE SEASON HUNTING

Jim Hamilton

Migration Routes

The snow continued to fall as I made my way up the narrow dirt road in the pre-dawn darkness. It had been snowing all night and as I neared the mountains, the flakes got larger and the snow depth was increasing. When I reached the trailhead there were 10 inches of snow covering the ground. I put my pack on and grabbed my flashlight and began heading up the trail. After hiking two miles, the sun started to make an appearance in the eastern sky. The snow depths at this elevation were pushing 20 inches and it was becoming more and more physically exhausting breaking a trail through it. This was one of those storms that you dream about getting during the hunting season. It was enough to get some of the deer migrating. This was the last day of the 2000 Wyoming deer season and my last chance for harvesting a trophy buck for the year.

It wasn't long before I spotted a group of deer up ahead feeding on a south-facing slope. I sat down and glassed the hillside and couldn't believe how many deer were visible. I had hunted this canyon just a week ago and had hardly seen any deer. Thanks to the early October storm, the canyon filled with deer literally overnight.

As the day went on I continued to find more and more bucks. Several bucks in the mid 20-inch range and a couple in the 27- to 28-inch class, but nothing the size I was holding out for. Just before dark I was glassing a nice, 28-inch buck with a couple of extra points on both sides when three people rode up on horseback. They couldn't believe that someone was this far back in on foot with this much snow on the ground. We all watched the buck for a few minutes and I told them that I didn't want to take the buck. I watched as they tried to get up on the buck, but the buck slipped over the ridge and out of sight before they could get a shot. I put my pack on and began my hike back to the truck.

I didn't pull the trigger that day, but it was still a successful hunt to me. Over the

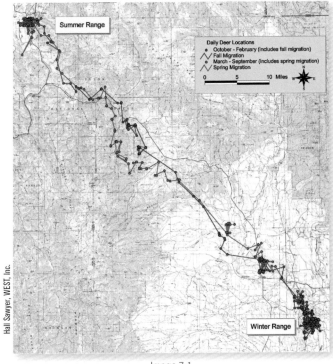

Daily Deer Locations
- October - February (includes fall migration)
/\/ Fall Migration
- March - September (includes spring migration)
/\/ Spring Migration

0   5   10 Miles

Summer Range

Winter Range

Hall Sawyer, WEST, Inc.

Image 7-1

course of the last 10 years, I have spent a lot of time during the spring identifying migration routes. I knew this particular drainage would have deer funneling into it with that much snow accumulation on the ground, but unfortunately, that was the last day of the season. If I would have had one or two more days, I know I could have found a wall hanger traveling through.

The majority of the deer in the Rocky Mountain States migrate between their summer and winter ranges. Given that fact, it shows you how important it is to identify migration routes and to use this knowledge during late-season hunting. Bucks will use these migration routes year after year. This information is of no use during early and mid-seasons, but during the latter part of the hunting season, it's priceless.

Deer are at a severe disadvantage this time of the year while migrating. The main reason for this is they are constantly moving which makes them a lot easier to spot. This is a lot different than when they were using their summer core area of only two square miles. This time of year they will cover that much distance in one day.

I have heard many stories of mass migrations back in the 50's and 60's. Many states had seasons that ran very late and coincided with the deer's migration. There were times that you could see hundreds of bucks per day. Thankfully, most of the game and fish departments don't let this happen nowadays. I sure would have loved to have hunted back then to witness some of those migrations.

Image 7-1 shows the spring and fall migration routes of a deer in western Wyoming. As you can see, there is not much difference between the spring and fall routes. This demonstrates how important it is to identify the migration paths in the spring and to put that knowledge to work for you during the late season.

Jim Hamilton

Transitional Ranges

One of the most common misconceptions I see people have is they think that deer complete their migration from their summer range to the winter range in only a few days. This is not the case. Deer can take up to two months to complete their journey. Image 7-1 is proof of that. Normally, deer will hold up along the way in areas known as transitional ranges. How long they occupy these areas usually depends on the weather. In the scouting section of this book, I cover in detail how to identify transitional ranges. That knowledge becomes very valuable late in the fall.

I harvested my Wyoming droptine buck by hunting a transitional range that I had identified during my spring scouting. The area is fairly low in elevation and contains very few deer during the early season, but when the snow starts to pile up, you can always count on finding some bucks taking up residence.

It was the last week of the season and as I made my way up the narrow two track road, the snow kept getting deeper and deeper. I parked my truck at the end of the road and grabbed my rifle and pack and started heading straight up the ridge through some small patches of scattered pines. The snow was now coming down horizontally as a stiff westerly wind sent chills through my entire body. I had just broken out into a sagebrush opening which was surrounded by small stands of aspens. I had been hiking all morning and finally had made it to the top of a ridge that ran from east to west. The ridges southern exposure was mostly made up of small aspen patches and sagebrush, as well as a couple of east-facing slopes that were covered by pines.

I had identified this area as a transitional range several years earlier during a spring scouting trip. The southern exposure is always covered with bucks during May and June and is used during the fall as well during years of heavy snowfall.

This particular year the hunting season ran through the end of October and there was about eight inches of snow covering the frozen ground. I had cut several sets of fresh tracks during my ascent, but nothing that looked very big. I continued still-hunting to the west, glassing the small finger ridges that fell off into the main drainage below. Finally, after several hours of hunting, I cut a single large set of tracks that were heading to the north which was just what I was looking for. I followed the tracks up out of the trees and into a sagebrush opening on top of the ridge. The tracks nearly disappeared several times because of the blowing snow, but I managed to keep on them as they continued over the top and entered the timber on the north side of the ridge.

I remained on the tracks for the next hour as they headed west and then went around the western point of the ridge and headed in the direction of a large basin on the south side of the ridge. I knew of a good point to glass the basin, so at that point I left the tracks and headed toward the top of the basin to a good vantage point that I have glassed from in the past.

By now the snow had died down, but the wind was still steadily blowing out of the west. I sat down under a large dead pine tree and began glassing. I started glassing where the buck's tracks entered the basin and within minutes, spotted the buck thrashing a small shrub with his antlers. I watched the buck for several minutes and was rather disappointed in the buck's typical frame. He had weak forks on the right front and back left, absolutely killing his score. I had no intention of taking the buck at that point until he turned his head and I saw the 8-inch drop tine that corkscrewed down off his right antler. I have always loved drop tines and had always wanted to harvest a buck that had one. With that being said, the buck is now hanging on my wall.

The key to harvesting that buck was identifying and knowing when to hunt transitional ranges. Earlier in the season this area wouldn't have contained any deer, but with the extreme cold and snowy weather, deer were forced to utilize the area.

It has been my experience that deer normally use more than one transition area along their migration route. The first is usually located at a considerably lower elevation than where the deer have been living and is located about midway in their

migration. There is normally a lot of cover, with some open south-facing slopes. The north-facing ridges are usually totally covered with pine trees which make them very difficult to hunt. Spot and stalk hunting is usually out of the question in most of these places. Still-hunting and drives for bucks usually provide the most success. Although drives are extremely effective, I refuse to hunt that way. I would much rather go one on one with a buck. It is much more satisfying.

Image 7-4 is a close-up view of a certain section of Image 7-1. This close-up view represents what I am calling a midway transitional range. You will notice that the deer spent several days in this area. The area is rather large, but one thing that you need to keep in mind is that this is only one deer. There will be literally thousands of deer utilizing these same areas during their migrations. How long they spend there will often be determined by weather conditions. The nicer the weather, the longer they will remain in these areas. If the weather is cold and there are good accumulations of snow, deer will tend to spend less time there and will move out onto their winter range sooner.

Identifying transitional ranges in the spring and then applying that knowledge in the fall paid off for me with this beautiful droptine buck.

Deer usually start occupying these areas in mid to late October. During this time of year, there have already been several snowstorms and the temperatures are really starting to cool down. Because of this, deer start to utilize the more open, south-facing slopes. When hunting transitional ranges, my preferred method is still-hunting. At this time of the year, you can find bucks up at any time of the day. They are a lot more active than they were during the early and mid-seasons.

The second transitional area is

Hall Sawyer, WEST, Inc.

Image 7-4

This photo shows the type of transition area that I concentrate on during the late season. This time of the year, bucks love to hang out in areas that have a good mixture of quakies and pines.

located at a much lower elevation and is usually occupied by the deer just before they dump out onto their wintering grounds. These areas are where the last of the trees meet the sagebrush flats. These areas are very open and are normally made up of sagebrush ridges covered with small patches of quakies. These small patches represent the last available cover the bucks will have before finishing their journey to their wintering grounds. Deer will occupy these transition ranges the last part of October and early November.

Rick Costello of Big Piney, Wyoming was lucky enough to draw a late October deer tag which allowed him to hunt in an area that deer normally use as a transitional range. It is an area that is just like the one we just talked about. It is made up of small patches of trees and sagebrush openings. Following is Rick's story of how he managed to harvest a beautiful droptine buck while hunting the transitional range.

Rick's transitional range buck is a 7x7 with a 7½ drop tine. The buck has an outside spread of 32½ inches and scores 204⁷/8 B&C.

Small Timber Patches, Big Bucks

By Rick Costello

The news from my doctor on that August day in 1998 was not good. The prosthesis from my hip replacement four years ago had come loose and I needed surgery to replace it. I decided to try to get through the hunting season and the doc agreed that postponing my surgery would not be a problem.

Hunting season is my favorite time of the year. I am a Wyoming native who started my boys hunting when they were six years old. The beauty of it is that we are still hunting together 25 years later. In the early years, my wife, Sharon, didn't go. However once she got hooked, she loved it even though she doesn't carry a gun. The memories and experiences that we have shared have been incredibly rewarding. To say we've grown into a very close family would be an understatement.

My youngest son, Brian, lives in Montana, while Shane, my oldest boy, lives about 40 miles from me. Last spring, Shane talked me into trying for a special deer permit. I applied and drew, but he didn't. "Don't worry," he said, "I'll get my deer early, and then we'll concentrate on yours."

Shane took a tall, heavy 6x6 that had G2s that measured 17 inches in length and 14-inch G3s on opening morning. Each base circumference was just under six inches. The buck's official gross non-typical score was a very respectable 195²/8 B&C.

My season opened two weeks later, but after several hunting trips to elevations from

7,000 to 10,000 feet, I had seen only small bucks, does and fawns and was starting to get discouraged. Prior to the last weekend of the season, I was happy to get a call from Brian saying he would be home to help me on the final days of my hunt.

Early Saturday morning found us on high ridges glassing likely areas. It felt great to have my whole family together on a hunt. Perhaps this would change my luck. On the way home at dark, however, we were all a little discouraged having failed to see even a single buck worth considering. We had hunted the highest and lowest terrain in the area, so we decided to check out some of the middle elevations the following day.

Daylight the next morning, the boys were pushing patches of trees for me, while Sharon moved the truck along the primitive roads to decrease the wear and tear on my hip. When they were part way through the fourth patch, I heard them yell, "Good buck!"

I heard the timber breaking near the top of the ridge about 250 yards away as I knelt down and got ready. Suddenly, a buck broke from the trees, but ran right along the top edge of a thin timbered strip that covered him enough to prevent my getting a good shot.

When the boys came out, we found the huge tracks of the buck heading into the next timber patch. We decided the best place for me was on top of the ridge, where I would have a better view of his likely escape routes. The boys would go to the far end of the patch and approach into the wind.

Shortly after my sons came into view on the ridgeline, they began waving for me to join them. When we got together, I learned they had spotted three bucks in the middle of a small patch of brush 800 yards away. We decided to pursue the bucks even though it was going to be tough to get very close.

Moving carefully, we sneaked through a draw and got within 400 yards. The deer were really tough to see, as all that showed through the brush were the tops of their antlers. Each of the three was facing a different direction and together they seemed to have any area of approach covered.

The big one's G2s appeared to be very tall, and when he turned his head to reveal a four-inch cheater off his left antler, I suspected he had more goodies that he was hiding from us.

There was a small ridge with some cover about 200 yards from the buck that would provide the best shooting position. To get there would mean crawling on our bellies through several places where we would be in partial view of the buck. Brian stayed put with his glasses on the deer while Shane and I took turns crawling.

Twenty hip painful minutes later, we were at the small ridge. The bucks had kept their heads buried so we didn't know if they were aware of us or not. We motioned Brian over to us so we could make yet another plan.

I had gotten into a prone position and kept my 7mm Remington magnum with the 3x9 Redfield scope on the big one's antlers. As the shadows grew longer, we felt it would only be a matter of time until they got out of their beds. I just had to be ready when the time came.

After more than two hours of watching the bedded bucks, it was getting harder to stay relaxed and comfortable. I knew something had to happen in the next 30 minutes or it would be too dark to shoot.

Finally, I told the boys to blow their deer calls. If he stood up or moved, I would be ready. They did. He didn't. Out of desperation, they even tried their elk calls. Nothing!

Finally, I said, "I'm on him and ready, stand up and yell." They did. Nothing! They even chucked some rocks his way. Nothing!

I decided to have Brian run down the draw and try to push the buck from his sanctuary.

Late Season Hunting

When Brian got into position, everything looked different and he could see only one long ridge and nothing else. Methodically, he moved ahead until he finally spotted us, whereupon Shane motioned for his brother to move to the right and proceed.

My heart rate increased with each step Brian took toward the buck. Suddenly, it happened! All of the bucks were charging to my left at a 45-degree angle. A split second later the 7mm roared and the deer staggered, but kept going. When I fired a second shot, dirt blew up in front of the deer and he turned to run straight toward us. At 30 feet, the buck began to slow down and I dropped him with one final shot.

It was nearly dark as we converged on the fallen buck, a 7x7 with cheaters on both sides and a 7½-inch drop on the right antler. A Game and Fish analysis of one of his teeth later revealed his age to be 9.3 years.

An hour later, we were heading to town with the 32½-inch buck that grossed 204⅞ B&C. It was the end of a perfect day of hunting a cagey and patient trophy mulie with my best friends.

Jim Hamilton

Weather

Weather during the late season can vary greatly. Some years it will be extremely hot and dry, while other years it can be very cold with feet of snow. Generally speaking: the more inclement the weather, the better the hunting. I honestly feel that this time of year gives you your best chance at harvesting a huge mulie.

The elevation I hunt at this time of year varies greatly. It is usually dependant on the weather conditions. If it is hot and dry, I will hunt at relatively high elevations. I will concentrate on the secondary ridges that the bucks were utilizing during the mid-season. Bucks will continue to use these ridges until late October or early November. At that time, the bucks will drop down in elevation to the smaller, flatter ridges that offer protection until the bucks dump out onto their wintering grounds.

269

Fog! The dreaded three letter word. If there is one thing that puts a glitch in my hunting method – it is fog!

Fog

If there is one thing that puts a glitch in my hunting method, it is the dreaded three-letter word—*fog*! When you rely on glassing as much as I do, fog is your worst enemy. What usually happens is you will either get rain or snow showers in the afternoon which leaves the ground soaked just as the sun sets. The storm will normally end during the night, but the high humidity level created by the rain or snow, won't allow the moisture to evaporate. This results in fog the next morning. If you're lucky, it will warm up enough to burn off. Other days, it will remain all day long. Although fog is my worst enemy while hunting, I still hunt in it. Oftentimes when it is valley fog, you can climb above it and have great glassing. If I do get on top of the mountain and it is still socked in, I will try to wait it out. I have literally sat on top of the mountain all day long waiting out the fog. Even when it doesn't totally lift, oftentimes it will thin out momentarily, allowing me a couple of minutes to glass at a time. A lot of the time, it will remain all day and then clear out about an hour before dark, giving you some good glassing time.

Oftentimes when the fog doesn't look like it is going anywhere, I will choose to do some still-hunting. If there is snow on the ground, I will slowly work my way around the mountain, while looking for tracks. Pay attention to the size of tracks you are seeing, as well as what direction they are traveling. This is a good way of identifying areas that the bucks are hung up in. If I find a large single set of tracks, I may choose to follow them in hopes of jumping the buck from his bed. Either that or I will return the next day and glass the area where I saw the tracks.

Snow—The Great Equalizer

If there is one thing that increases your odds of taking a trophy mule deer, it is snow. I feel that snow has led to the demise of more trophy bucks than any single other factor. This is for several reasons. The first is visibility. It is easy to spot a buck several miles away with a fresh new blanket of snow. Deer are also a lot more active when there is snow on the ground and the temperatures have cooled down. But the main reason it puts the odds in your favor is because of the added bonus of being able to see tracks. It doesn't matter how cagy and smart a buck is, he still has to leave a set of tracks behind. Tracks tell you a lot. When you come across fresh tracks on a trail, you instantly know how many deer are in the group and what direction they

I feel that snow has led to the demise of more trophy bucks than any single other factor.

are traveling. I was able to harvest my Wyoming droptine buck by tracking him in several inches of new snow into a large basin and then glassing him from above.

This time of year I am looking for single sets of tracks. Bucks are getting ready for the rut and don't like the company of other bucks during this period. I still check out all tracks, but generally the biggest bucks are by themselves at this time. Nothing gets me more excited than coming across a fresh single set of large mule deer tracks.

A couple of friends of mine, Gil Winters and Ron McBee harvested a B&C buck a few years ago after locating a huge set of single tracks crossing the road after a fresh snow.

Gil's 32-inch wide buck has a net score of 191⅛ B&C.

Tracks

By Gil Winters

On this particular day, I was hunting with my brother Brad and three friends, Ron McBee, Brian Green and Bill Nolan. We have all had pretty good success in hunting mule deer in the past. Bill has killed a buck that gross scores 209⅛ and nets 201 B&C, Ron has killed a buck that gross scores over 200 typical that has double drop tines and a couple of years earlier, I had harvested a 194⅞ net B&C buck with my bow.

Well before daylight, we were all in position to do a push through a large stand of timber. It was the second to the last day of the deer season and there were several inches of fresh snow blanketing the ground. I was well familiar with the country because I had spent a week earlier in the season pursuing a large non-typical that a friend had seen while bowhunting.

The snow was deep and the walking was extremely tough. We continued our drive until 11:00 a.m., which was the time we agreed to meet back at the truck. After comparing notes, our efforts only produced numerous does and three small four point bucks. Not much, considering the amount of country we had covered.

After the morning hunt, Brad and Bill decided to head back to camp and kick up their feet for a while. Ron, Brian and myself, decided to drive around and look for tracks. The weather really had the animals on the move and in a two hour period, we had gotten out and checked hundreds of sets of tracks. Unfortunately, none of them appeared to be the size of deer we were looking for. Then, about 1:00 p.m. we drove past a single set of tracks and I told Ron that we had better go back and check them out. Ron backed up the truck and I saw his face light up when he looked at the tracks. After looking at the tracks, we all three agreed that the track was huge and that the buck may be packing the size of headgear we were looking for.

The tracks were heading into a large canyon and we felt that there was a good chance that the buck was still in the area. The plan was for Brian and I to take the truck to the far side of the canyon and get set up on a good vantage point and then 20 minutes later, Ron would follow the tracks into the canyon.

The snow was coming down horizontally as we parked the truck and loaded up our gear. We didn't know it at the time, but Ron had already started into the timber. Before we were in position at the vantage point that we had picked out, the buck came blowing down the side of the canyon approximately 200 yards away. He was flat covering some country. It was truly amazing watching that magnificent animal coming off the hill. Brian, being a little fleeter of foot, ran to a small knob to where he could get set up to shoot. Brian fired a couple of shots, but both missed their mark.

The buck came to a clearing and hesitated to cross it, allowing me enough time to touch off one shot. The buck instantly fell to the ground, but regained his footing and headed straight downhill. Brian headed for higher ground to get a better look at the canyon, while I took up the blood trail. I followed the buck's tracks downhill for quite some distance, before he turned and went up the other side. As I continued following the trail, I kept glassing often. A short distance later, I glassed the buck bedded underneath a tree and put him down for good with one shot.

The buck was larger than we could have imagined. The buck's antlers were over 32 inches wide, and after the mandatory 60-day drying period, had a net score of 191$\frac{1}{8}$ B&C.

After a fresh snow, not only do I glass for bucks, but I also glass for tracks.

Late Season Glassing Tips

This time of year I almost exclusively use Phase I, II and III glassing. With cold temperatures and snow on the ground, deer are usually fairly visible and I don't need to use Phase IV. About the only time the spotting scope comes out this time of year is when I spot something with my binoculars and I need to see more detail.

Unlike the early and mid-seasons, a buck doesn't have a core area that he remains in for any certain amount of time. A look at any of the migration graphics in this book confirms that. This time of the year you might see a buck one day, and he could be miles away the next. So if you do spot a buck while glassing, do everything you can to close the deal as soon as possible. The buck may be on a totally different mountain come the next day.

After a fresh new snow, I not only glass for deer, but I also spend just as much time glassing for tracks. Continue following the tracks with your binoculars to see where they are headed. A lot of times you can see them entering a patch of timber, but not exiting. In the preceding photo, I glassed a fresh set of tracks that came over the ridge and entered a small patch of timber. The exciting thing was that the tracks did not come out the other side. It took two hours of waiting before the buck came out, but unfortunately, he didn't quite meet my standards. This can be a very effective way of finding bucks after a fresh snow.

Image 7-9 shows a typical secondary ridge that I like to glass during the late season. During the mid-season, I would be concentrating my glassing efforts only on the upper portion of the ridge, but during the late season, I spend time glassing the entire ridge, as well as the basin below. Bucks are moving a great deal at this time of the season and you can just about spot them in any kind of terrain as they are passing through.

Image 7-9

As with any other time of the season, I like to be at a good vantage point at first light to glass. If there is a large amount of snow on the ground, I will mainly glass the south-facing slopes. These slopes are normally fairly open and are covered with scattered pines and several patches of quaking aspen. I feel that I have a huge advantage over the bucks once they start utilizing these patches. This is because I can get on an opposing slope and glass the entire patch easily. This time of year the quakies don't have any leaves and it is relatively easy to spot deer. I honestly believe that the bucks feel concealed and well hidden while in the quakies—if they only knew. I used this exact method to harvest a Boone and Crockett typical in Colorado in 2003.

When glassing from an opposing slope, it is amazing how well you can see into the patches of quakies on the other side. The bucks feel very concealed when they are bedded in the patches of trees – If they only knew.

275

Quakie/Pine mix

Image 7-11

When glassing this type of country during the late season, there are two types of terrain you should pay particular attention to because they tend to be areas that bucks favor. If you'll look at Image 7-11, it shows the first type of terrain I will spend most of my time glassing. It is the area where the pines and quakies overlap and they are mixed. Bucks love these areas. I believe they like the security of having the pines only a couple of jumps away.

Image 7-12 shows the second type of terrain I like to concentrate on, where the end of a ridge runs out and starts to fall off, especially if there are any small benches. Bucks love to bed on the ends of the ridges and benches overlooking the drainage below.

End of ridge/benches

Image 7-12

Late Season Hunting

I honestly feel that the late season gives you your best chance at putting your tag on a trophy sized mule deer. He is not the same animal that he was during the early and mid-seasons. His mind is now on other things, such as migrating, rutting and just trying to get enough food in his belly.

KEYS TO SUCCESS

Migration Routes & Transition Ranges – If you are hunting an area where the season runs into November, you really need to focus your efforts on migration routes and transition ranges. When migrating, deer will often hang up in transition areas for several days, or even weeks, depending on the weather. This time of year you really need to start paying attention to any does you might see because generally, the bucks are usually nearby.

Hunt the Quakies – As snow accumulates on the north-facing slopes, deer will start to inhabit the south-facing slopes more and more. This is because food is plentiful and it requires less energy to feed in the shallower snow. Concentrate your efforts on south-facing slopes that have a good mix of quakie patches, scattered pines and sagebrush openings.

Snow – The Great Equalizer – I consider snow to be the great equalizer. I feel that snow has led to the demise of more trophy bucks than any one other factor. You need to use it to your advantage while hunting. Not only does a fresh snow cover make it a lot easier to spot deer while glassing, but the largest advantage it gives you is you are able to see how many deer are inhabiting the area by the fresh tracks in the snow. I not only look for tracks as I hike up the trail, but while glassing I am always looking for fresh tracks that just might lead me to a magnum buck.

Still-Hunting

Although glassing is my preferred method of locating bucks during the late season, this is one part of the season that I don't mind doing some still-hunting. It is definitely a good way to make the day a lot more exciting, but the downside is that you are continually spooking deer all day long.

The way I still-hunt a mountain depends on the terrain. I am what I call a "terrain hunter." What that means is I like to let the lay of the land dictate how I hunt it. I will not have a set plan going into it, I will simply make decisions on how I am going to hunt it as it comes.

Normally I like to stay near the ridgetops. This is because I like to glass a lot even

Image 7-13

when I am still-hunting. I will generally follow the contour of the ridge, stopping to glass all new terrain as it comes into view. I don't mean just up close either, I am glassing good distances away. This time of year with all of the snow on the ground, bucks are relatively easy to spot at great distances.

As I slowly follow the ridgetop, I make notes of any tracks I come across, as well as what direction they are headed. This is important. This time of year if you find that all of the tracks are heading in the same general direction, you can bet they are heading in the general direction of their wintering grounds. If I continue hunting the area the rest of the day without any success, I will hunt a different place the next day in the same direction that all of the tracks were heading.

Still-hunting in deep snow can be very exhausting. Image 7-13 shows a drainage that took me six hours to hike into. I started hiking at 6:00 a.m. and didn't get there until noon. I was exhausted when I finally reached the top. I saw a lot of tracks that day, but evidently the deer were smarter than me. Most of them had already headed to lower elevations.

North-facing slopes generally have good snow accumulations during the late season which makes finding food rather difficult.

Hunting the Quakies

If I am hunting an area where the season runs into late October or early November and there is snow on the ground, I almost exclusively hunt stands of quaking aspens. These are magnets for bucks this time of year. Why is this? I can sum it up in one word – Food. As snow accumulates on pine covered north-facing slopes, food becomes especially hard to find. In order to get enough food, mule deer start seeking out the more open south-facing slopes covered by patches of quaking aspen. A healthy aspen grove will generate the forbs and forage that deer like at a rate of approximately 10 times that of the average conifer forest. That is huge. While aspen stands provide important forage for the deer all year long, they become especially important this time of the year when the snow accumulations keep piling up.

Deer seem to prefer the smaller, younger stands of aspens. They will consume the buds, twigs, bark, sprouts and fallen leaves. I have watched numerous times as bucks will paw through the snow to get at the yellow aspen leaves laying underneath. There are also several plants that grow in the aspens that are not edible to the deer at any other time of the year except after the first frost. What happens is, in the fall, frost breaks open herbaceous plant cells, which are normally poisonous to the deer, and they will lose their toxins with the loss of cell fluid. These plants, such as false hellebore and cow parsnip, become an important part of the deer's diet in the late fall.

I put this knowledge to work on my 2003 Colorado hunt. After a seven-hour drive, my hunting partner Scott Mansor and I had arrived in Colorado the day before the opener. It had been three years since we had hunted this particular spot, so it was

During the late season, bucks will start seeking out the south-facing slopes where the food is more accessible and plentiful.

good to see the area and get familiar with the terrain again. The only disappointing thing was that there wasn't any snow on the ground, unlike three years earlier when we had 18 inches of snow to greet us. But since it was November, we knew that that could change in a hurry.

Well before daylight, Scott and I were making our way toward the long ridgetop that we wanted to glass from. The ridge offered a commanding view of the southern exposure of a large creek drainage. The hillside was covered with several small aspen patches and had numerous sagebrush openings. Several inches of snow had fallen during the night and the wind was blowing unbelievably hard as we made our way to the top. About a half mile into the hike, Scott split off and dropped down into the timber, while I continued to the top of the ridge. I arrived at the top at daylight, but the combination of wind and snow made it impossible to do any glassing. My only option was to drop into the timber out of the wind and do some still-hunting. I continued hunting all day without laying eyes on a single deer. Disappointing yes, but we still had six days of hunting left.

The second day wasn't much better. We tried a different area several miles away hoping to locate where the deer might be hung up. There were numerous snow showers that dropped several inches of snow, but the temperatures were too warm and the snow would melt shortly after. We saw a few more deer but only one buck—a small two point. Not much, but at least I had laid eyes on my first buck of the hunt.

Since we hadn't seen much during the first two days, Scott and I decided to hunt a little higher in elevation the third morning. There were eight inches of snow on the ground as we made our way down an open hillside at daybreak. When we reached the timbered ridge below, we split up. Scott took the top of the ridge, while I dropped down about midway. I hadn't walked 200 yards when I spotted a buck bedded down 75 yards in front of and below me. I could only see his right antler, so I slowly moved to my left to get a better look. He was wide. The buck was 33 inches wide and tall. Unfortunately, the buck's antlers were spindly and had weak forks. An awesome buck, but not what I was after.

We continued working the timber patches all morning and into the afternoon. We saw numerous small bucks and at one point I was second-guessing my decision

281

My Colorado buck scores 197²⁄₈ gross and nets out at 191³⁄₈ B&C typical.

to turn down the wide buck earlier that morning. That thought didn't last long though. At 1:00 p.m. I sat down and started glassing a small patch of quakies on the opposite side of the canyon and within minutes I spotted what looked to be part of a deer antler. I moved about five feet to my left and took another look. From that angle I could see the entire left antler of the buck. When I finally got a look at both antlers, I couldn't believe what I was looking at. The buck was one of the largest typicals I have ever seen while hunting. I was confident that he was large enough to make the B&C record book. Unfortunately he was bedded in a spot that didn't offer any shot. I ranged the buck at 350 yards and was relieved he was within range because it was impossible to get any closer. All I could do was sit and wait. Scott was only 75 yards down the ridgeline so I motioned for him to come up.

We intently watched the buck for 20 minutes and he did not move an inch. I got nervous when I looked farther up the ridge and noticed two other hunters sitting on a rock outcropping watching the same ridge the buck was on. I was confident they couldn't see the buck from the angle they had, but I was worried nonetheless. Finally the buck stood up. I still didn't have a shooting lane, so we waited once again. The buck stood motionless for five minutes. In the mean time, a little snow flurry had turned into a total whiteout. The buck was no longer visible. Now I was really worried. I was afraid that the opportunity of a lifetime was slipping away. During the whiteout, Scott kept his binoculars glued on the spot the buck was standing in, while I was covering my video equipment. After covering the camera I grabbed

Note the size of the neck and body on my B&C buck.

my rifle and found a solid rest on a small dead quakie. The snow started to thin out and to our relief, the buck was still standing there. A moment later, Scott said, "He's making his move." Before he even finished saying it, I fired. The buck leaped straight in the air and took off toward some thick timber. The quakies were so dense that it was tough finding a shooting lane. I looked ahead of the buck and saw a large gap in the quakies, which would offer me my only shot before the buck reached the pines. When the buck reached the gap, I fired. The buck fell instantly. Scott yelled, "He's getting up." I fired again and the buck was down for good.

After loading all of our gear into our backpacks, we dropped down into the bottom and worked our way up the other side to where the buck finally came to rest. As I walked up on the buck, I realized I had just shot the buck of a lifetime.

I didn't get much sleep that night as I kept thinking back on all of the great hunting memories I have had over the years. There was one memory in particular that I kept going back to though. It was just two months earlier in the high country of Wyoming on a backpack hunt with my good friend, Doug Ayers. As we sat looking over miles and miles of great mulie country, Doug (knowing how bad I wanted to harvest a B&C buck) said, "I know a lot of mule deer hunters, but none that hunt any harder than you do. If you keep hunting like you do, you will get a B&C mulie." Not totally convinced, I replied, "I hope you're right." As it turns out he was. Thanks Doug, I just wish you could have been along on the hunt to share the experience with Scott and I.

Packing my Colorado buck straight uphill was hard, but I could still smile!

The buck is extremely heavy and is 27 1/2 inches wide. The buck has been officially scored at 197^2/$_8$ gross and nets 191^3/$_8$ B&C. The biggest factor in harvesting this buck was spending a lot of time glassing. That's the great thing about late season hunting, you can glass deer all day long. Make sure you spend a lot of time looking through your optics, even while still-hunting. You will hear me preach this throughout this book time after time, but I honestly feel that glassing is one of the most important things you can do to increase your chances of taking a trophy mule deer.

Although I would rather glass the quakies rather than still-hunt them, occasionally there will be patches of quakies where the lay of the land won't let you glass them. You have no choice other than to still-hunt through them. When still-hunting these patches of aspen, I normally like to hunt them from top to bottom or from side to side, but the main thing is to have the wind in your favor. The bucks normally hang on the edges of the quakies, not far from stands of thicker timber. The mistake I see most hunters make in the timber is that they don't use their binoculars enough. Even in the timber I am constantly glassing my surroundings hoping to spot any

284

When still-hunting the quakies, I still use my binoculars often. Even in the thick timber, you will be amazed at how far and how much more you will see when using your binoculars.

deer before they spot me. Try it, you'll be amazed at how far you can see through the trees and how many more deer you will start to see.

In large quakie patches I will travel at a little bit faster speed than the smaller ones, especially if I am not seeing any tracks. Once I come across tracks, I only take a couple of steps at a time and then I stop and glass. After I pick everything apart, I will repeat this process.

I killed my Colorado B&C buck during the first week of November. During this time of year you need to start paying attention to groups of does when you are glassing. Bucks might not be rutting yet, but I guarantee you they won't be far away. When I spotted my Colorado buck I actually had spotted a group of about eight to 10 does feeding amongst the quakies. As I broadened my scan of the mountainside with my binoculars, I located the buck bedded at the base of a large quakie. Although he was by himself, he was only a couple of hundred yards away from the group of does. Any other time of year and I would have totally ignored the does, but this time of year they become a very valuable part of the formula.

Bill's kids, Jake and Natalie hold the Buck's sheds that Bill picked up in 2004. The Buck's sheds should become the NASHC new world record for matched typical mule deer.

Better Late Than Never

By Bill McEwen

On a cold, cloudy day in March 2004, I was shed hunting in one of my favorite areas. The snow was still deep. It was almost impossible to walk, unless I stayed on the game trails where deer and elk had packed the snow during the winter. There were no deer, elk or fresh tracks in the area. Suddenly, I saw part of an antler protruding from the snow about 40 yards away. It appeared to be a fresh, brown elk antler. I stepped off the game trail and started post-holing that way. I realized that it couldn't be an elk antler. It was too early for elk to lose their antlers. When I pulled the antler from the snow, I felt a rush of excitement. It was an enormous typical deer antler. My excitement was tempered by the thought of long days and weeks of frustration that I would likely encounter while trying to find the match. There was no doubt that I would make every possible effort to find it. Then, I noticed the tip of another antler poking out of the snow only three feet away. Just an inch of bone was visible. Could it be? I reached down and pulled out the perfect match to the first giant antler. Shock and disbelief was followed with pure joy and deep satisfaction. I had found a matched set of fresh brown typical antlers that far exceeded any other set I had ever found.

I developed a deep appreciation for nature, wildlife and wild country when I was very young. Both of my parents had backgrounds and careers in wildlife and science. My dad took me into the outdoors for all kinds of activities all the time when I was growing up in Colorado. The sights, sounds and smells of the Colorado mountains, foothills and plains became hardwired into my brain. Some of my earliest memories are of hiking with my dad and then later, excitedly telling my mom exactly how many deer we saw. Eventually and inevitably I developed a special passion for hunting. Over the years this passion has frequently bordered on obsession. These days I live with my beautiful wife and two wonderful children. We live in the middle of some of the greatest mule deer country on earth.

Hunting seasons are relatively short compared to the time one can spend shed hunting. I started shed hunting as a teenager and became more involved with each passing year. Now at age 45, I find I have to hike regularly to keep my body in the same condition that came naturally when I was younger. For me, shed hunting is the perfect way to exercise and have fun at the same time. By the spring of 2004, I had been shed hunting for over 30 years. I have picked up literally thousands of deer antlers. I knew very well how rare and special this set of sheds was.

When I got home I scored the set of sheds. The score I came up with, combined with an average inside spread, would make a net typical score of well over 200. I was thrilled to have found such an incredible set of antlers. However, I couldn't help but think, "Wouldn't it be great if I could somehow find this buck during hunting season, or at least find his sheds again the next spring," these thoughts were frequent through the next year. Hunting season in 2004 passed without me or anyone else laying eyes on the big buck. Was he still out there? The question was answered in January 2005, when a friend photographed the buck. There was no doubt it was him and his antlers were as good or better than the previous year. He had a very distinctive lopped tip on his right ear. I would be able to recognize him if I saw him, even without his antlers. I had high hopes for finding his sheds. I spent plenty of time looking but to no avail. Numerous other shed hunters made it virtually assured that somebody found them, but I never did hear any confirmation. Oh well, I could still dream of crossing paths with him during hunting season. It seemed the buck summered in the high country and did not arrive on the winter range until after hunting season. The deer in this region utilize vast areas of summer range. There are wilderness and other roadless areas. Heavy timber, tall brush and sheer size of the landscape, make hunting an individual buck on the summer range a needle in a haystack proposition. It would take an incredible early storm to bring him down to winter ground during hunting season. Finding him in the high country would take a miracle but at least I could fantasize about the possibility.

One day in August 2005, the phone rang. It was a man with the Denver chapter of SCI. He told me I had just won a Colorado statewide raffle tag for deer. I wanted to believe him but didn't dare to. I had to assume it was somebody playing a particularly nasty practical joke. After multiple confirmations and receiving the actual license, I let myself accept that I really had won. I always buy a ticket or two for the raffle but I assumed that I would never win. As I pondered the possibilities there was one primary thought. This was the miracle I needed to bag the giant typical buck that I had the sheds from. The raffle tag allowed me to hunt anywhere in the state from late August through January 31st. There was plenty of time to wait for bucks to reach the winter range. I decided that I would use the raffle tag to primarily look for the big typical. I knew of no other bucks of that quality. Although I would love to travel around the state following up on tips and rumors, I did not have the time or the money to do that.

I did a little hunting in October. As expected, I didn't see many big bucks then. I started getting serious after the third rifle season ended. It was now mid-November. A hefty snowfall and the influence of the rut made for prime hunting conditions. Every day numerous big bucks

Bill's late season buck is 29 inches wide and gross scores 191⅝ B&C.

were sighted. I had set my standards at the highest level. I would not shoot a buck unless it was the giant typical or another equally as good. I passed up some great nontypical bucks that would score well over 200 gross. I had been fortunate enough to kill a few bucks like that in recent years. I wanted the giant typical.

In the early part of December the rut rapidly diminished. Bucks started to become harder to find. A high-pressure dome of arctic air settled over western Colorado. Temperatures plunged to well below zero. Hunting in these conditions became difficult and uncomfortable, even a little dangerous. I kept plugging away through it all. I hiked into and hunted one hotspot after another. I knew enough honey holes that I couldn't possibly hunt them all, even with all the time the raffle tag allows. Every week I returned at least once to the winter range where the big typical should eventually show.

On December 9th, it was bitter cold but brilliantly sunny. Billions of ice crystals sparkled under the afternoon sun. I was moving through scattered junipers on a flat ridgetop. A deer ahead caught my eye. A quick look through binoculars told me everything I needed to know. Here was the giant typical buck that I had the sheds from. It was instantly obvious that it was him. However, I did not shoot right away. It was also obvious that his antlers had suffered some regression in the length of his tines. Most of the regression was on his left antler, especially his G4. I reflected for a few moments on just what this unexpected development meant to me. I decided it didn't matter. This was the buck I was hunting. He was still hugely massive and magnificent. He wouldn't score as great as before, but he was old. It would be good to take this buck now that his life was nearly over. The shot was an easy one, just a little over 100 yards. When I knelt next to the old warrior, I knew I had made the right decision.

The buck had evidence of his long life written all over him. His lopped ear and scarred face were evidence of many battles. The molars on his jaw were worn smooth like polished stones. I sent an incisor to a laboratory for a precise age. The result that came back was 11 years. That is truly old for a mule deer buck. He had evaded hunters all those years by simply avoiding them. He likely stayed at high elevation in thick cover every fall until after hunting seasons were over. I felt a little guilt over crossing him up with the raffle tag. I'm comforted to know that many young bucks and does are surely his offspring. His health, vigor and resourcefulness should live on for years to come. Hopefully some of his descendents will grow antlers of the same magnitude as well. His antlers are 29 inches wide and officially score $191^5/_8$ gross, 184 net. The mass is what is most impressive. The bases are $5^6/_8$ inches at the first measurement. The heavy mass carries throughout the entire rack. The sheds officially netted $179^4/_8$ without a spread. With the inside spread added to the sheds score, the buck would have scored $203^6/_8$ net in the fall of 2003. Judging from the photographs it appears he scored at least that high again in the fall of 2004. He lost almost 20 inches in net score in his last year. Often people kill a four-year-old buck with big antlers, and say, "If only he could have been a year of two older, he would have grown even bigger." It's not often somebody kills a buck that's 11 years old and knows for a fact that he was bigger in previous years.

Deer hunting in much of western Colorado has been very good since the late 1990's. My friends and I have been taking monster bucks while all the while we were hearing people say that the good old days were gone for good. Relative to my lifetime, these are the good old days. Big, old mule deer bucks are still a rare and precious thing though. More needs to be done to limit hunting pressure to make sure a few bucks can reach old age. It is hunting that is the biggest cause of buck mortality and it is the factor that is most easily controlled.

Having the Statewide Raffle Tag was something that I never imagined would happen to me. It was quite a ride. The excitement of winning the tag and thinking of the incredible possibilities were followed by a huge amount of self-induced pressure. The actual hunting was fun and enlightening as hunting always is. However, the seemingly endless season was a severe test of physical and mental endurance. When I pulled the trigger, the finality of it was like a friend died. The local legend of a buck was now dead. The hunt of 10 lifetimes was over forever. I was thrilled with my buck and now that some time has passed since the hunt, I am even more satisfied with the whole experience. I hunted 28 days. I saw 373 bucks during that time. I witnessed a fascinating glimpse into the world of mule deer during a time when I'm normally not out very much.

The Bottom  Line

Migration routes are great places to hunt if your season runs late enough in the year. Bucks will utilize the same routes, year after year. I have several places that I have identified as migration routes and during years of heavy snowfall, I can always count on finding a lot of bucks moving through the area.

Transition ranges and migration routes pretty much go hand in hand. Transition ranges are areas along a buck's migration route where he will tend to hang up for a certain amount of time while he is migrating. How long they utilize these areas is usually dependant on the weather.

Weather during the late season can be both frustrating and rewarding. The dreaded three letter word "fog" is my worst enemy while hunting. I rely on glassing so much that it definitely hinders my hunting technique. Although I dislike the fog, I will still-hunt in it. This is a great time to do some still-hunting to locate tracks and find out which areas the deer are using and in which direction the deer are traveling.

The rewarding weather usually comes in the form of snow. I consider snow as "the great equalizer." I feel that snow has led to the demise of more trophy bucks than any other factor. It doesn't matter how cagey an old buck is, he still has to leave a telltale set of tracks behind.

As snow accumulations start piling up, food can be increasingly hard for bucks to locate on the north-facing slopes. This time of year bucks will start utilizing the south-facing slopes that have a good mixture of quaking aspen and pines. Quakie patches have a lot of food which the bucks really welcome this time of the year.

290

SECTION 8

ON THE HORIZON

Wyoming Living Legends

When the hunting season is long over, I enjoy pursuing monster bucks with a video camera on the winter range. This is one of my favorite times of the year because I get a close-up look at all of the trophy bucks that eluded me during the previous hunting season. Not only that, I can watch and study them to better understand their behavioral tendencies.

I filmed for several years and put together a video series called *Magnum Mulies*. It all started with *In Pursuit of Magnum Mulies* which was released in 2000. Then, in 2001, I released the second in the series, *Magnum Mulies 2 – The Pursuit Continues*. Finally, in 2003, I released the third and final installment in the series, *Magnum Mulies 3 – The Final Pursuit*. The video series was a great success and all three videos are now sold out and will no longer be reproduced.

Over the years, I have been fortunate enough to film some of the largest bucks that have ever been filmed. One clearly stands out as my favorite, a buck that I named Goliath. I was able to follow Goliath over the course of two years and was lucky enough to get both sets of his antlers. He was nearly 40 inches wide and had an amazing 210-inch typical frame.

Two other bucks that roamed the Wyoming winter range were Morty and Popeye. I didn't film these two bucks because they were on the winter range before I started filming for my series. I did get to watch Popeye on many occasions and can still picture him standing out in the sagebrush.

Mike Eastman started calling these three bucks the Wyoming Living Legends. Indeed, over the years, they have definitely reached legendary status. Mike commissioned artist Brent Todd to put all three of the bucks on canvas making their way to their wintering grounds. I feel fortunate to have been able to watch Popeye and Goliath for several years on the winter range. Following are their stories of how they became so well known and loved by mule deer enthusiasts everywhere.

Popeye

One day at work I was visiting with another individual by the name of Ed Boe, and as usual the conversation soon turned to the subject of big bucks. Ed told me of a buck that he had seen on the winter range that had one of the largest sets of antlers that he had seen in several years. Since Ed spends a lot of time out on the winter range looking at deer, he had my attention to say the least. Being the big buck fanatic that I am, there was no way that I was going to let this conversation end until I had directions to where this buck was wintering. After getting the directions, time seemed to slow down. It took the clock forever to reach the magical hour of

Popeye • 1995

Mark McCord

4:00 p.m., which marked quitting time. When I finally got off work, I drove home and grabbed my binoculars and then made a beeline for the area that the buck was in. Excitement soon turned into disappointment. Darkness was now settling in and I had yet to catch a glimpse of the buck that I had come to see. On the bright side, tomorrow was the start of the weekend, which would give me plenty of time to locate the buck.

The next morning found me back where I had left off the evening before. I had been driving for close to 30 minutes when I came to an intersection in the road. The left fork continued heading west up the small canyon to where it dead-ended, while the right fork switchbacked up the steep south-facing slope, coming to an end at one of the many gas wells that dotted the country. Because this deer winter range is so vast, I elected to take the right fork because it would provide the better vantage point from which to glass the many sagebrush covered ravines. Before I made it to the top of the hill, three bucks appeared about 100 yards above and to the left of me. As I brought my truck to a stop, the bucks continued feeding across the slope heading to my right. The two bucks on the right were respectable bucks, but the buck on the left was the one that I had come here looking for. Stretching nearly 40 inches wide, his rack was one of the most beautiful that I had ever seen. This was the first time that I had laid eyes on this fantastic buck, but it was not to be the last.

The first year that the buck was spotted was the 1992-1993 winter. He came in with five points on the right antler and six on the left. Nothing spectacular, but he was only four years old. The right shed was later picked up by Albert Ellis of Jackson Hole, while the left was picked up by one of Ed's friends, who would later give the antler to Ed. Over the next few years, his antlers grew to tremendous proportions and so did his popularity.

The 1993-1994 winter is when Ed Boe first saw the buck. The rack sported 10 points on the right, and six on the left. He showed a great amount of horn growth from the previous year. Ed spent seven to 10 days watching the buck that year before he dropped his antlers. It paid off as Ed was able to get the right antler, while the left was picked up by an unknown antler hunter. The right antler scored 87⅞ Boone and Crockett points. Doubling this measurement and figuring in an inside spread would have given his typical frame a gross score of right at 200. His non-typical points for that year totaled around 20 inches.

During the 1994-1995 winter, Ed found himself laid off from work, so when the buck showed up, Ed spent nearly every day for two months watching the buck, but he was not alone. The popularity of the buck had started to spread. It was not uncommon to see 10 trucks at one time parked along the road trying to catch a glimpse of the now famous deer. The buck came in this year with 10 points on the right and nine points on the left. His typical frame gross scored 207⅝ Boone and Crockett points and he had a total of 37⅝ inches in non-typical points. Luck was on Ed's side that year, as he managed to pick up both the right and left antlers.

Surviving yet another hunting season, the buck returned during the winter of 1995-1996. His antlers continued to grow from the previous year. He had seven points on the right and seven points on the left and his antlers spread 40 inches wide. His typical frame gross scored 218⅝ and he had a total of 19 inches of non-typical points. By now the buck had been in several videos and hunting magazines and was known by almost everyone who was into trophy mule deer hunting. People were coming from various states just to see the majestic buck. The buck had become so popular that he was even given the name "Popeye," which is very fitting because when you first see him, the eyes pop right out of your head.

The only time that Popeye had been seen was in the winter. Speculation grew as to where he lived during the summer and fall, and almost everyone had developed their own theories as to where he went. But that is all they were—theories. Then it happened. During the summer of 1996, he was spotted by several people while on his summer range. Mark McCord was even lucky enough to sneak to within 20 yards of him and snap some of the most amazing photos that you will ever see. Like wildfire, word spread that Popeye had been spotted and that the following hunting season might bring an end to this magnificent legend. This gave many a sick feeling in their stomachs, knowing that the buck might never return to the winter range again.

At the end of the 1996 deer season, there was still no word of Popeye being harvested by a hunter. Did he survive? Would he make it back to the winter range again? It would be a long wait until December to find out if he did indeed make it through another deer hunting season. Then, just like clock work, Popeye showed up just as he had in all previous years. At eight years old, his antlers were about the same in size as the year before. He had 11 points on the right and six points on the left, with an outside spread of well over 40 inches. His typical frame grossed $219^{7}/_{8}$ Boone and Crockett points and he had a total of $32^{4}/_{8}$ inches in non-typical points. If he hadn't broken off the G1 on the left antler, his typical frame would have scored well over 220 typical.

The 1996-1997 winter was probably the harshest winter that Popeye had to face throughout his life. With his age and the harsh winter conditions, it is believed that Popeye died that winter shortly after shedding his best set of antlers. It still amazes me that bucks such as Popeye can elude hunters and predators for that many years only to die of old age. Congratulations, Popeye, on one hell of a run.

No one person is more responsible for Popeye's popularity than Mike Eastman. Mike lives in Powell, Wyoming where he publishes *Eastmans' Hunting Journal* and *Eastmans' Bowhunting Journal*—the absolute best western big game hunting magazines on the market since 1987 and 2000, respectively. For over 40 years, Mike has observed mule deer on the winter range and Popeye has graced many pages of *Eastmans'*, capturing the hearts of trophy mule deer enthusiasts across the nation. Mike has also produced the Mule Deer Stalker video series, which contains four videos on trophy mule deer. The next best thing to seeing Popeye in person is to watch him on the *Best of Mule Deer Stalker* DVD.

Popeye has also been the subject of many pieces of art work. Artists such as Brent Todd of Salt Lake City, Utah, and Chris Lacey of Reno, Nevada, have used Popeye as their subject in many drawings and paintings. Chris has also done a bronze of Popeye.

Out of the five years, Ed Boe has managed to collect three full sets and a couple of single antlers of Popeye. It is truly one of the most awesome collections of antlers that one will ever see.

Goliath

It had been a relatively slow day as far as filming goes. Since daybreak I had traveled nearly a hundred miles and had yet to capture any good bucks on film. Tired of bouncing down the dusty roads, I was about ready to call it quits for the day when my luck took a turn for the better. Just as the sun was setting, I spotted a buck chasing a couple of does back and forth about midway up a large, sage-covered ridge. I raised my binoculars and couldn't believe the caliber of buck standing before me. Not since the famous Popeye had I laid eyes on a buck of this size. Unfortunately, he had broken off his entire front fork on his right antler. Still, he was a world class mule deer.

Over the course of the winter I continued looking for trophy mule deer to film, but always found myself returning to check on the monster buck, which I was now calling Goliath. Why Goliath? Well, there are two reasons for this. The first is fairly obvious. He was true giant. The second...Who killed Goliath? That's right, it was David. I was hoping I could find him during the next year's hunting season and possibly harvesting him.

Later that spring, I managed to pick up his sheds and if he had not broken off his right front fork, he would have gross scored 210 B&C typical points. His outside spread was 38½ inches wide and his G2s were an amazing 21⅜ inches long.

The following summer I scouted without locating Goliath, and I didn't have any better luck finding him during the 1999 hunting season. I heard about several large bucks that were harvested, so I tracked them down to see if any of them were Goliath, but luckily none of them turned out to be him. I would just have to wait for winter to arrive to see if he was still alive.

Goliath • 1999

December came and I found myself checking out Goliath's favorite rutting spots, eventually locating him during my second trip. He was less than five hundred yards from where I had first seen him the year before. In hot pursuit of a doe in estrus, he only had one thing on his mind, and it wasn't me. I took advantage of his preoccupation with a doe and watched him for several hours in awe of the size of his antlers. He managed to beat all the odds and survive another year.

I was fortunate enough to get his antlers again that year. His typical frame scored 210 B&C typical, and he picked up more mass and his outside spread stretched out to 40 inches wide.

The summer of 2000, I searched high and low, but was still unable to turn up Goliath's summer hideout. Before I knew it, the hunting season was over and I still hadn't been able to locate this great buck. All was not lost though. I was looking forward to seeing him on the winter range a couple of months later. Unfortunately, that would not happen.

I was talking with a friend that informed me he had heard Goliath had been harvested by a hunter from Utah. When I got home from work that day, there was a message on my phone from David Woodhouse of Spanish Fork, Utah informing me that he had indeed harvested Goliath during the 2000 hunting season in Wyoming. He had showed the buck to Doyle Moss who instantly recognized the buck from my Magnum Mulies videos and told David he should give me a call. I called David back that night and confirmed that he did indeed kill Goliath. Following is David Woodhouse's story of taking Goliath.

The author with Goliath's 1999–2000 mounted sheds.

David harvested Goliath during the 2000 season in Wyoming.

A Legend Falls

By David Woodhouse

During the second weekend of the 2000 Wyoming deer season, I was looking for big bucks with my father, Tom Woodhouse. After hunting hard over the opener we had not planned on coming back until later in the season, but with a big storm bringing snow, we could not resist returning to the mountains.

A cold Saturday morning found us back where we had left off the week before. Conditions were perfect as we hunted the area under a huge, bare rocky mountain with fresh deer tracks all around in the six-inch-deep snow. Though we saw many does, small bucks and a few bighorn sheep, no big bucks were seen.

Back at camp, we decided to try to find the buck that had left the huge set of tracks we had seen on opening weekend. It was still snowing as we climbed the mountain to a vantage point from which we would glass and wait. I spotted two does right away, and another bull moose (I believe I saw more bull moose than buck deer on this hunt!). Dad and I glassed for a couple of hours until I got restless and decided to go over one more ridge and look into the next canyon before dark. Dad said he would head back to the truck and drive around to pick me up at the bottom.

I had to hurry through one open canyon and up the other side to make it before dark. I had picked out an ancient, weathered pine as a marker, and that's what I headed for. When I reached my landmark and carefully looked over the ridge, no deer were visible in the clearings below or to the side. But as I looked across the canyon in front of me, the first thing I noticed was a deer coming out of the timber and heading up the basin at the top. This wasn't just any deer, but the largest buck I had ever seen!

It was snowing and I don't remember the time, but it was growing dark. I quickly judged the range at 350 yards as I removed my pack and found a rest for the Ruger .270. Placing the crosshairs on the huge mule deer, I squeezed the trigger. The buck never even moved—I had missed!

What a beautiful sight he was as I sat up and took another look at the buck. A little calmer by then, I found a better rest and held the crosshairs a bit higher. Breathing calmly, I settled down and fired once more. Nothing! The deer was nowhere to be seen. But then as I pulled my binoculars out and glassed the basin, I saw that he was down and not moving.

Marking the spot, I hurried around the basin to the dead deer. In the darkness, I used the flashlight to clean the buck and guide Dad up to my location. I knew deer of this size were around, but I had not expected to see any, let alone harvest one. We brought the deer down as far as possible in the dark and then returned the following morning to bring him the rest of the way. Leaving him on the mountain made for a very restless night!

My Wyoming buck scored 206⅝ SCI. The rack is just over 34 inches wide and an honest 24 inches tall. His cape was scarred and cut, and he had an inch long slit in one ear. He obviously fought some battles during his long life.

In December, I showed the picture to Doyle Moss, a friend of mine. After looking at it for a minute, he said, "This buck's name is Goliath, and he is a video star and legend. Go get the video Magnum Mulies and look at the cover." I did, and he was right. David Long had been filming and following Goliath for two years. Goliath's once magnificent cheaters are just bumps now and his main beams have lost some of their size, but his mass is greater than before.

The Future of Mule Deer

The glory days of the 1960's for mule deer must have been something else. All of the stories I hear and read about 30-inch bucks everywhere make my imagination run wild. What it must have been like to have hunted back then. Will those banner mule deer days return to the West? Unfortunately the answer is a definite "No." Too many things have changed since then that will not allow the mule deer numbers we had back then.

Although we will never see those kinds of populations again, that doesn't mean that everything is gloom and doom for the mule deer in the western United States. Before we can fix the declining population levels of the mule deer, we must first find the cause. Wildlife agencies across the West are scrambling right now to try and figure out the cause of the decline.

Population declines happen when deaths exceed births—it's that simple. Unfortunately, there are so many factors that play into the scenario of things that it is not easy to pinpoint exactly why the populations are currently trending downward. One thing we must keep in mind is that the cause for the decline is widespread, not localized. All western states have seen declining mule deer populations.

Bad winters can have a devastating effect on mule deer populations. The notoriously bad winter of 1992-1993 wiped out nearly half the mule deer numbers in certain areas. How does this affect trophy mule deer numbers? Well, in 1992 there were 20 typical bucks and eight non-typical bucks harvested in the Rocky Mountain States that were large enough to make the all-time record book. The following year there were only 10 typical bucks and 5 non-typicals that qualified.

That is a 46.5% reduction in B&C entries. Another good example is the Wyoming Game and Fish Department's Grey's River check station. In 1992 they checked 297 bucks through the station and in 1993, they only checked 42 bucks. Those kinds of numbers are staggering.

So why are the mule deer populations declining? Personally I feel there are three factors, besides bad winters, that play important roles in the decline of trophy mule deer—habitat loss, hunting pressure and poaching. While hunting pressure and poaching mainly affect the numbers of trophy bucks, habitat loss affects the entire mule deer population.

Habitat Loss

Habitat loss is definitely one the major contributors in the decline of the mule deer population in the West today. When most people think of habitat loss, they think of the loss due to development of the land. While this is an important factor, there are other contributors such as fire suppression and overgrazing. I am not a biologist, nor do I claim to be, but it doesn't take a genius to realize that not only are the mule deer losing habitat, but the quality of the existing habitat is being degraded as well.

The major contributor to the degradation of the mule deer's summer range is fire suppression and overgrazing by domestic livestock. Many public land areas I have hunted have so much downfall, that deer avoid these areas. Not only do deer avoid them, the extremely thick timber doesn't have much food. A lot of this habitat goes unused. I feel areas like this would greatly benefit by a controlled burn. Recently burned areas are great food plots for mule deer.

The overgrazing of livestock is very evident as well. Many small stream banks that I have hunted near have been beaten down to barren dirt by large numbers of cattle. There is very little food and the areas that are nothing but dirt, are easily eroded. This damage, which is done in a short amount of time, can take years and years to recover. This area that is situated along the bank of a river or stream, known as riparian habitat, is one of the most important habitats for mule deer in the West. Because riparian habitat is so diverse and dense, it is often the first area to show signs of impact from overuse. Overgrazing by domestic livestock is the number one factor in our decreasing amount of riparian habitat. These areas are used extensively during migrations in the spring and fall, as well as during fawning in the month of June. Image 8-5 shows just how important the riparian habitat is and how often deer utilize it.

Image 8-5

The image is from a GPS-collared mule deer doe that recorded her position every three hours from late May thru mid-October. The interesting thing is, even after arriving at her summer range, she made regular two- to three-mile trips to the Snake River (riparian habitat) throughout the summer, but particularly during parturition in June. The riparian habitat was critical to her during fawning.

Throughout the years it has been documented that Forest Service biologists have recommended reductions in domestic grazing on public lands. Finally, the agency is listening to those biologists. On March 20, 1996, the

USDA Forest Service and the USDI Bureau of Land Management, in partnership with USDA Natural Resources Conservation Service (NRCS), agreed to implement a strategy to "Accelerate Cooperative Riparian Restoration and Management." The initial focus of this effort was grazing management in 11 western states with directions to expand the program over time. The three major roles for the National Riparian Service Team (NRST) are as follows: training and information sharing, consulting and advisory services & program review and evaluation. Hopefully, under guidance from the NRST, these agencies can implement livestock grazing plans that will bring back some of our streamside habitat that has been severely degraded by overgrazing from domestic livestock.

Unfortunately, winter range habitat is not what it used to be either. A study conducted in 1988 near my hometown of Big Piney, Wyoming, showed that 60% of the large sagebrush was in fair to poor condition, while other shrubs such as mountain mahogany and bitterbrush were in even worse shape. Most of the shrubs were found to be 50 to 100 years old, which greatly reduces their ability to produce browse. According to the report, poor habitat conditions were a result of fire suppression, overgrazing and drought.

A plan has been implemented to help remove some of the older brush, which will make way for new growth in the form of grasses, forbs and shrubs. Several methods have been implemented – dragging large chains to break down older brush, controlled burns and mowing the brush with bush hogs to kill it. This is not a quick fix however. It can take up to 20 years for shrubs to come in where the sagebrush has been thinned.

Habitat restoration is something we can all be involved in. Everyone needs to do their part. Contact the game and fish agency in your area and see if there is anything you can do to help. Many agencies have volunteer programs that allow the public to participate in habitat restoration projects.

Hunting Pressure

Public land mule deer are receiving as much hunting pressure right now as they ever have—even in the backcountry. Years ago, there used to be several spots I could go to and not run into any hunters, but nowadays, such spots do not exist. Equipped with better equipment and more mule deer knowledge, guys are penetrating the backcountry in their pursuit of trophy mule deer. General, public land hunting nowadays, is mediocre, at best.

A glance at the current record book shows that there are still plenty of B&C heads being taken every year. But if you look even closer, you will find that the vast majority of these bucks are coming from areas that have an extremely limited amount of tags available. Most of these areas have extremely low draw odds, often running at less than a 10% chance of drawing. Some areas are even less than 1% for some of the most highly sought after tags.

Even with all of the limits on tag quotas, I feel that they need to be limited even more. Not only do the tag quotas need to be reduced even more, I feel that one of the largest problems is that several states allow hunting well into November, and some as late as December. It is a shame how many big bucks die in Colorado and Idaho during late hunts. Yes, I am guilty of applying for these late tags just like everyone else, but I still wish that they would do away with them. I think the quality of hunting would greatly increase in these states if that were to happen.

Times are definitely changing in the world of trophy mule deer hunting and all in all, I think that the game and fish departments are doing a good job of keeping up with those changes. Like it or not, I think that we need to see even more limits on tag quotas in the Rocky Mountain States as well as doing away with all of the late rut hunts.

Poaching

Poaching is probably the most direct cause of the decline of mature mule deer bucks. Even with habitat restoration and proper game management, poaching can single-handedly wipe out your large bucks in a short amount of time. There may have been a day when poaching was only done by your "Average Joe Hunter" on a very rare basis, but nowadays, poaching is very organized and involves very large operations.

I live by one of the best mule deer winter ranges in the West. I have had the pleasure of watching some of the biggest mule deer bucks to ever roam the state of Wyoming. These winter ranges allow you to get a good look at all of the bucks that eluded you during the hunting season. This time of the year the bucks will let you drive right up to them and take photos or simply admire them. Unfortunately, some individuals are out there for another purpose – poaching. Bucks are very vulnerable at this time of year and there are a few lowlifes that take advantage of this during the winter. Every year on the winter range near my home there are several deer carcasses found with the head cut off.

Generally, when someone thinks about poaching, they think about a deer being shot illegally out of season. As you will see in the following stories, some of the best mule deer are taken illegally during the hunting season. It is unfortunate that these magnificent animals had to die at the hands of poachers.

I feel this part of the book is especially important because poaching is having a huge effect on our trophy mule deer population. I contacted all eight game and fish departments for the Rocky Mountain States and asked them if they would be kind enough to provide me with a story and photo of a trophy mule deer poaching case that took place in their states. Fortunately, all of the departments were more than glad to help. They all feel the need to inform the public of the quality of animals which are being poached these days. Here are several poaching cases that have taken place in the West over the past few years:

Colorado

Year: 2002

In the summer of 2002 a large non-typical mule deer buck was videotaped on the Uncompahgre Plateau west of Montrose, CO. News and photos (from the video tape) of the UP buck spread like wildfire through the communities around the plateau. Wildlife officers kept an eye on the buck through the summer, but when the deer moved from summer range to winter range, he was not seen again.

During winter range patrols in December, 2002 wildlife officers talked to a local man who bragged about seeing a huge buck in the trunk of a "friend's" car. The officers immediately suspected that it could be the UP buck. They began asking around and eventually were given the name of a local man who was bragging about killing a record book buck. Colorado licensing records showed that the man did not have a deer license for 2002 and so the officers went to the man's house to interview him. He was not at home, but two of his relatives were and gave consent for the officers to search the residence. The search turned up nothing, however questioning of the relatives revealed that the suspect had something to hide.

A couple of days later, the suspect met the wildlife officers at the CDOW office in Montrose and admitted to having the head from the large deer. However, he claimed that he had found the deer rack while riding up on the forest and claimed that the deer was already dead when he found it. The officers didn't buy this story, and after further questioning, the man eventually confessed to seeing the deer while moving cattle and shooting it with a handgun that he carried on his hip. He claimed that it was the smaller of three bucks in a group.

The man then went out to his car and returned with the antlers from the 39-inch wide buck which had been hidden in a pile of sawdust.

The man pled guilty to hunting without a proper and valid license, unlawful possession of a mule deer and was assessed the "Samson" trophy surcharge for possession of the huge deer. The handgun used to poach the deer was also forfeited.

The 39-inch Uncompahgre Plateau buck was filmed during the summer by a local resident before being poached later that year on the winter range.

Idaho

Year: 2004

By Robby Denning

It was early November 2004. Snow had been falling in the high country for several weeks and the deer migration toward the desert country of Fremont County, Idaho was underway. Fish and Game officer, Charlie Anderson, was on patrol when a tip came in that a large buck had been illegally killed in the last several days in his patrol area. The season was open for 800 tag holders, but according to the tip, the person who shot the buck didn't possess one of the easy-to-draw tags. Apparently, the suspect had conned his younger brother of the ripe old age of 12 to tag the buck for him. Cases like this are extremely hard to prosecute, but poaching is poaching and Charlie quickly solicited the help of five other officers in the region.

When most people think of poachers, they envision someone killing easily accessible bucks on the winter range. This indeed is how many big deer are stolen from law-fearing hunters, but as it turns out here, this isn't always the case. Poachers can do their evil deeds even when the season is open.

Charlie soon learned that the 12-year-old tag holder had recently graduated from a Hunter Education Course taught by Charlie himself. He knew that this boy's family had a history of breaking game laws and transfer of a tag (highly illegal) to another person was not above their doing. Through his research, he put together a theory about how this deer was killed and transported to town.

The older brother possessed a valid cow elk tag for the same unit, giving him reason to be in the field during the deer hunt. School records also showed that the younger brother had been pulled out of class for two hours the day the buck had been shot. Charlie theorized that the older brother shot the buck while elk hunting and then took his brother out of school to tag the deer before coming back to town. Because Charlie had a prior history of investigating this family, he elected to have the other officers question the boy about the incident.

The officers pulled the boy out of class, but waited for his father to be present before starting questioning. To think that a big brother would put a young boy in such a precarious position saddened the officers. Once the questioning started, the boy became confused and frustrated. His father soon spoke up and told the officers that the person they really needed to talk to was his older son, the boy's big brother.

The older brother arrived with an air of confidence, but the presence of the officers was overwhelming. Soon, he confessed to the crime. He had indeed seen the buck while he was elk hunting, shot it, then pulled his little brother out of school to tag the giant deer, all as Charlie had suspected. It had only been a week since the buck was killed, but the Fish and Game already had a confession and the poached buck in their possession, all thanks to the willing citizen who reported the crime.

Before trial, Charlie had an official scorer measure the buck. The green score was 252⅝, with an outside spread of 32 inches. The antlers also had over 40 inches of mass as determined by the "H" measurements on the Boone and Crockett scale—a truly giant buck. The judge in the case levied only an $800 fine, five days in jail, and a two year loss of hunting privileges. The Fish and Game had pushed for a much stiffer sentence, but the judge went light because the

Robby Denning standing next to the massive 252⅝ B&C buck.

perpetrator didn't hinder the investigation.

Considering what this poacher took from the hunters of Idaho, his sentence is like a lashing with a wet noodle. There were 800 other tag holders for this hunt who deserved the chance to legally harvest the buck. Charlie tried to get the judge to view the antlers at trial but was unsuccessful. Later when the judge, a hunter himself, did see the antlers, he admitted that the fine and penalty were not enough.

We hunters, especially trophy hunters, have the highest obligation to follow the laws of the land that were designed to protect the resource we so dearly love, ultimately benefiting us all. There will always be those who ignore the laws and sometimes escape justice. However, as long as we have officers like Charlie Anderson and citizens willing to report violations, their crimes will never be easy to commit.

Montana

Year: 2005

What started out as a kidnapping plot ended up in the illegal possession of a trophy mule deer. A Simms, Montana resident was arrested in March of 2005 for allegedly plotting to kidnap the son of CBS's Late Show host David Letterman. The tip came from an acquaintance of the suspect who had been told of the plan. The suspect had been doing some painting on Letterman's Rocky Mountain ranch near Choteau, Montana and had allegedly told his friend that he was going to kidnap the toddler when Letterman returned to the ranch for a visit.

On Wednesday, March 16, 2005, the Choteau, Montana game warden was contacted by the Great Falls, Montana agent of the Federal Bureau of Investigation, who had been investigating an individual on federal fraud charges. They had also received a tip from a concerned citizen who mentioned the possibility of a trophy mule deer buck that had been poached on the Rocky Mountain front west of Choteau.

A search warrant was issued on Friday, March 18 pursuant to fraud charges for the suspect's Simms, Montana residence by the Teton County Sheriff's Office and the FBI. While searching a barn located on the premises, the officers found and videoed several large elk racks, as well as a world class set of mule deer antlers. The antlers were all hidden underneath a tarp in the rafters of the building.

This is a photo of the buck which was found on an undeveloped roll of film in the suspect's camera during a search of his home.

Three days later, the video which was taken during the search was turned over to the Montana Fish, Wildlife & Parks. The combination of the antlers being hidden in the barn and the concerned citizen's statement, the Fish, Wildlife & Parks made an application for a search warrant. After being granted, the warrant was served on Monday, March 28.

The mule deer rack was seized, as well as the film which was found in two cameras. The film in one of the cameras had not yet been exposed, but the other had been. It contained several photos of a live deer in the background, but the last two pictures on the roll were of the mule deer in question laying dead on the ground.

When questioned about shooting the deer, the suspect stated that he did not shoot it, someone else did. The suspect did plead guilty to a felony theft charge and the "possession of an illegally taken game trophy animal." In exchange with this plea, the Teton County Attorney dismissed the solicitation of kidnapping charges against him.

The buck was later scored by an official B&C measurer at 207⅞. The buck exceeds the current Montana state record which was taken in 1983 and scored 205⅜.

Nevada

Year: 1996

Nevada game wardens spent several years compiling information about illegal activity on Granite Mountain near Gerlach, Nevada. The Department of Wildlife has received information on the poaching of trophy quality mule deer in the Gerlach

area for several years. It was only after enough information was gathered that Nevada's game wardens were able to analyze the information in order to determine who was connected to who, who was involved in the actual illegal killing of wildlife, who was assisting in covering up the criminal activity, and where some of the illegal wildlife was being stored.

In July of 1996, more than 25 individuals were interviewed, including both suspects and witnesses. Initially, these interviews involved 16 officers from several law enforcement agencies including Nevada Department of Wildlife, U.S. Fish & Wildlife Service, California Fish & Game, and the Washoe County Sheriff's Office.

As a result of these interviews, several photos and three deer heads were seized from three individuals, and enough information was obtained to initiate a grand jury investigation. As a result, an indictment was issued against a Santa Rosa, California resident for the Unlawful Possession of a Mule Deer. That individual ultimately pleaded guilty to the charge and was sentenced to 30 days in jail, $5,000 civil assessment, $1,000 criminal fine, forfeiture of his four-wheeler, rifle and deer mount.

New Mexico

Year: 2003

With an antler spread of 37½ inches wide, the buck was definitely attracting the attention of the locals. Residents would watch the buck in amazement of the tremendous 11x9 rack. Unfortunately that all ended in late November or early December of 2003. While elk hunting in the area that the big buck was calling home, a local Aztec, New Mexico resident couldn't resist the temptation of the monster buck.

After no further leads in the case, G&F officials had one of the locals who had been watching the buck, draw a sketch of the antlers to put on their website, hoping that someone would recognize it.

Two tips to Operation Game Thief played a huge role in the solving the case. The first tip led officers to the buck's carcass on December 5, 2003. The second tip, which came in one year later, led game and fish officials to the suspect.

The suspect's confession to poaching the buck, removing its antlers and leaving the carcass to rot, resulted in being sentenced for illegal killing, illegal possession and unlawful transportation of big game. He received a $1,500 fine and was ordered to reimburse the state $250 for the deer. In addition, he forfeited his rifle, lost his hunting privileges and was ordered to serve 323 hours of community service

Utah

Year: 2004

What started out as a routine traffic stop, ended up being a lot more. On November 15, 2004 at approximately 4:00 p.m., the Summit County Dispatch called for any available wildlife unit to aid a Utah Highway Patrol trooper who had made a stop

The beautiful 37½-inch buck had a total of 20 points.

just south of the Silver Summit exit on westbound State Road 40.

A short time later, conservation officers arrived at the location and the trooper explained the situation to them. He said that he had stopped the vehicle for some equipment violations and that he noticed that the passenger in the vehicle, who was dressed in camouflage, had blood on his hands. When he inquired about the blood, he was told by the passenger that he had killed a deer. The Trooper went on to say that the deer head was in the backseat of the vehicle and that he had taken possession of a firearm that was located in the vehicle, and secured the firearm in his patrol car.

After being filled in, the Conservation Officers proceeded to contact the individuals inside of the vehicle. When asked who had killed the deer, the passenger in the vehicle stated that he was the one who had killed the deer. The driver of the vehicle claimed that he knew nothing about the deer and that he was contacted by a friend to pick up the passenger and take him to Salt Lake City.

Inside of the back seat of the vehicle the officers could see the tips of antlers sticking out from beneath some jackets. One of the officers asked the passenger to remove the deer from the back seat so that they could have a good look at it. The passenger removed the jackets and set the deer head and antlers outside of the vehicle on the ground. The head and cape were wrapped in a white plastic bag and there was not a carcass or any meat from the deer in the vehicle. The passenger stated that he had not yet retrieved the meat from the mountain. The cape of the deer was still quite warm to the touch, indicating that the deer had not been dead very long.

The passenger stated that he had killed the buck about four hours earlier on the Wasatch Extended Archery Area, which incidentally, was approximately 10 miles away and that his archery equipment and vehicle were still in the Salt Lake City area. When asked why he was in this particular area at this time, he stated that a friend had dropped him off and that he was hunting coyotes. When asked about the driver of the vehicle, he stated that he was just a guy who was giving him a ride back to Salt Lake City and that the driver had nothing to do with the deer head.

The officers noticed that there was no tag visible on the deer's antlers. When asked where his tag was for the deer, the passenger stated that the tag was inside of the deer's ear. Upon inspection, indeed there was a tag in the deer's ear: a 2004 Montana Resident Antelope Tag. The license was issued in the passenger's name and had been notched and validated for November 15.

At this point, the officers told the passenger that his story was not making much sense. It was very unusual for him to be in this area with a freshly killed deer, no carcass, with a rifle, no vehicle and the deer tagged with a Montana Antelope License. Finally, after realizing there was no way out of his predicament, the passenger stated that he was going to be straight up with the officers. He finally confessed to shooting the deer with his rifle. He pointed to a ridgeline to the east of the highway and said that he had killed the buck on the other side of the ridge.

At this time, the passenger was taken into custody. Inside the suspect's backpack, officers also found night vision optics and other miscellaneous gear. A search of the suspect's rear pants pocket, turned up six 7mm Remington Mag. cartridges. Four of the cartridges had not been fired, while the other two had been fired and were the

The seized rack had a spread of 30⅞ inches, thus qualifying it as a "trophy" under Utah law.

spent casings. The officers retrieved the deer head, along with the rifle from the Trooper's patrol vehicle and the suspect was transported to the Summit County Jail by the Trooper.

After arriving at the jail, the suspect stated that he had come to Utah three days prior, to hunt deer in the Wasatch Front Extended Archery Area. After hunting along the Wasatch Front and running into people everywhere, he and a buddy came to the location where he killed this deer to hunt the area with bows. He said that they saw several big bucks, but they must have been hunted hard because they were not able to get anywhere near bow range of the bucks. The next day he had a friend drop him off in the same area where they had hunted the day before, so he could hunt coyotes with his rifle. That is when it happened. He stated that the biggest buck that he had ever seen in his life stood up in front of him and he got caught up in the moment and shot the deer.

The suspect said that he went to the deer and proceeded to cape it out and cut the deer's head off. He said that he did not gut the deer because he got nervous and he knew that he had made a huge mistake. He then hiked out of the canyon with the head and his rifle and met the driver, who was to give him a ride to Salt Lake City. When asked what role the driver had in the crime, the suspect stated that he did not even know him and that this was the first time that he had ever met him. He said that a buddy had arranged for him to come and pick him up, and that the driver knew nothing about the killing of the deer until he saw him with the head.

On November 19, 2004, the mule deer buck's antlers were measured by an official measurer for the Boone and Crockett Club. The antlers measured 30⅞ inches wide, thus qualifying the deer as a trophy deer under Utah law. Due to the fact that the deer qualifies as a trophy deer, the crime qualifies as a third degree felony and restitution was set forth as $8000.00.

Wyoming

Year: 2000

By Brady Vandeberg

A survivor, he lived out his long life mostly in the dry breaks just south of the Powder River east of Kaycee, Wyoming. He avoided hunters in the open barren country by bedding down in the shade of an old dry wash and staying put even when a four-wheeler would rumble by only yards away.

Few locals even knew he was around. Occasionally, stories would surface about a great deer, with massive antlers spreading twice his body width, seen crossing the road by dark of night in vehicle headlights. I was fortunate enough to see this great deer the winter before he died. He was on the river with a group of does. When he rose out of his bed and turned away, laying his ears back, it seemed as if his antlers just kept going and going. He was wise enough to stick to thick cover away from roads during the daytime so I let him be, hoping he would be content and not wander to an area where someone who couldn't resist the temptation would kill him out of season.

Then came the drought of 2000. The summer was hot and dry and not much grass grew in the hills. The ranchers were having a tough time and so were the deer. The old buck was getting on in years and was forced down to the river with the rest of the deer to take advantage of the grass that grew in the shade of the cottonwood tress.

When hunting season opened on October 1st the old buck avoided hunters as best he could by traveling down the river and finding a piece of ground with little human pressure. That is where he spent his last few days.

A young ranchhand that had just moved to Wyoming wanted to hunt deer in the worst way. Not yet a resident, he asked his employer to buy a deer tag and let him shoot the deer, which is illegal in the state of Wyoming. The employer agreed and on the third day of the season the ranchhand went down to the river bottom and saw a big mule deer buck. The ranchhand was pleased for this was a respectable buck with five points per side. Tagging the deer with his employer's tag, the ranchhand loaded the deer on his four-wheeler and headed back to his house. That's when he saw the monarch. This was a dream buck. A deer like he had never seen before.

Immediately he planned how he would put this great deer on his wall. His wife had never killed a deer before so he thought it would be great to have her kill this buck. The only problem was that she was not a resident either. The pair approached their neighboring ranchers who had been good to them and helped them settle into their new home. They told the story of this great mule deer and asked if the neighbors would buy a deer license to tag the deer if his wife killed it. The neighbors had no interest in hunting anymore so they obliged and the hunt was on.

The third day of the season was almost the last for the big buck but the new hunter was not comfortable with a quick shot and some wary does warned the deer of danger. His luck would not continue on the fourth day of the season. The big buck made the mistake of staying in the same area and it didn't take long for the pair of hunters to find him. The wife took aim and with the echo of the shot, the great deer fell to an illegal hunter.

Officer Brady Vandeberg holding the tremendous 39-inch Powder River Monarch.

This violation might have gone undetected but a deer that size draws attention and admiration so it wasn't long before people began to talk. I began hearing rumors of a huge deer with a 39-inch spread that had been killed on the river. I began tracking down stories and heard that the wife of a ranchhand had killed it. Knowing that she wasn't a Wyoming resident, I checked the nonresident hunting license draw information and quickly determined she had not applied for nor received a Wyoming deer license in 2000. Seeing the ranchhand in town one night, I asked if someone had killed a big deer east of town and he said his neighbor did but he was able to talk her into trading it to him for two bum lambs. I explained that he would need to get a game tag for the deer and asked if I could see it. We made arrangements to get him the game tag and sure enough it was the big deer I had seen the year before.

As fall turned into winter, I kept hearing many different rumors and too many stories with too many variations, the whole thing just didn't feel right. After many interviews with the ranchers and ranchhands, none of them admitted to any wrong doing. When confronted with the prospect of going to court and having a long, drawn out trial, the ranchhand finally confessed that his wife actually killed the deer and they used the neighbor's license to tag it. Additionally, he admitted to killing the first buck.

Both the ranchhand and his wife pleaded guilty to killing the two buck deer and cooperated with the Game and Fish Department in wrapping up the case. They lost their hunting privileges and were fined over $1200.00. Both deer racks and all of the meat was seized. Both landowners who provided the deer licenses were also charged with illegally transferring a deer license and paid fines.

Wildlife Violator Compact

The Wildlife Violator Compact (WVC) is one of the best poaching deterrents there is. The concept first came to life by the member states of the Western Association of Fish and Wildlife. Wildlife commissioners and law enforcement administrators from several states liked the concept and began to format it after similar programs, such as the Driver's License Compact. The first drafts were individually completed in 1985 by the states of Colorado and Nevada. Eventually the drafts were joined and thus the WVC was born. During the 1989 Legislative session the WVC was passed into law in Colorado, Nevada and Oregon.

Today there are 18 member states that participate in the program. Under the compact, if a person is arrested for violating a law that protects wildlife while he or she is in a state other than his or her state of residence, the person is given the same procedures to follow to comply with the citation as a resident of the issuing state is afforded. This includes the right to sign a recognizance stating that he or she will comply with the requirements of the citation, without being required to post bond or appear immediately before a court.

The compact requires a member state to notify another member state when a resident of that other state has been issued a citation for a wildlife violation and has failed to comply with that citation. Under the compact, when a member state is notified of the noncompliance, the member state is required to notify the violator and initiate action to suspend the violator's license and approval privileges. The compact also requires member states to notify a violator's home state if the violator has been convicted of a wildlife violation, and the home state is required to treat that conviction as if it occurred in the violator's home state. The compact requires member states to make reports to other member states about wildlife convictions and suspension actions. The bottom line – if you get convicted of a game violation and lose your hunting privilege in any of the 18 states, you lose your hunting rights in all member states as well.

Unfortunately, only a small amount of poachers are actually caught. There simply are not enough game wardens to cover the amount of territory that needs to be covered. We all need to help. If you see anything suspicious or know of an incident involving a trophy buck, or any game animal for that matter, make sure and contact the proper authority. Here is a list of state poaching programs along with phone numbers for the Rocky Mountain States to report game violations:

State	Program Name	Phone
Arizona	Operation Game Thief	1-800-352-0700
Colorado	Operation Game Thief	1-877-265-6648
Idaho	Citizens Against Poaching	1-800-632-5999
Montana	TIP MONT	1-800-847 6668
Nevada	Operation Game Thief	1-800-992-3030
New Mexico	Operation Game Thief	1-800-432-4263
Utah	Help Stop Poaching	1-800-662-3337
Wyoming	Stop Poaching	1-800-442-4331

Our Younger Generation

Mule deer hunting has always been a big part of my life, but I have always said that I would never force any of my kids to hunt. If they showed an interest, that would be great. If they chose not to hunt, I would be fine with that as well. My youngest daughter, Nicole, showed an interest and took it upon herself to sign up for a hunter safety course. I remember the day she passed the class very well. She didn't have to say anything. It was fairly obvious she had passed by the way she was running out of the building screaming. She was only 10 at the time, but she knew that in two years time, she would be going on her first mule deer hunt. She had informed me that she wanted to shoot a bigger buck than all of the boys in her class; I told her we would see what we could do.

The year had finally come. A little over a month after Nicole's twelfth birthday, hunting season was upon us. This particular day, we awoke at 4:00 a.m. and were on our way out of town by 4:30 a.m. When we arrived at the trailhead, we had an hour and 20 minutes before sun up, which meant we could be near the top of the ridge at first light. Nicole had had an eight hour volleyball tournament the day before, so she was kind of having a hard time getting her legs underneath her. We stopped fairly often, which resulted in us not making the top of the ridge before first light.

When we were within 500 yards of the top, we spotted a couple of does feeding in an opening, but because of the contour of the hillside, we couldn't tell if there were more deer with them or not. It didn't take long to figure out there was a buck with them because four shots rang out from directly above us. The hunter either had a semi automatic rifle, or he set a new world record for firing four rounds from a bolt action rifle. I turned to Nicole and said, "He didn't get that deer. Anytime someone rushes their shots that fast, there is no way they are going to be accurate."

I was bummed. We had hiked all this way just to have someone beat us to the deer by a couple of minutes. We continued climbing straight up the ridge, and in a matter of minutes, we spotted four bucks about two hundred yards directly to our right. They were on top of the ridge that paralleled the one we was on. There were three four points and a two point. Unfortunately, they had us pegged. I laid my pack

Nicole's first high country buck had an outside spread of 27 inches.

on the ground and just as Nicole was settling the crosshairs on the bucks, they disappeared over the ridge to the north.

I figured the bucks wouldn't go very far and if we could get to the top, there was a stringer of trees that we could walk behind until we got far enough north to see into the next basin. As we topped out, we saw an outfitter with his hunter who had set the new speed record for four consecutive shots heading in the opposite direction we were going.

Once behind the line of trees, we traveled approximately 250 yards to a spot that would allow us to look into the basin that the bucks disappeared into. When we were close to the edge, I told Nicole to stay put and using the last tree as cover, I peeked over the edge and there they were. One buck was bedded down and the remaining three were standing looking back in the direction from which they had come. I eased away from the edge and gave Nicole a thumbs-up.

I chambered a round for her and slipped off my pack. We belly crawled up to the edge and I had her lay the gun over the pack to use it as a rest. The largest buck was standing on the right and was providing her with a great broadside shot. I figured the bucks to be at a little over 200 yards and straight down the extremely rough and steep hillside. I told her to make sure and take her time getting ready for the shot. I even reminded her of the guy that shot four times just a few minutes earlier. The bucks looked to be getting impatient and I was worried that they were going

316

to disappear over the ridge just as they had done earlier. While I kept thinking to myself that she needed to get the shot off, I kept telling her, "Take your time. Don't rush."

She told me that she couldn't quite get the crosshairs to hold steady so I told her just before pulling the trigger to take a deep breath and hold it. She took a deep breath but still didn't fire. She had to let the breath out. On her second attempt at taking a deep breath, she pulled the trigger. I watched through the binoculars as the buck leaped high into the air and spun 180 degrees and vanished out of sight followed by the three remaining bucks. I told Nicole, "He's hit. You got him."

We sat there talking for several minutes talking about whether she had hit the buck or not and I told her I was confident that she had connected. The only question in my mind was how well was he hit. I started looking at how far away the bucks had been when Nicole shot and I was starting to worry that it was a little bit farther than I had originally judged. I opened up the top compartment on my backpack and grabbed my rangefinder and took a reading of the tree that the buck was standing next too. I was shocked when it revealed it was 350 yards! That is 100 yards farther than I had originally thought. I was still confident that she hit the buck hard.

We slowly started working our way down the upper portion of the ridge that the bucks disappeared over, while constantly keeping an eye on the openings to the north of the small timber patch we were entering. When we started getting close to where the bucks had been standing, we ran into the small two point. He looked confused and lost. I told Nicole that that was a good sign because often bucks that lose a buddy often hang around not knowing what to do. However, there was no sign of the three larger bucks.

When we arrived in front of the small patch of trees where the bucks had stood, we started scouring the hillside for any sign of blood. There was none. Now I was really confused because I knew she had hit the buck. I started looking closely at the fresh tracks but could only find two sets. This told me that I had the wrong set of trees. We walked down to another patch of trees that looked similar about 40 yards down the ridge. There were several sets of fresh tracks and once again I felt we had hope. I dug out my rangefinder and ranged back up to where Nicole had shot from and it read 348 yards. This was indeed the right location. In a matter of seconds, I found fresh blood on a small rock and said to Nicole, "You hit him. Now, let's find him."

We had only been looking for a few seconds when Nicole located the blood trail heading straight down off the steep mountain. We had only followed the blood trail for about 15 yards when I noticed a gray patch in a small patch of trees below us. I put up the binoculars and there he was, piled up. I turned to Nicole and yelled, "You got him. He's down." We gave each other several high fives and then hugged one another. We both had tears in our eyes as we made our way down to the buck, whooping and hollering all of the way. I was extremely proud of her accomplishment. The buck had an outside spread of 27 inches.

After a short photo session, it took us two pack trips to get the buck off the mountain. We completed our second pack trip at 6:00 p.m. It had taken us 10 hours to make the two trips. We were tired and sore, but both of us still had smiles on our faces. We accomplished our goal of getting her a high country mule deer in the backcountry. I can honestly say that I was more excited for her that day than I ever have been for myself on any of my deer. That day will always remain very special to me, and oh yeah, by the way, Nicole's buck ended up being bigger than all of the boys' in her class that year.

I can't emphasize enough the importance of getting young people involved in hunting. It is important that they learn proper hunting ethics and the importance of wildlife conservation at an early age. Our kids of today will be our wildlife conservationists of tomorrow. It is important that you give them the opportunity at an early age. I am thankful that my dad gave me that opportunity when I was young.

Hunting, it is a great tradition – be sure to pass it on.

The Bottom  Line

Over the years, I have been fortunate enough to have seen many magnum mulies in the high country. I have been lucky enough to harvest several of them, while many others were able to elude me. Some of them have flat taught me a lesson or two. That is what keeps me coming back. Trophy hunting mule deer is an extreme challenge that I welcome every fall. It pushes me to the limits, both physically and mentally, and I plan to accept that challenge for years to come.

There is no such thing as an unsuccessful hunt. I firmly believe this. If I felt that I needed to kill a deer in order for a hunt to be successful, I would quit hunting and take up something else. If you can't bear the thought of going several years without harvesting an animal, don't take up pursuing monster bucks. There will be a lot of tags that go unfilled in your quest for that buck of a lifetime. Don't get me wrong though, every time I set out on a hunt I am going to give it 110% by hunting as hard as I possibly can to try and harvest a monster mulie. If I don't harvest a buck, it is not because of a lack of effort–guaranteed!

I feel that with every season that goes by, I have gained more valuable knowledge of mule deer behavior and feel I have become a better hunter. To become a better hunter, not only do you need to gain more knowledge, you need to be able to apply that knowledge on future hunts.

Hopefully you will be able to take something from this book that will make your future high country hunts more enjoyable. One thing is for sure, pursuing mulies in the high country will give you memories that will last a lifetime. My good friend Mike Eastman, summed it up well when he said, "Hunting the high country gets in your blood. There's something about watching a 30-inch mulie bounce along a 10,000-foot ridge with nothing except deep blue sky between the tines of his rack. Visions like these engrave themselves into the trophy hunter's memory of stone."

I hope you have enjoyed this book as much as I have enjoyed writing it.

David W. Long